Retiring Right

Planning for Your Successful Retirement

Lawrence J. Kaplan

AVERY PUBLISHING GROUP INC.
Wayne, New Jersey

ABOUT THE AUTHOR

Lawrence J. Kaplan is an authority in the field of personal financial management and retirement planning. He received his M.A. and Ph.D. in economics from Columbia University. He has served as Professor of Economics at John Jay College of the City University of New York for the past twenty years and has served as an officer of a Welfare Fund which administers the benefits programs for over 15,000 New York City employees.

Dr. Kaplan is the author of six books on personal finance and investing. Following his own advice, he has just retired from teaching and plans to lecture extensively to groups, organizations, and colleges. Dr. Kaplan resides with his wife Jeanne in Manhasset, New York.

Cover design by Martin Hochberg and Rudy Shur
In-house editor Susan Capasso
Page layout Diana Puglisi
Typeset by ACS Graphics Services, Fresh Meadows, NY

Library of Congress Cataloging-in-Publication Data
Kaplan, Lawrence J. (Lawrence Jay)
   Retiring right.

   Bibliography: p.
   Includes index.
   1. Retirement—United States—Planning.
2. Retirement income—United States—Planning.
I. Title.
HQ1062.K35   1987   646.7′9   87–1403
ISBN 0–89529–365–X (pbk.)

Printed in the United States of America
9 8 7 6 5 4 3 2 1

CONTENTS

Preface, v

Introduction, vii

1   First Facts About Retirement and Planning, 1
2   Understanding Your Social Security, 11
3   Checking Your Pension Benefits, 29
4   Savings, Investments, Life Insurance, and Annuities, 57
5   Budgeting, Credit, Inflation, Taxes, and Tax Shelters, 99
6   Estate Planning: Wills, Trusts, Probate, Estate and Gift Taxes, 133
7   Handling Legal Affairs, 169
8   Making the Retirement Housing Decision, 185
9   Interpreting Medicare and Medicaid, Other Health Insurance, and Nursing Homes, 213
10   Preparing for the Inevitable, 247
11   Working and Playing in Retirement, 265

Appendices
A   Inventory of Personal and Financial Data, 281
B   Resources, 307
C   Suggested Readings, 311

Index, 317

With love for my wife, Jeanne who was always there, and for my children Harriet, Sanford, and Marcia who were there even though they were away.

PREFACE

As more and more people confound the chronologists and survive to become senior citizens, the need to improve the quality of their lives becomes more apparent. Yet the quality of life does not improve itself; it requires careful thought and planning. Most people, however, in their forties, fifties and sixties tend to postpone decisions that will affect the rest of their lives. How easy to procrastinate on crucial issues, how easy and how unwise, when only a little effort is needed to enhance the days and years ahead. Now is the time to gather the background material, concepts, and understanding that will enable you to control your own future and your finances.

Over the years, while serving as an officer of a welfare fund, I have had the opportunity to observe individuals approaching retirement. In most cases they are unaware of the basic considerations relating to retirement until the reality is upon them. These people seldom recognize that thinking and planning ahead can make the difference between successful retirement and one marred by faulty decisions. This is true even for those who consider themselves knowledgeable in the field. To plan properly requires knowledge of financial planning, the very heart of successful retirement; in addition, successful planning involves some knowledge of pensions, savings and investments, life insurance, budgeting, taxes and tax shelters. It also requires a knowledge of the basics of Social Security, Medicare and supplemental health insurance to provide coverage for major gaps in protection. Furthermore, individuals should be aware of estate planning, the role of wills and trusts, and some basic legal considerations—including various forms of property ownership and protection of assets in late or second marriages. Retirement housing, work and leisure plans, are equally significant. Finally, retirees and their spouses should also know how to plan realistically to make it easier to cope with life's inevitable losses.

Many books currently on the market attempt to supply necessary information, but a review of these works indicates that many of them fail to grapple with the core of issues. In some the coverage is cursory; others are encyclopedic. Some completely omit important components of a practical retirement plan or are out-of-date. Many provide no index, depriving the reader of a convenient way to locate specific information. To overcome these weaknesses in the available literature, I have sought to cover the major areas in sufficient depth to provide the reader with the clear understanding of the issues. In additionn, technical words and terms are defined in a glossary at the end of each chapter. Most important, *Retiring Right* offers you, the reader, the opportunity to personalize the material through self-study. Many chapters provide self-study sections that will enable you to develop an individual retirement program. Such interaction between book and reader is also provided in Appendix A, which will help you to set up an inventory of personal and financial data, Appendix B will direct you to important resources, and Appendix C (a selected bibliography) to delve more deeply into particular subject-matter areas.

The Tax Reform Act approved by Congress and signed by President Reagan on October 22, 1986 is the most significant change in the philosophy and structure of income taxation since 1913 when the 16th Amendment to the United States Constitution authorized the income tax. The Tax Reform Act of 1986 brought dramatic changes to several key areas of retirement planning, including, among others, the tax liability of older Americans, Individual Retirement Accounts, pension vesting rules, the use of tax shelters, income shifting for the funding of education (Clifford Trusts), and gift giving (the Uniform Gifts to Minors Act). These changes sparked the need for a revised edition of this book.

This edition not only incorporates information regarding changes in the income tax law, but also a new section on retirement havens abroad. The new Federal Employees Retirement System that is effective January 1, 1987, and several new Federal laws enacted in 1986 that affect retirement planning are discussed here as well.

For his assistance in reviewing changes made by the Tax Reform Act of 1986 I thank Paul J. Malagoli, Chartered Financial Consultant (Ch.F.C.) and Chartered Life Underwriter (C.L.U.) of the Equitable Life Assurance Society of the United States, and I also thank Professor Emeritus of Economics Louis Fier of Brooklyn College. For their help in updating Social Security and Medicare data for 1987, I owe a debt of gratitude to the Social Security Administration office in Mineola, New York, in particular to Martin Stein, District Manager, JoAnn Katz, Assistant District Manager, and Richard Berman, Operations Officer. Finally, I thank my editors at Avery Publishing Group, whose team effort expedited publication of this revised edition.

The content of the book has been reviewed by lawyers, accountants, and experts in various fields, to whom I owe a debt of gratitude. Two officers and colleagues of the Professional Staff Congress– City University of New York Welfare Fund, the late Professor Ralph G. Ledley, Chairman of the Fund, and the late Professor Martin K. May, Vice Chairman, encouraged me while this project was in the formative stages. Professor Ledley reviewed the first draft of two chapters: Estate Planning (Ch. 6) and Handling Legal Affairs (Chapter 7); Professor May helped to shape Chapter 4, which deals with savings and investments. Bruce D. Smith, Assistant Vice President of the Teachers Insurance and Annuity Association–College Retirement Equities Fund, made valuable suggestions in his review of the chapters on pensions (Chapter 3) and Medicare (Chapter 9). In addition, Judge Arthur Adler reviewed Chapter 2, Understanding Social Security.

I also owe a debt of gratitude to some of my friends and colleagues at the John Jay College of Criminal Justice of the City University of New York, who kept a candle glowing in the dark hours of this project—President Gerald W. Lynch, Vice President John J. Collins, and Professor Judith Bronfman, Director of Governmental and Community Affairs. Professor of English Shirley Schnitzer completed a thorough editing of the next-to-final draft of the book and Marie Simonetti Rosen, Director of Publications, kept the project moving. I owe a special debt to Professor of Government and Public Administration, Gary D. Helfand, who recognized the merits of this work and steered me in the right direction.

Lawrence J. Kaplan

INTRODUCTION

WHY PLAN FOR RETIREMENT?

If you're under 55, you probably haven't given much thought to retirement. It seems as if getting old is something that happens only to other people. You tell yourself that you'll plan for retirement when the time comes—that there is no need to think about it now. Right?

Wrong! If you want the so-called golden years of your life to be truly golden, you must prepare for them now. The sooner you get started, and the more you investigate and understand your own situation, the better your actual retirement will be. Planning for your retirement will enable you to reach the following goals.

Eliminate Fear and Uncertainty and Achieve a Sense of Security

Many people approach retirement in fear and trepidation. This is quite natural because everyone fears the unknown. By thinking about the future and planning for it, you can reach the retirement stage of your life with the kind of knowledge and financial and emotional preparation that enables you to know what to expect. The unknown becomes known, and the fear and uncertainty of retirement are replaced with a sense of security.

Prepare for the Unexpected

As you move along in life, problems constantly present themselves. Without a plan that looks into the future, each crisis is purely a chance event. If you have planned ahead, in the event of an unexpected problem such as a sudden illness in the family, or a downturn in the economy which affects your savings or investments, you will be better able to cope with the difficulty and make the necessary adjustments.

Gain Flexibility

By starting your planning early, you will give yourself enough lead time to prepare for the things you would like to do when you retire. You will have the time to prepare for a second career, if you want one, or to learn a new hobby or sport for your retirement years. If your choice is incorrect, you will have enough time to modify your plan and try something else.

Make the Right Decisions

If you plan for retirement, you do not have to make hasty, ill-considered decisions. For example, housing plays a large role in shaping your retirement. By investigating numerous housing locations and living arrangements during your pre-retirement years, you will be able to base your ultimate housing decision on a seasoned judgment.

Each of us approaches retirement with different needs, interests, and attitudes. The goal of all of us, however, is successful retirement. That means a sound financial plan, psychological and social stability, and stimulating and satisfying activities that provide us with a sense of accomplishment and a feeling of usefulness.

The purpose of this book is to help you develop a total, individualized retirement plan that will generate maximum satisfaction, security, and fulfillment. To this end, the book features self-study guides in every chapter that will enable you to personalize your retirement plan, applying the concepts or principles discussed in the text. By completing these self-study guides, you will acquire a thorough understanding of yourself. It is only through such an understanding that you can chart a course for becoming a happy retiree.

Chapter 1
First Facts About Retirement and Planning

What is retirement? Retirement may be defined as a withdrawal from one's office, service, or business, bringing with it a lifestyle that is less structured and that offers a great deal of additional free time. If we assume that the life cycle consists of four stages—childhood, the teen years, the mature years, and the retirement years—then the retirement years are the culmination of the working years. This stage of the life cycle can bring an individual to the highest level of development, to the period when he or she harvests and enjoys the fruits of a lifetime of labor. Or it can plunge a person into boredom, restlessness, depression, and even despair.

WHO ARE THE RETIREES?

Our youth-oriented society generates many misconceptions about the 65 and over population, which is usually retired. These myths are so pervasive that many older people themselves accept them as truisms. Popular myths include the following: most older people live in old-age homes, nursing homes, or mental hospitals. As a group they are lonely, socially isolated, bored, and no longer able to enjoy life. If they have jobs, they are unproductive and cannot learn new things. And, in terms of economic status, they are the most poverty-stricken group in the country. Are these allegations true? Not at all, as you will see by the following description of Americans age 65 and over.

Numbers

The total population of the United States was about 233 million in 1980. Based on the Census Bureau's latest projections, it will grow to about 255 million by 1990 and about 275 million by the year 2000. In 1986, the 65 and older population constituted about 12.2 percent of the total, or about 29 million. As the population born in the post-World War II baby boom ages and joins the ranks of the elderly, the 65 and older group may reach 35 million by the year 2000.

Life Expectancy

A baby born in the year 1900 could not anticipate a very long life—only 46 years for males and 48 years for females. As of 1980, however, our life expectancy has risen to 70 years for males and 78 for females, or a lifespan of about 25 years more than that of our great-grandparents.

1

Income

The majority of people 65 or older have incomes well above the official poverty level which a recent Census Bureau report estimates at about $9,300 or less for a family of four. This same Census Bureau report shows that only 15.3 percent of people 65 and older are classified as poor, or living below the poverty line. The percentage would probably be even lower if noncash benefits for the poor, such as food stamps, Medicare, and Medicaid were counted. Nevertheless, elderly Americans living below the poverty level are struggling to feed and house themselves.

The majority of the elderly are living comfortably. Social Security benefits are indexed to keep pace with inflation and are almost tax-free. At the same time, children are grown and on their own, most mortgages are paid off, and work-related expenses no longer tax the budget.

Employment

The labor force was 107 million in 1980 and is projected to grow about 1.3 percent a year, reaching 122 million in 1990. The trend to retire before the age of 65 appears to be slowing down. Federal law states that it is illegal for an employee to be fired, denied a job or a promotion, or demoted because of age, and that protection extends to one's 70th birthday. In 1980 about one-fifth of all elderly men were employed, but about 85 percent indicated that they wanted part-time jobs.

As for the myth that elderly workers are unproductive, studies of the labor force reveal that the elderly perform as well as or better than younger workers even though it has been noted that perception and reaction speed have declined. While it may take an elderly employee a little longer to learn something new, older workers can learn new things as well as young workers.

Housing

Housing surveys show that the elderly live in homes that are older than those occupied by the rest of the population. But that is because they had purchased their homes about 30 or 40 years before retiring. The overwhelming majority of the elderly live in safe, standard housing. At the same time, those below the poverty line are not all living in proper housing. Some live in shabby hotels, broken-down tenements, or, worse yet, on the streets. A significant percentage of the homeless in America are over 65. It has been estimated that 30 to 40 percent of the elderly living in nursing homes are there because they cannot care for themselves and have nowhere else to go.

Physical Health

The health of 80 percent of the 65 or older group is excellent, good, or fair. The Census Bureau reports that less than 5 percent of the elderly live in old-age or nursing homes. Among the healthy elderly, a significant decline in activities and interests occurs only among those who are 85 or older, a population numbering 2.8 million in 1986, or about 9 percent of the elderly. The overwhelming majority of elderly people are well and living normal lives. However, as retired people know, health care becomes a much more important cost item after age 65. It is estimated that health care for the elderly costs three to four times what it costs for other Americans.

Mental Health

Although as many as one-third of the elderly may experience stress or have an occasional bout with depression, the proportion is not substantially different from that of the younger population. The significant fact is that not more than 10 percent suffer from senility. Perhaps another small percentage suffers from defective memory, but about 80 to 85 percent of the elderly enjoy good to excellent mental health.

Social

While almost one-third of the elderly live alone, the majority have friends and relatives and actively participate in various functions sponsored by their religious congregations and other voluntary organizations. They are neither socially isolated nor lonely. Studies show that most older people prefer some degree of separation from their children even if their lifetime ties were always close. They are generally happy, have high morale, and enjoy living.

MAJOR CATEGORIES OF RETIREMENT PLANNING

Retirement planning can be divided into six major categories.

1. **Financial Planning.** Financial planning is concerned with understanding your major sources of retirement income, including Social Security (Chapter 2), pensions (Chapter 3), and savings and investments, life insurance and annuities, and miscellaneous sources of potential income (Chapter 4). Your potential income from these sources becomes the basis for developing a retirement budget. Useful skills in planning a budget are knowing how to calculate your net worth, use credit, cope with inflation, apply tax benefits for older citizens, and use tax shelters (Chapter 5).

2. **Estate Planning and Preparing for the Inevitable.** This area of planning involves the objectives, tools, and steps of estate planning and the role of wills, trusts, and probate. It is also concerned with minimizing estate, inheritance, and gift taxes. Part of the planning process involves arranging a funeral, making a checklist of things to do after a death, and learning how to survive a loss (Chapters 6 and 10).

3. **Legal Affairs.** Some of the legal concerns of retirement planning are the various forms of property ownership, a late or second marriage, bankruptcy, setting up a new business, and how to choose and use a lawyer (Chapter 7).

4. **Physical and Mental Health.** This category entails the maintenance of good health. An important related aspect is interpreting Medicare—how it works and what you need to supplement it. You should also be familiar with other forms of health insurance such as Health Maintenance Organizations and Blue Cross-Blue Shield (Chapter 9). Psychological health involves making adjustments in the transition from work to retirement; problem areas of some retirees, such as alcoholism and drug abuse; mental illness among the elderly; and retirement planning for good mental health.

5. **Housing.** This area entails an assessment of your housing needs: deciding whether to stay where you are or to move elsewhere; considering whether to buy or to rent; evaluating condominiums, cooperatives, mobile homes, and other housing alternatives; and taking into account all the financial aspects of the housing decision (Chapter 8).

6. **The Retirement Lifestyle.** This category deals with work options and challenges at or after retirement, such as a second career, full-or part-time work, volunteer work, and job hunting. It also covers the entire area of leisure planning (Chapter 11).

These six components comprise a total retirement plan.

STEPS IN THE PLANNING PROCESS

The five steps involved in the retirement planning process are presented below.

1. **Analyze the Present.** Analyze your present situation by assembling all the relevant facts and information for each of the major categories of retirement planning. This will give you a starting point from which you can then project into the future.

2. **Expand Your Research Efforts.** Broaden your sources of information. Talk to retirees you know in order to acquire first-hand knowledge of the problems they faced in making the transition to retirement. You may also wish to talk to counselors who are trained to offer guidance and assistance. Another major resource is your library, whose senior citizen collection of books and articles is usually quite extensive.

3. **Set Retirement Goals.** Write down some of the goals you would like to achieve in retirement.

4. **Use this Book as a Self-Study Guide.** Read the book and answer the self-study questions at the end of each section. This will enable you to understand your own needs and interests so that you can personalize your retirement plan.

5. **Update Your Plan Periodically.** Review your plan from time to time and update it as the need arises. Obviously, if your present situation changes, you must make adjustments which reflect these changes.

A TIMETABLE FOR RETIREMENT PLANNING

When should you start to plan for your retirement? Actually, you took your first step in the retirement process when you got your first full-time job: you began your contributions to Social Security, and you joined your employer's pension plan. Thus, you set in motion the accumulation of your nest egg. But during this early period of employment, most people are immersed in job and family responsibilities, and retirement is just too far off in the future to think seriously about it.

So—a realistic time to start the retirement planning process is *at least ten years before* your estimated retirement date. Ten years of lead time will enable you to make corrections and adjustments in the major planning areas. In your financial plan, for example, you can check your annual net worth analysis against your financial goals. If you find your income is inadequate, you have enough time to change jobs, to earn more money in a second job, to save more, or to change your investment portfolio. These options are generally foreclosed to individuals already in their sixties. In addition, by thinking ahead and planning ahead, you may be able to avoid the trauma of *retirement shock*, a psychological condition resulting from being totally unprepared for the new retirement lifestyle.

But all is not lost if you do not start ten years in advance. You can start five years or even one year in advance and still benefit. In fact, the guidelines suggested in this book will be helpful to you even if you are already retired. But remember—an early start gives you more flexibility than a later one.

SELF-STUDY: MY RETIREMENT GOALS

Record your preliminary retirement goals. Of course, all of these are a first approximation and are subject to change as you progress in the retirement planning process. (The list omits financial, estate planning, and legal areas.)

1. Physical and Mental Health

a. *Physical* What is your plan for a program of physical activity: a sport, an exercise program, other physical activity (such as walking, dancing, gardening, etc.)?

_____

_____

_____

b. *Social* How do you plan to make new friends—become more active in political, cultural, or social activities?

_____

_____

_____

c. *Religious*   What is your plan, if any, for becoming active or more active in religious activities?

_____

_____

_____

2. Housing   What is your retirement housing plan—stay where you are or relocate; be an owner or a renter; live in a single-family home, a two-family home, or a multi-family home; a condominium or a cooperative; or in a retirement village?

_____

_____

_____

3. Retirement Lifestyle

a. *Employment*   What is your employment plan after retirement—no work at all; full-time or part-time work; same type of work or a different occupation? What training or retraining, if any, is required?

_____

_____

_____

b. *Leisure*   What is your leisure plan—specific hobbies; travel; volunteer work?

_____

_____

_____

c. *Educational*   What is your plan for continuing education—individual courses of interest or a structured program leading to an undergraduate, graduate, or professional degree?

_____

_____

_____

d. *Cultural* What is your plan for developing a greater interest and involvement in the arts and letters—theaters, concert halls, libraries, or museums?

_____

_____

_____

e. *Artistic* If you have artistic or musical talent, how do you propose to develop these abilities?

_____

_____

_____

MAKING THE RETIREMENT DECISION

Unless you are forced to retire, you reach a time in your working life when you yourself must make the decision to retire or to remain on the job. Aside from a health-related retirement, the most important factor affecting the decision is probably economic, revolving around the question: will my retirement income be sufficient to enable my spouse and myself to live reasonably well? A significant related question is: will my retirement income be adequate five years from now or ten years from now?

Because they are concerned with inflation and general economic uncertainties, some older Americans are putting off their retirement. Others retire and then return to work. A recent Congressional study indicates that 65 is no longer the standard retirement age. The median age for workers to start drawing pensions is 62 with almost 60 percent receiving pensions before age 65. Whether this trend will continue is not presently clear.

Reasons for Retiring

There are many incentives to retire. The anticipation of a reasonably sufficient retirement income is the strongest incentive. Up until the mid-1970s this fact was reflected in the official statistics on the number of people working. Between the early 1950s and mid-1970s the number of men and women aged 65 and over who were still in the work force was reduced by half. Inflation during this period was not a problem, and the economy was enjoying continued prosperity. Related to this are three additional factors which are discussed below.

The Social Security program encourages older workers to retire by providing a pension at age 65 or at ages 62, 63, or 64 with actuarially reduced benefits. Early retirement between the ages of 62 and 64 began for women in 1956 and for men in 1961. The number of people opting for early retirement increased significantly when these changes in the Social Security law were approved.

A second factor encouraging retirement is the knowledge that Social Security benefits will increase as the cost of living increases. Known as the escalator provision, this periodic adjustment in benefits enables Social Security income to keep up with inflation.

A third factor which encourages older workers to leave the job market is the growth of private pensions. Over the last 30 or 40 years, private businesses have initiated a variety of retirement benefit programs for their employees. Most of the beneficiaries find that these private pensions, supplemented by their Social Security, provide a comfortable retirement income.

A variety of other reasons for retirement are worth noting:

- Some retirements are prompted by poor health or by unsatisfactory working conditions.
- Some are mandated by the employer because of age; federal law now designates age 70 as the mandatory retirement age.
- People retire in order to realize and expand their talents more fully; to pursue new interests; to develop new or existing skills; to achieve new knowledge; or to begin a second career.
- Others want to have leisure time to develop closer relationships with their children, with other family members, or with friends.

Reasons for Continuing to Work

For a long time, the retirement age was considered to be 65, but government policy is supporting a change. Under the Federal Age Discrimination in Employment Act, the mandatory retirement age has been raised from 65 to 70. The thinking behind the law is that individual ability to do a job should be the basis for continued employment and most people agree.

The 1979 amendment to the Social Security law offers further encouragement for retiring at a later age. Under this amendment, potential retirees can receive an increase in benefits for each year that they postpone retirement beyond age 65—three percent a year instead of the former one percent.

The inflationary threat is another reason for continuing to work. Many older workers think that their dreams of retirement are unaffordable. They worry about their economic future. Even though Social Security's cost-of-living escalator clause offsets the impact of inflation, most private pensions are not raised automatically as prices rise.

A final reason for remaining at work is that many jobs that used to be strenuous and physically draining are easier to perform now that machines have been developed to perform the tasks. Similarly, boring and repetitive types of work are being eliminated by automated robots on assembly lines. These changes are encouraging older workers to stay on the job.

GLOSSARY

Estate Planning. The process of designing a program for the effective management, enjoyment, and disposition of assets at the least possible tax cost.

Financial Planning. Consists of analyzing your net worth (assets minus liabilities), setting financial goals for the future, and then deciding what you must do to achieve those goals.

Life Cycle. Consists of four stages of growth: childhood, the teen years, the mature years, and the retirement years.

Retirement Planning. A process which involves the projection of individual needs and goals into the future, including a sound financial plan; a plan for management and disposition of assets at death; the legal implications of retirement; a plan for staying physically healthy and making the necessary psychological adjustments; a housing plan; and a plan for work and/or leisure.

Chapter 2
Understanding Social Security

SOCIAL SECURITY BASICS—THE BACKGROUND OF SOCIAL SECURITY

The philosophy of the American government for almost 150 years of its existence was that responsibility for the care of the poor and the aged was a private matter that belonged to the family. State and local communities did help on occasion in cases of dire need. When the Social Security Act was signed into law by President Franklin D. Roosevelt in August 1935, responsibility for the aged was transferred from the individual family to society. This was a giant step forward for the United States, taken long after the industrial nations of Europe had adopted some form of retirement benefits for their citizens. Today, in spite of a recent financial crisis, our Social Security program is an integral part of the American economic system.

The Social Security Amendments of 1983 have expanded coverage so that almost all Americans who work and their dependents and survivors are covered. Federal workers, previously excluded, are now required to join the system if they were hired on or after January 1, 1984. Also included are the President, his cabinet, members of Congress, and Federal judges. In addition, the 1983 amendments require the estimated one million employees of nonprofit organizations such as hospitals and charities to join the system. State and local government workers who previously had the right to drop out of Social Security are now barred from leaving the system once they join it.

The Social Security Act became effective January 1, 1937. Currently about 36 million men, women, and children are receiving $174 billion in annual Social Security benefits which are spelled out in the law, and over 124 million workers are making contributions. The original law provided only for old age retirement benefits. Even before the benefit portion of the program became operative, Congress amended the law in 1939 to provide retirement benefits for a worker's dependents and survivors. The 1939 amendments also provided for payment of monthly benefits in 1940, two years earlier than the original law had specified. In the early 1950s the Social Security law was extended to cover self-employed individuals as well as farmers and domestics. Disability insurance was added in 1956, and Medicare for those 65 or older was added in 1965.

YOUR SOCIAL SECURITY PAYROLL DEDUCTIONS

The benefits paid by Social Security are derived by taxing earnings. For every dollar you pay, your employer contributes an equal amount. If you are self-employed, you pay about twice what the individual employee pays because no one matches this contribution. The amount of money collected by the Social Security system depends on two factors: the tax rate, which is a percentage figure; and the earnings base, which is the maximum amount of earnings that can be taxed. This limit on taxable earnings is called the *maximum taxable amount*, and you pay no taxes on amounts higher than this maximum. Table 2.1 presents *tax rates* and *maximum taxable amounts* for the 1980s. The data for 1986 through 1990 are specified in the Social Security Amendments of 1983.

Table 2.1

Social Security Tax Rates and Maximum Taxable Amounts for the 1980s

Year	Employer and employee tax rate[a]	Self-employed tax rate[a]	Maximum taxable amount
1980	6.13%	8.10%	$25,900
1981	6.65	9.30	29,700
1982	6.70	9.35	32,400
1983	6.70	9.35	35,700
1984	6.70	11.30	37,800
1985	7.05	11.80	39,600
1986	7.15	12.30	42,000
1987	7.15	12.30	43,800
1988	7.51	13.02	b
1989	7.51	13.02	b
1990	7.65	15.30	b

[a]Data for 1986–1990 are from the Social Security Amendments of 1983.

[b] To be determined each year based on increases in average earnings of all employees in the country (whether or not under Social Security).

Although the increases in the tax rates and taxable amounts mean that workers in the higher income brackets will be paying more into Social Security, they will also be able to count on greater benefits later. This is because benefit amounts are based upon earnings credited for Social Security.

The money you pay into Social Security is not specifically held for you until you retire. Almost all of the taxes paid into the system by today's workers are paid out to today's Social Security beneficiaries. So when you retire, your benefits will have to be paid by those working at that time. The system is known as *pay as you go*. This requires that taxes be increased as benefits are increased. One of the reasons for increasing taxes is that the ratio of workers to beneficiaries has declined and is expected to continue to decline. In 1950 the ratio was sixteen workers to one beneficiary. Today, it is about three to one, and by the year 2020 it will be two to one.

When Congress decides to increase the Social Security tax rate or maximum taxable amount, it simply amends the *Federal Insurance Contributions Act* for employees and employers and the *Self-Employment Contributions Act* for the self-employed. The letters

FICA which appear on your paycheck stub stand for the Federal Insurance Contributions Act and identify your Social Security payroll deductions. Social Security taxes are collected by the Internal Revenue Service which transmits them to the United States Treasury.

How to Check Your Earnings Record

To protect your investment in Social Security, it is important for you to check your Social Security earnings and quarters covered as recorded in your personal account. You want to be sure that the government's records are correct. To obtain a free statement of earnings credited to your Social Security record, phone your local Social Security Administration office. To make it easy for you, Figure 2.1 is a reproduction of the Social Security form, "Request for Statement of Earnings." Photocopy it, fill it out, and mail to: Social Security Administration, Wilkes-Barre Data Operations Center, P.O. Box 20, Wilkes-Barre, PA 18703. You will receive an official statement from Social Security listing your earnings credited to your account and your quarters of coverage.

It is important to verify these Social Security records every year or two, because the law sets a time limit of three years, three months and fifteen days after the year in which the wages were paid or the self-employment income was earned for making corrections easily. Mistakes can be corrected after this time limit, but it is more difficult to do so. The importance of accurate Social Security records increases as you get closer to retirement.

How to Qualify for Social Security

To qualify for Social Security you must satisfy three requirements:

1. You must have reached *retirement age.* At any point from age 62 on, you can retire and receive a monthly benefit for life.

2. You must be *fully insured.* Fully insured means that you have met the *quarters of coverage* requirement. A quarter is one-quarter of a year, or three months. The four quarters of coverage in a year are January 1–March 31, April 1–June 30, July 1–September 30, and October 1–December 31. For 1987, you must have earned a minimum of $460 within one of the specified quarters to earn one *quarter of coverage.* To keep pace with inflation, the minimum earnings per quarter are adjusted annually. The exact number of quarters of coverage you need to be fully insured depends upon your age. If you reach 62 in 1987, you need 36 quarters of coverage, as indicated in Table 2.2. If you have ten years of work credit, or 40 quarters, you are fully insured and will never need more. For any type of benefit, you must have a minimum of six quarters, but the benefit would be scaled down. "Fully insured" does not mean that you get the highest monthly benefit. It merely means that you have enough quarters of coverage to be eligible for benefits when you retire, or for your survivors to receive benefits when you die.

Figure 2.1

Request for Statement of Earnings

	FOR SSA USE ONLY	
REQUEST FOR STATEMENT OF EARNINGS (PLEASE PRINT IN INK OR USE TYPEWRITER)	**AX**	●
	SP	●

I REQUEST A SUMMARY STATEMENT OF EARNINGS FROM MY SOCIAL SECURITY RECORD

	Full name you use in work or business			
NH	First	Middle Initial	Last	●

	Social security number shown on your card		Your date of birth			
SN		●	**DB**	Month	Day	Year	**A**

	Other Social Security number(s) you have used		Your Sex	
MA		●	**SX** ☐ Male	☐ Female

	Other name(s) you have used (Include your maiden name)
AK	

Specifications for This Form Were Secured From the Social Security Administration

- - - - - - - - - - - - - *FOLD HERE* - - - - - - - - - - - - - - - - -

PRIVACY STATEMENT

The Social Security Administration (SSA) is authorized to collect information asked on this form under section 205 of the Social Security Act. It is needed so SSA can quickly identify your record and prepare the earnings statement you requested. While you are not required to furnish the information, failure to do so may prevent your request from being processed. The information will be used primarily for issuing your earnings statement.

I am the individual to whom the record pertains. I understand that if I knowingly and willingly request or receive a record about an individual under false pretenses I would be guilty of a Federal crime and could be fined up to $5000.

Sign your name here: (Do not print)	Date
▶	

I AUTHORIZE YOU TO SEND THE STATEMENT TO THE NAME AND ADDRESS BELOW: *(To be completed in all cases)*

	Name of the addressee		
PN			●

	Street number and name		
AD			●

	City and state		Zip Code	
		ZP		

Form **SSA-7004 PC**   OP 1   (9-82) Previous Editions are Obsolete

3. You must file an application, since benefits are *not* paid automatically upon achieving retirement age.

Table 2.2

Work Credit Required for Social Security Retirement Benefits

If you reach age 62 in	You need credit for this much work	
	Years	Quarters
1983–1986	8	32
1987–1990	9	36
1991 or after	10	40

Filing an Application

If you are planning to retire, you should apply approximately three months before the retirement date. The application must be filed at your local Social Security office. Your benefits will become effective as of the month you reach retirement age. Benefits are retroactive only for the twelve months before the date of filing. Therefore, a delay for any reason, even a disabling illness, may cause loss of benefits.

What records will you need? The records you submit to establish your right to benefits should be certified documents bearing the official seal of the agency from which you obtained them. Photocopies are not acceptable. The Social Security representative will return the document to you after making a copy for their records. Documents in foreign languages are acceptable.

The following records are needed for retirement benefits:

- Social Security card, or a record of the number.
- Proof of age. Usually a birth certificate or a baptismal certificate made before the fifth birthday.
- Form W-2. The Form W-2 should show your earnings for the year prior to the year in which you are applying for Social Security retirement benefits. If you are self-employed, bring a copy of your last Federal income tax return.
- Proof of marriage. Your marriage certificate is required if you are applying for benefits as a spouse. A divorced woman needs proof of divorce in addition to proof of marriage.
- For a child: Social Security number; proof of age; if adopted, proof of adoption; if stepchild, marriage certificate of natural parent and stepparent.

COMPREHENSIVE BENEFITS FOR YOU AND YOUR FAMILY

Social Security provides a package of benefits for you and your family that would otherwise be unaffordable. This package includes retirement benefits, disability benefits, and survivors' benefits. Supplemental Security Income, a fourth program, is payable to the blind, disabled, and people aged 65 or older whose principal sources of income are insufficient to provide a minimum standard of living. Medicare, a fifth program, provides hospitalization and medical expense benefits upon reaching age 65. (Discussed in Chapter 9.)

Retirement Benefits

Retirement benefits are available for you, your spouse, your children, and your parents.

For You. The earliest age at which you can receive Social Security benefits is 62. But if you retire at age 62, you will have to settle for only 80 percent of your full benefits, known as your *primary insurance amount.* The primary insurance amount is the largest benefit a worker can receive upon retiring at age 65. If you retire at age 63, you will get 85 percent of your primary insurance amount, and at age 64, 93 percent. If you retire at age 65 or later, you will get 100 percent of your primary insurance amount. It is important to keep in mind that the lower percentage you receive if you retire between 62 and 65 is the percentage you will continue to receive forever after. If you stop working altogether before age 62, or stop working before 62 and subsequently rejoin the work force, you will not forfeit your ultimate right to retirement benefits. However, you will still have to wait until at least age 62 to collect benefits. Furthermore, your benefits would be reduced because your Social Security contributions would have been lower.

For Your Spouse. If a spouse has not worked at all and therefore is not entitled to his or her own Social Security benefits, then the spouse at age 62 would get 37.5 percent of the worker's primary insurance amount; at age 65, the spouse would get 50 percent of the worker's primary insurance amount. If a spouse has worked to some extent, but his or her earnings entitle him or her to less than 50 percent of the worker's benefit, the spouse would nevertheless receive 50 percent. If the spouse has worked sufficiently to be entitled to a benefit greater than 50 percent of the worker's benefit, then the spouse would collect a benefit equivalent to his or her own earnings. In other words, when a husband and wife have both worked and paid Social Security taxes, each is entitled to his or her own full benefits based upon earnings and years of service.

For Your Children. Each dependent child and grandchild is entitled to receive 50 percent of the retired worker's primary insurance amount. A dependent child is one who is under 18 years of age, who is a full-time student between 18 and 22, or a child of any age if under a disability which began before age 22.

For Your Parents. A dependent parent who is at least 62 is entitled to receive 50 percent of the retired worker's primary insurance amount.

Disability Benefits

You can plan for retirement and even ultimately death, but you are unable to plan for sudden catastrophe—an illness or injury which might immobilize you for several months or many years. When total disability occurs, the economic impact on the individual and family members is generally severe. As protection against such risk, disability insurance is probably the most important form of Social Security coverage.

With this type of insurance, you and your family are assured of a monthly income if you should be disabled for an extended period. Social Security computes these benefits as if you had retired in the year the disability began. The program provides major protection against potential financial disaster.

Disability benefits were added to the Social Security Act in 1956, and in the years since then Congress has substantially liberalized these provisions of the law. Today, the U.S. government through the Social Security system provides a non-cancelable disability policy to almost all its citizens. Such a policy purchased from a private insurance company would be prohibitive in cost except to very wealthy individuals.

Disability Defined

An individual is considered to be under a disability if the following conditions prevail:

1. You are unable to do *any substantial gainful work* anywhere in the national economy because of a physical or mental impairment.

2. The physical or mental condition is expected to last, or has lasted, for at least 12 months, or is expected to result in death.

Therefore, if you are disabled and cannot engage in your usual work, or any other work, you and your dependents are eligible for disability benefits at any age.

Disability Benefit Amounts

The amount of your monthly disability payment is the same amount you would receive at retirement. The disability insurance benefit, therefore, is equal to your average covered monthly earnings over a period of years determined by your birthdate. It is calculated just as your retirement benefit would be calculated.

For disabled widows, disabled surviving divorced wives, and disabled widowers between 50 and 62, reduced benefits ranging from 50 percent to 82.9 percent of the deceased spouse's full benefit, may be paid if the disability prevents any *gainful work*. Widows and widowers would be found disabled if they satisfy the requirements of an impairment listed in the *Listing of Impairments* available in any Social Security office.

Total family benefits for disabled workers who first became entitled to disability benefits after June 1980 are limited to the lower of either of the following: (1) 85 percent of the worker's average indexed earnings before becoming disabled; or (2) 150 percent of the worker's disability benefits.

No benefits can be paid for the first five months of disability. This is the required waiting period. The first payment, therefore, is for the sixth full month of disability.

If you become disabled, contact your local Social Security office.

Qualifications for a Disability Benefit

To qualify for a disability benefit you must have earned 20 quarters (five years) of coverage sometime during the ten years before you were disabled. If you become disabled before age 31, you will need only half the quarters between the time you are 21 and the time you are disabled, with a minimum of six quarters.

To collect benefits, you must file an application and include proof of disability; you must be willing to accept vocational rehabilitation when required.

Survivors' Benefits

When you die, regardless of your age at death, those who will qualify for your benefits include: your spouse at age 65, or as early as age 60 if reduced benefits are taken; your unmarried children under age 18, or 22 if students; and your dependent parents age 62 or older.

For Your Spouse. If you should die, your surviving dependent widow, widower, or divorced spouse can begin to collect a benefit at age 60. The benefits range from 71.5 percent of the deceased worker's primary insurance amount when the survivor is age 60, to 100 percent when the survivor is age 65. A surviving dependent divorced spouse must have been married to the worker for a minimum of ten years in order to qualify for benefits, and if remarried, is not entitled to any benefits. There is no reduction in benefits paid to widows or widowers over 60 who remarry. If the widow or widower would get a larger benefit based upon the new spouse's earnings record, the larger amount would be paid.

For Your Children. Your unmarried children or grandchildren who would ordinarily qualify for the 50 percent benefit when you retire would each get benefit amounts equal to 75 percent of your primary insurance amount if you should die.

For Your Parents. If you leave two dependent parents, both over 62, *each* can collect 75 percent of your primary insurance amount. If only one is alive and over 62, he or she gets 82.5 percent.

Lump-sum Death Payment. If a worker dies, up to $255 is paid to the person who is the widow or widower of the deceased and has been living in the same household with the deceased at the time of death.

Are My Survivors Eligible for Benefits If I Am Not Fully Insured? Yes. Your family may be eligible for benefits even if you are not fully insured when you die. You may be *currently insured,* which means that you earned six quarters of Social Security credit in the three years before your death. If you are currently insured, your surviving children get benefits if they are (1) under 18; (2) any age, if disabled before 22; or (3) full-time students from 18 through the quarter or semester they become 22. Your widow, widower, or divorced wife can also collect if caring for children who are under 18 or disabled before 22.

Supplemental Security Income

Supplemental Security Income (SSI), a new federal program, became effective January 1, 1974, to "assure a basic level of cash income to the aged, blind, and disabled under conditions that promote self-respect and dignity." The program is designed for people in financial need and provides eligible individuals with monthly payments from the Federal government. Even though the Social Security Administration runs the program, SSI is not the same as Social Security. The two main differences are as follows. Although SSI is administered by the Social Security Administration, which runs Social Security benefit programs, SSI is financed from general funds of the U.S. Treasury rather than from the contributions of workers, employers, and self-employed people. Secondly, SSI limits the value of the assets and income you are permitted to have and still be eligible for payments, while Social Security imposes no limits on the amount of money or property you can have to receive Social Security payments. However, you can receive both Social Security and SSI if you satisfy the eligibility requirements of each.

SSI payments are made monthly by the Federal government. The gold-colored checks are sent out during the first week of each month, and the millions of people who receive them call them *gold checks.*

How SSI Works

If you apply for SSI, you will be asked two questions. First, what is the value of your assets? These include the things you own such as property, savings accounts, stocks, bonds, jewelry, and other valuables. You will also be asked what your income is. The program sets limits on the value of your assets. A dollar limit is placed on each asset you own, but assets that are basic necessities of life are not counted. A home, for example, does not count as an asset, and the government does not ask for a lien on it. A car is not counted at all if it is used for transportation to a job or to a place for regular treatment of a specific medical problem.

You can also have some income and still be eligible for SSI. A maximum is set on the amount of income you may earn in a month. An evaluation of your monthly income includes money you may be receiving from Social Security, Veterans Administration, workers' compensation, pensions, annuities, gifts, and other income.

For the year 1987 a single person can own assets of up to $1,800 and still be eligible for SSI. A couple can own assets of up to $2,700 and still be eligible. Your personal effects or household goods do not count as assets if their total equity value is $2,000 or less. If the total equity value exceeds $2,000, the excess counts. The equity value is what you can sell the item for, less the amount of any legal debt against it. If you own one car, only the portion of the current market value which exceeds $4,500 may be counted as an asset.

How Much SSI Pays

Maxiumum monthly payments vary depending upon whether the recipient is an individual or a couple and whether the recipient is living alone or with others. In 1986 payments of up to $336 a month could be made to an individual and up to $504 to a couple. The monthly check may be lower than the maximum if the recipient has other income. Special payment rates have been established for blind and physically and/or mentally disabled persons. The specific amounts can be obtained from your Social Security office. The amount of the SSI check varies from state to state because each state contributes a different amount to the benefit provided by the Federal government.

OTHER ASPECTS OF SOCIAL SECURITY

As the time to collect Social Security retirement benefits draws near, the same relevant questions are frequently asked by the prospective recipients: whether to retire at 62 or wait until 65; and whether it is necessary to stop working in order to receive Social Security benefits. In addition, beneficiaries are curious about the method for calculating retirement benefits; cost-of-living adjustments (COLAs); and the tax and legal status of benefits. Explanations of these aspects of Social Security follow.

Should You Retire at 62 or Wait Until 65?

Earlier in this chapter, it was described how your benefit is reduced if you retire at age 62. It is important to carefully consider the advantages and disadvantages of working until you are 65 or taking a lower benefit at 62. At 65 you will receive your full basic benefit, while at 62 you will receive only 80 percent of your benefit. The decision, however, should not be based on 80 percent versus 100 percent because your basic benefit will be higher if you continue working until 65.

First, you can credit more earnings toward Social Security than was possible years ago. The most that could be credited twenty years ago was $4,800. Even though that amount can now be indexed, by waiting until 65 you will have even more high-credit years on your record, that is, years in which you earned a higher salary and contributed more to Social Security. This would boost your average earnings and thus your basic benefit.

Second, no matter how long you work, a fixed number of years is used to calculate your average earnings. That number is based on your year of birth. (See Table 2.3.) If, for example, you were 62 in 1987, the number of years used is thirty-one and your basic benefit would depend upon your thirty highest earning years whether you retire now or continue to work until 65 or even 70. However, by waiting until 65 rather than retiring at 62, three more low-earning years can be omitted from your benefit computation.

Table 2.3

Years of Earnings Used to Compute Your Retirement Benefit Under Social Security

Year you were born	Year you reach 62	Years needed
1917	1979	23
1918	1980	24
1919	1981	25
1920	1982	26
1921	1983	27
1922	1984	28
1923	1985	29
1924	1986	30
1925	1987	31
1926	1988	32
1927	1989	33
1928	1990	34
1929 or later	1991 or later	35*

*Maximum number of years that count

On the other hand, the principal advantage of retiring at 62 on a reduced benefit is that you will have collected several thousand dollars over the three-year period, and so you would be ahead. By deferring retirement until 65, it will take you a number of years—known as the break-even point—to catch up to the total benefits already received. By postponing retirement to 65 or 70, you are taking a gamble on your life expectancy. There is no easy answer for this decision.

Some people prefer the financial and psychological benefits of working full-time as long as possible. To this group, retirement is not too appealing. If you find yourself in this group, you will also find that Social Security offers you several incentives to remain on the payroll. First, your eventual benefit will be higher. Second, if you work until 70, you will receive full benefits regardless of how much you earn. And, third, if you work beyond age 65, you will be entitled to a special bonus for each year of work performed. This bonus, known as the *delayed retirement credit*, increases your benefits by 3 percent for each year between the ages of 65 and 70 in which you do not get benefits, or ¼ of 1 percent for each such month. For example, if you continue to work to 70, your benefits will be increased 15 percent.

Must a Recipient of Social Security Retirement Benefits Stop Working?

No. Retirees 65 through 69 years old could earn $8,160 in 1987 without losing any of their Social Security benefits. If you were under 65 in 1987, you could earn up to $6,000. Recipients of benefits lose $1 of Social Security benefits for every $2 of income they earn in any year in excess of the annual earnings limits, even if they actually work only one month. For example, if you are 67 years old and earn $10,000, you are $1,840 in excess, which is $10,000 minus the $8,160 allowed. You must pay $920 (one-half $1,840) to Social Security in a lump sum or in three installments, whichever method of payment you choose. The Social Security Amendments of 1983 liberalized the earnings test starting in 1990, stretching the penalty of $1 for every $3 earned above the base.

When an individual becomes 65, he or she qualifies for the higher maximum permitted earnings. The difference between the ceilings for those under 65 and those 65 through 69 is aimed at discouraging early retirement, particularly for those between 62 and 65.

The reduction of benefits because of excess earnings does not apply after a worker reaches age 70. This exemption takes effect in the month that the individual becomes 70 years of age.

The earnings limits for recipients of Social Security benefits are raised each January to reflect the rate of inflation.

Method for Calculating Retirement Benefits

A new method for calculating Social Security retirement benefits, spelled out in the 1977 amendments to the Social Security law, became available for public use on January 1, 1979. Individuals retiring between 1979 and 1983 used the old method or the new method, whichever yielded a higher benefit, but starting January 1, 1984, only the new method is used.

Under the new method, benefits are based on indexed earnings which reflect the impact of inflation and the current higher levels of living, as compared with the 1950s and 1960s when average annual earnings ranged from $2,800 to about $6,000. For example, if a worker's actual earnings for 1956 were $3,000, this amount would be adjusted by means of a formula to about $8,000 or $9,000, a more realistic figure. These adjusted earnings are averaged together and another formula is applied to the average to obtain the benefit rate. All of these computations are handled by computer.

This method is intended to insure that benefits will reflect changes in wage levels over your working lifetime. This is important because average wages in our economy can change greatly over a 30- or 40-year period. Using this method of computation, if you reached age 65 in 1987, your monthly retirement benefit could be as much as $789.

Cost-of-Living Adjustments (COLAs)

Whenever you retire, your main concern will be protecting your retirement income against inflation. Fortunately, some protection is built into Social Security payments in that they will rise each year on a scale which is tied to increases in the cost-of-living. The U.S. Congress approved these automatic increases in Social Security benefits starting in 1975 using the U.S. Consumer Price Index as the guideline. The adjustment is made once a year.

In the past, this cost-of-living adjustment was made effective July 1, and the dollar increase was included in the July benefit check. The Social Security Amendments of 1983 postponed the payment of cost-of-living increases for six months, from July 1983 to January 1984. January is now the permanent date for COLA increases in each year starting January 1984. As a result of this change, the Social Security system will save an estimated $39.4 billion dollars through 1989.

The 1983 Amendments include a fail-safe provision designed to protect the system against periods of high inflation. This stabilizer will become effective for the years 1985 through 1988 if reserves in the old-age and disability trust funds ever fall below 15 percent of the money needed to provide payments for a year. If that occurs, automatic COLA increases will be based either on the rise in the Consumer Price Index or the average gain in wages, whichever is lower. In 1989, the stabilizer percentage will rise from 15 to 20 percent.

It is comforting for benefit recipients and potential retirees to know that the financial structure of the Social Security system is now sound, and also, that benefit payments will continue to rise as living costs increase.

Tax and Legal Status of Benefits

In the past, Social Security benefits payable under the old-age, survivors, and disability programs were exempt from Federal income taxes and usually from state and local income taxes. For the first time since benefits were paid in 1940, some recipients will be required to pay an income tax on their Social Security benefits. Starting with income earned in 1984, the 1985 Federal income tax was levied against part of the Social Security benefits received by retirees whose gross income, including half their Social Security benefits, exceeds $25,000 for single taxpayers or $32,000 for married taxpayers filing jointly. In calculating gross income, Social Security recipients must also include income from tax-exempt municipal bonds.

As for the legal status of benefits, they are not subject to garnishment or attachment, except for delinquent Federal taxes, child support, or alimony payments.

IMPORTANT TIPS

You should do several things to assure that you receive all the benefits to which you are entitled. The steps to take are explained below.

1. **Estimating Benefits.** In retirement planning, it is important to estimate your expected Social Security retirement allowance in advance. Therefore, as you approach your retirement date, you should visit or write to your local Social Security office to have their experienced staff make the final and exact calculations for you.

2. **Applying for Benefits.** Under Social Security law, you will not receive your benefits automatically. You must apply, and should take this initiative within the three-month period before the month in which you reach retirement age. Your benefits will become effective as of the month you reach retirement age.

3. **Proofs You Need to Receive Your Benefits.** The documents required to apply for Social Security benefits include Form W-2 Wage and Tax Statement for the previous year, your Social Security card or number, birth certificate or baptismal certificate to prove your age, marriage certificate if you are applying as a spouse, and children's birth certificates if you are applying for them.

4. **Informing Other Family Members.** Inform your spouse and children of the Social Security benefits for which they may be eligible under various conditions. If anything happens to you, it is important that they are made aware of the Social Security benefits to which they may be entitled. Be certain also that your family members know where your proofs and documents are located.

5. **Maximum Benefits.** If you retire at age 65, you will receive 100 percent of your *average monthly covered earnings.* If you retire at 62, you will receive only 80 percent of this amount. In general, therefore, it is advisable to retire at 65, if possible. Present law provides that persons who delay retirement beyond age 65 receive a delayed retirement credit of 3 percent per year (or ¼ of 1 percent for each month) in additional benefits. The 1983 amendments boost this by one quarter of a percentage point each year beginning in 1990, until it reaches 8 percent in 2009.

6. **Statement of Earnings.** Periodically, mail a "Request for Statement of Earnings," including a request for quarters of coverage, to:
   Social Security Administration
   Wilkes-Barre Data Operations Center
   P.O. Box 20
   Wilkes-Barre, PA 18703
   If you do not choose to use the form reproduced in Figure 2.1 in this chapter, you can obtain this information by writing a letter stating your Social Security number, date of birth, name, and full address.

7. **Compare Statement with W-2 Forms.** When you receive your "Summary Statement of Earnings" from Social Security, check the annual figures shown against your W-2 forms or other earnings records to be sure they are accurate.

GLOSSARY

Average Indexed Monthly Earnings (AIME). Social Security benefits are based on indexed earnings, which reflect the impact of inflation and higher earnings levels at present as compared with the 1950s and 1960s, when average earnings ranged from $2,800 to $6,000. For example, if a worker's earnings in 1956 were $3,000, this amount would be adjusted to about $9,000. These adjusted earnings are averaged to obtain a benefit rate that is more in line with today's earnings. This method is used for all people retiring on or after January 1, 1984.

Cost of Living Adjustments (COLA). An annual increase in Social Security benefits designed to protect retirement income against the inroads of inflation. The Social Security Amendments of 1983 established January as the month for the annual COLA increase.

Death Benefit. When an individual dies, whether working or retired, Social Security pays a one-time, lump-sum death benefit of $255 to a surviving spouse of the deceased living in the same household. If there is no spouse, children may be eligible.

Disability. Applies when you are so severely physically or mentally disabled that you are unable to do *any substantial gainful work,* and when the condition is expected to last at least 12 months or is expected to result in death. You and your dependents are eligible for benefits at any age if you become disabled.

Disability Insurance. A Social Security benefit which protects you, your spouse, and your children during your working years by providing benefits if you are unable to work for an extended period of time because of an illness or other disability. The amount of your disability benefit is your *primary insurance amount* at the time you become disabled. There is no reduction in your primary insurance amount if you start receiving the benefit before age 65.

Early Retirement. Retirement before age 65. You can retire as early as age 62 if you are *fully insured.* If you retire at 62 you will receive 80 percent of your *primary insurance amount,* losing 5/9 of one percent for each month that you receive your benefit before age 65. This reduction is permanent, and does not increase to the full primary insurance amount at the normal retirement age. At age 65 you are entitled to 100 percent of your primary insurance amount.

Earnings Limitation for Employees (Retirement Test). If you continue to work after your Social Security benefits start, you are subject to the *earnings limitation,* under which your benefits are reduced by $1 for every $2 you earn over the earnings limitation. No earnings limitation applies when you reach the age of 70.

Federal Insurance Contributions Act (FICA). This is the Federal law that sets the *tax rate* and the *maximum taxable amount*. To increase Social Security taxes Congress merely amends this law.

Fully Insured. This means that you have met the *quarters of coverage* requirement. The exact number of quarters of coverage you need to be *fully insured* depends on your age. If you have ten years of work credit, or forty quarters, you are fully insured and will never need more. (Fully insured does not mean that you get the highest monthly benefit. It means that you are eligible for benefits when you retire, or that your survivors can get benefits when you die.)

Gold Checks. Monthly payments to beneficiaries of the Supplemental Security Income program. The checks are gold-colored, and the recipients, who are needy people with limited income, refer to them as gold checks.

Hospital Insurance (HI). One of the two separate programs in the Social Security structure. The other is the Old-Age, Survivors, and Disability Insurance program. Each program sets an individual tax. The two taxes are added together and collected as one amount whether you are an employee or self-employed. The Hospital Insurance program pays for hospitalization, which is Part A of Medicare. When you become eligible for this benefit, you no longer pay the tax unless you are still working.

Indexing. The current method for figuring Social Security retirement benefits. Actual earnings for past years are adjusted or indexed to account for changes in average wages since the year the earnings were received. These adjusted earnings are averaged together and the benefit rate is calculated from this average.

Late Retirement. If you reach 65 between 1982 and 1989, but continue to work, thus delaying the start of your benefit, you receive a bonus, or *delayed retirement credit*, which increases your benefit 3 percent for each year you work. If you continue to work to 70, your benefit will be increased 15 percent (5 years x 3 percent a year).

Maximum Family Benefit. There is a limit on the total amount of benefits that all members of one family may receive based on the earnings record of one worker. This limit varies with the *primary insurance amount*.

Maximum Taxable Amount. The limit on your earnings that are taxed each year. You do not pay any taxes on earnings over the *maximum taxable amount*.

Medicare Aid. An extension of Medicare coverage to people under 65 who have been entitled to Social Security disability payments for twenty-four consecutive months or more, and to people requiring kidney transplants or dialysis treatment.

Old-Age, Survivors, and Disability Insurance (OASDI). One of two separate programs in the Social Security structure. The other is the Hospital Insurance program. Each program sets a tax. The two taxes are added together and collected as one amount whether you are an employee or self-employed. The OASDI tax pays for monthly benefits to entitled beneficiaries.

Pay-As-You-Go. Almost all of the taxes paid into the Social Security system by today's workers are paid out to today's Social Security beneficiaries. This requires that taxes be increased as benefits are increased.

Primary Insurance Amount (PIA). The largest benefit a worker can receive upon retiring at age 65. All Social Security benefits are based on the *primary insurance amount.* Beginning in the year 2003, the age at which full benefits are payable will slowly rise from 65 to 67 in 2027.

Quarters of Coverage (QC). A minimum number of calendar *quarters of coverage* is required in order to be *fully insured,* that is, eligible for the various types of Social Security benefits.

Replacement Ratio. The percentage of your pay that is replaced by your Social Security retirement benefit.

Retirement Insurance. A Social Security benefit which enables you to retire at age 62 or over, and to receive a monthly benefit for life.

Self-Employment Contributions Act. The Federal law that sets the *tax rate* and the *maximum taxable amount* for the self-employed. An amendment to this law can change the tax rate and/or the maximum taxable amount.

Social Security Program. A Federal program established in 1935 to provide retirement, survivors', disability, and medical benefits through a payroll tax paid both by employers and employees.

Students' Benefits. A Social Security program which provides monthly payments to full-time students between ages 18 and 22 because of the death, disability, or retirement of a parent, or in some cases, a grandparent who worked long enough under Social Security.

Supplemental Security Income (SSI). A separate Social Security program that provides a basic cash income for people in financial need who are 65 or older, and for the needy of any age who are blind or disabled.

Survivors' Insurance. A Social Security benefit which is a form of life insurance that provides income to your dependent spouse, your dependent children, and your dependent parents (if they are 62 and over) in the event of your death.

Tax Rate. The percent of your earnings which are paid by you and your employer each year into the Social Security program. A self-employed individual pays a higher rate. Tax rates are set by Congress.

Widowers' Benefits. A Social Security program which provides monthly benefits to a father if his wife died while insured under Social Security, and if he has not remarried and cares for an unmarried child under 18, or an older child who was disabled before age 22.

Chapter 3
Checking Your Pension Benefits

Analysts in income security for the elderly refer to a three-tier system. The Social Security system is the most important and covers the greatest number of people. It is therefore the first tier (Chapter 2). The second tier consists of pensions, both private employer pension plans and public pension plans for career government employees. The third tier consists of a variety of income sources such as income from investments and private savings (principally home ownership) which in combination supplement Social Security and pensions. Individuals or couples who can count upon adequate income from these three tiers are indeed fortunate and can look forward to a secure retirement.

TYPES OF PENSION PLANS

Private employer pensions, subsidized and regulated by the government, are usually an automatic accompaniment of working in a particular job. The Federal government regulates private pension plans by granting favorable tax treatment to plans which meet certain standards. Approved plans are government subsidized to the extent of about $10 billion a year, representing the amount of taxes the companies would have paid if the tax exemptions were not provided.

The plans set up by self-employed people, known as Keogh plans, and Individual Retirement Accounts (IRA) for individuals who wish to accumulate retirement savings, are voluntary plans. Under Keogh and IRA plans, the individual decides if he wants to set up such a plan, how much to put into it (within statutory limits), and how the funds should be invested (again within statutory limits). Because these plans are subsidized by the government through tax deferment, there are penalties on the withdrawal of funds before retirement age.

Today, probably 90 percent of all government employees, including Federal, state, and local, both military and nonmilitary, are covered under some form of career public pension plan. Some of these employees are also covered by Social Security. Perhaps 40 percent of the people over 65 will eventually get some retirement income from private employer pensions. Career government plans will pay benefits to about 10 percent of people over 65, and an additional small percentage, mostly higher-income people, will get significant retirement income from Keogh plans and IRAs. In combination, these provide an important supplementation to Social Security. This chapter analyzes private and public pension plans.

PRIVATE PENSION PLANS: GROUP

The development of private pension plans in industry reveals that growth was slow and often controversial. A major expansion of private plans occurred after World War II, particularly for workers in organized industries. Currently, about 50 million people, about half of all non-governmental employees in the United States, are covered by private pension systems. Because of abuses that became prevalent in the 1960s and 1970s, Congress passed the Employee Retirement Income Security Act, known as ERISA, in 1974 to provide some protection for private pension plan members. A Supreme Court decision in 1983 outlawed sex discrimination in pension plans, and in 1984 Congress passed the Retirement Equity Act to make it easier for women to participate in pension plans and to receive retirement benefits. A discussion of these developments as well as the basic features of private pension plans follows.

Background

Private industry in the United States in the nineteenth and early twentieth centuries was not too concerned about the provision of income for the old age of their employees. However, a few early private pension plans date back to the turn of the century. These include the Railway Express Agency, originally American Express Agency, in 1875; Consolidated Edison Company of New York, then Consolidated Gas Company of New York, in 1892; Carnegie Steel in 1901; and Standard Oil Company of New Jersey in 1903.

A growth period occurred between 1900 and 1920 when pension plans were established by the major railroads, utility companies, banks, mining companies, petroleum companies, and to some extent manufacturing firms. But even by 1920 fewer than 10 percent of the employees in nonagricultural employment were employed in establishments with pension plans. Of this 10 percent, very few individuals were actually eligible for coverage since many of these early plans were designed primarily for office employees and executives rather than for the so-called blue collar workers.

Before the Social Security Act of 1935, not many employers thought they had an obligation to do more than pay wages for work performed. Their philosophy was simply that they were buying work, and that they could not be good businessmen and also be held responsible for what happened to their workers in retirement. Organized labor tried to establish pension plans tied to unions but were unsuccessful. In fact, until the mid-1940s some unions actually opposed the establishment of private pension plans by employers. They thought of such plans as binding the worker to the industry and employer rather than to the union.

After World War II, circa 1945, there was a major expansion of private plans, particularly for workers in organized industries. By 1955 over 14 million workers were covered. The unions in this period supported the establishment of pension plans in industry to supplement the meager retirement allowances (averaging $25 a month) being paid by Social Security. Moreover, with wage and price controls in effect during World War II and for a time thereafter, pensions were one of the few things that unions could fight for to improve the living standards of their members. Industry discovered that a good pension plan would attract and hold employees. Currently, about 50 million people, or approximately half of all non-governmental wage and salaried workers in the United States, are covered by private pension systems.

In the 1960s and early 1970s many workers discovered to their dismay that their expectations for the receipt of benefits did not materialize. The rules were stacked in favor of the employer, and minor deviations such as a break-in-service or changing jobs nullified a member's right to a pension. Abuses were so prevalent that Congress took action in 1974 to provide some protection for pension plan members by passing the Employee Retirement Income Security Act, better known as ERISA.

The Employee Retirement Income Security Act of 1974 (ERISA)

This pension reform act, approved by the Federal government in 1974, established rules regarding eligibility for pensions, funding, and day-to-day operations which affect thousands of employers and millions of employees. As the name of the law implies, the primary goal of ERISA is to increase the probability that employees who are covered by a retirement plan during much of their working careers will in fact receive benefits upon retirement. ERISA covers nearly all pension and retirement plans created by private employers engaged in interstate commerce. Its provisions do *not* apply to plans sponsored by governments, charitable organizations, or firms exclusively involved in intrastate commerce. The law regulates only plans that are in existence. It does not require firms to initiate retirement plans for their workers, but existing plans must meet certain standards. Moreover, ERISA does not force companies to pay any minimum amounts to employees other than those specified in the plan.

ERISA was intended to put private pension programs on a secure financial footing and to assure millions of workers that they could depend on receiving retirement payments. It prescribes minimum standards with which covered plans must comply. Among the major items covered in the law are the following: vesting, benefits, financing, funding, survivors' benefits, and disclosure to participants. ERISA also established the Pension Benefit Guarantee Corporation (PBGC), which guarantees benefits to plan members even when a plan's assets are insufficient to fulfill its commitments. The framers of the ERISA law also provided for employees of companies which do not have pension plans. Such persons can set up their own retirement systems, called *individual retirement accounts* (known as IRA) that offer substantial tax benefits to encourage saving for retirement. A 1981 law expanded the concept of IRA to permit individuals who are already covered by a private or a public pension to set up an individual retirement account.

The Retirement Equity Act of 1984

The proponents of this law argued that women have been hurt economically by provisions of the ERISA law of 1974, which they say benefited men but not women. The Retirement Equity Act of 1984 has made it easier for women to participate in private pension plans and to receive retirement benefits, either their husbands' or their own.

Under this legislation, a spouse has to give written permission before an employee can choose a retirement plan that would stop pension payments upon the employee's death instead of continuing the payments to the surviving spouse. Under the 1974 law, an employee did not need a spouse's permission to waive payment of those benefits. Usually, payments to the employee will be slightly greater if payments to a surviving spouse are waived.

Another provision of the law requires payment of benefits to the spouse of a worker who was fully vested or had become eligible for the plan after working for a certain number of years, even if the worker died before the early retirement age of 55. The 1974 law required that employees be vested in a pension plan after ten years on the job.

In an effort to adjust private pension plans for women who enter the work force relatively early and interrupt their careers to have children, the new law lowers from 25 to 21 the age at which workers must be allowed to participate in such plans.

The 1984 law also requires that when pension plans calculate how long an employee has worked to be eligible for a pension at retirement, the pension plans must count years of service from the time the employee turns 18. Under the 1974 law, the age used for that calculation was 22.

The 1984 law also allows employees who have worked fewer than five years to stop working for five years without losing pension credit for earlier service, and it bars pension plans from counting a one-year maternity or paternity leave as a break in service.

In a divorce case, the new law authorizes a court to award a person part of a former spouse's pension as part of the settlement if the person has not remarried.

The new law will provide a more secure old age for thousands of American women who now are deprived of pension benefits by loopholes which do not recognize their contribution both inside and outside the home. In pension matters of the private sector, the new law is a major step toward true economic equity for women.

Equal Pensions for Men and Women

On July 6, 1983 the Justices of the U.S. Supreme Court issued a 5–to–4 decision, *Arizona Governing Committee v. Norris*, outlawing sex discrimination in pension plans. Up to mid-1983, retirement annuities paid men and women different amounts. This payment schedule was based on the fact that on the average, women live nearly eight years longer than men. Therefore, pension plan administrators reasoned that women should get smaller payments spread out over a longer period. The Supreme Court ruling requires that future pension checks of several million women be increased and that the checks for a larger number of men be reduced. Because the decision is based on employment-bias law, it affects only company pension plans and not those offered by insurance companies on the open market. The immediate impact will be on *defined contribution plans* in which employees or employers pay into retirement accounts.

Administrators of private pension plans will have to make the changes required by the Supreme Court in an estimated 450,000 pension plans. They have two choices: either to increase women's benefits to men's levels, or to set a new, equal figure between the two. The first approach would cost employers millions of dollars, while the second approach would cost employers less money but may encourage men, whose benefits would be cut, to withdraw from company-sponsored pension plans and to purchase annuities from insurance companies. With fewer men in company plans, the remaining men would have to bear a higher proportion of annuity costs, which may drive more men out.

The ruling applies to contributions paid into retirement plans after August 1, 1983, and is not retroactive. It also does not affect persons already retired and those whose pension plan contributions are complete by August 1, 1983.

Another impact of the decision may be that employers, fearful of sex-bias charges, will stop offering annuities for retirement and instead offer lump-sum payments at retirement.

The Supreme Court decision that retirement annuities must be equal for men and women will affect more than 10 million workers.

Age Discrimination in Employee Pension Plans

On October 21, 1986, President Reagan signed the Omnibus Budget Reconciliation Act of 1986 (OBRA), which addresses the issue of continuing retirement plan contributions after normal retirement age. OBRA amends the 1974 Employee Retirement Income Security Act (ERISA) and the Internal Revenue Code (IRC) to prohibit discrimination on the basis of age in employee pension benefit plans. The OBRA amendments require employers to continue pension plan benefit accruals and contributions after the normal retirement age. The OBRA amendments also prohibit pension plans from excluding eligible employees from participation if they were hired at or after the plan's normal retirement age. All OBRA requirements are generally effective for plan years beginning on or after January 1, 1988.

Basic Features of Group Pension Plans

The following information will help you to understand the crucial elements of your group pension plan. Essentially, there are two types of plans: the defined contribution plan and the defined benefit plan.

Defined Contribution Plan

In this plan the company or institution contributes a fixed amount each year to a fund that invests the money in a variety of ways. When you retire, your contributions and earnings which have accumulated over the years are used to purchase an annuity. The retirement income you will receive is determined by the size of the annuity bought by the money credited to your account.

An outstanding example of a defined contribution plan is the Teachers Insurance and Annuity Association–College Retirement Equities Fund (TIAA–CREF), founded in 1918 to provide retirement benefits for the staff of colleges, universities, independent schools, and certain other nonprofit and tax-exempt educational and research institutions. Today over 3,600 educational institutions have TIAA–CREF retirement plans. Some 800,000 participants are accumulating future retirement income in their annuity contracts, and another 138,000 participants are receiving annuity income benefits. The TIAA–CREF defined contribution retirement plans for higher education offer a fully portable, fully and immediately vested system. It is designed to permit, perhaps even encourage, the transfer of academic talent from one institution to another without concern about forfeiture of pension benefits.

Defined Benefit Plan

This type of plan establishes a formula for determining your pension, and it requires that your employer contribute enough into the pension fund over the years to insure that your retirement allowance equals the amount prescribed by the formula. The pension is usually tied both to years of credited service and to salary. Your retirement allowance will be best when it is based upon the earnings in your last year or in the final few years of service when you are likely to be earning most. Least favorable is a plan that gears your pension to the average earnings for all years.

The vast majority of retirement plans are of the defined benefit type. The retirement plans of business, industry, and state and local governments are almost universally defined benefit plans.

Other Features of Group Pension Plans

Some pension plans are tied in with Social Security benefits. These plans are called *integrated plans.* In some integrated plans, the participant's monthly pension amount is computed according to the plan's benefit formula, but then a percentage of the participant's monthly Social Security benefit is subtracted from the pension amount.

Both defined contribution and defined benefit plans may require or allow contributions by employees. If a pension plan is financed entirely by the employer, it is referred to as *noncontributory.* In a *contributory* pension plan both the employer and the employee share the cost in some prescribed proportion. The majority of corporate pension plans are noncontributory. Some plans are administered solely by unions and financed by union dues or assessments.

In contrast, most federal, state, and local government pension plans are *contributory.* In contributory plans, if you leave your employer before your rights have vested, you are legally entitled to take out your own contributions with interest. The employee share of costs in a contributory plan is usually between three and ten percent of wages and generally paid through payroll deduction.

If you are a participant in a contributory plan, you pay income taxes on the amount you put in. When you collect your retirement allowance, the amount you contributed over your working life is not taxed. However, you must pay income taxes on the contributions of the employer and on the interest earned by both your contributions and your employer's contributions.

According to rules developed by the Internal Revenue Service under provisions of the Internal Revenue Code, an employer who makes contributions to a *qualified pension plan,* one which meets a set of specified criteria, can deduct management's contributions to the plan from its taxable income as a business expense. Another tax advantage is that investment income of a qualified pension plan is allowed to accumulate untaxed. Qualification standards apply only to private pension plans and not to retirement plans of governmental or charitable organizations because those organizations are tax-exempt.

Eligibility Requirements for Group Pension Plans

Most pension plans require employees to meet certain eligibility requirements before they can participate in the plan. ERISA approves four age-service eligibility standards, depending on other characteristics of the plan: age 25 and one year of service; age 25 and three years of service; age 30 and one year of service; and three years of service but no age requirement. The last requirement applies to Keogh plans, those used by self-employed people for themselves and their employees. Keogh plans are discussed later in this chapter. These eligibility standards constitute the maximum restrictions. An employer has the right to make an employee a participant sooner.

For defined benefit plans, ERISA recognizes a special provision which you should be aware of, especially if you are in your fifties and contemplating a job change. The law permits a defined benefit plan to exclude from membership a person who begins work within five years of the plan's normal retirement age.

Credit for Years of Service

How you earn benefits is usually determined by the number of years you work for your employer. You must know exactly how your employer counts a *year of service* and how any breaks in that service can affect the benefits you have accumulated. You must check to be sure that you have earned the pension benefits you think you have, or that the *break in service* you may have taken has not jeopardized your benefits. Under most plans, you will have a year of service if you work at least 1,000 hours in a 12-consecutive-month period. Some plans, however, use other standards for measuring years of service. Your plan may provide that you will have a break in service if you do not work at least 500 hours in a 12-consecutive-month period.

Some plans give you credit for work performed before you became a participant, while others do not. Under some plans you stop earning pension credits when you reach the plan's normal retirement age even if you continue to work. Other plans give credit for years of service after retirement age. To avoid losing some or all of the benefits you have accumulated because of a break in service, read your *Summary Plan Description* (or SPD), a booklet issued by the employer explaining the pension plan's provisions, particularly for break-in-service rules.

In a defined contribution plan your accrued benefit at any point equals the amount credited to your account. If the plan puts the money into a cash value life insurance policy, the amount for which the policy could be surrendered represents your accrued benefit.

In a defined benefit plan the accrual process is different because your retirement allowance is not a special sum set aside for you in the pension fund, but a fixed monthly income that will be paid on retirement. For example, one arrangement would compute the benefit as follows: if the plan requires 30 years of service and you leave the company after 20 years of covered service, you are entitled to two-thirds of the estimated pension. Another arrangement computes benefits at a fixed percentage each year. The law permits a plan to use a flat rate of not less than 3 percent a year so that an employee accrues 100 percent of the projected pension after no more than 33⅓ years of covered service. ERISA also allows plans to apply different percentages for early and later years.

Time Required for Vesting

The term *vesting* means the absolute right of an employee to receive money from a retirement plan, even if he or she resigns or is fired, based upon the employee's own contributions and the employer's contributions. Employees' contributions vest immediately and can be withdrawn when the employee leaves the job. However, the rights of employees to employer contributions are generally subject to limitations, including service time requirements and amount limits. In some plans employer contributions vest immediately as earned, while in others vesting occurs in 5, 10, 15, or even 20 years.

The Tax Reform Act of 1986 accelerates minimum vesting requirements set by ERISA. The 1986 vesting rules become effective in 1989. Three of the more popular vesting plans are *Cliff vesting, graded vesting,* and *vesting upon entry.*

Cliff vesting. ERISA provided full retirement benefits after ten years of employment. The Tax Reform Act of 1986 provides full benefits after five years of employment, starting January 1, 1989. Short of ten years under ERISA or five years, employees get nothing.

Graded vesting. ERISA provided 25 percent vesting after 5 years of service, 5 percent for each additional year up to 10 years, plus an additional 10 percent for each year thereafter, or 100 percent vesting after 15 years of service under the old law. The 1986 law requires that companies vest workers 20 percent after three years, then 20 percent per year until they are fully vested after seven years. This is shown in the following table:

ERISA		Tax Reform Act of 1986	
Through December 31, 1988		Effective January 1, 1989	
Years of service	Non-forfeitable percentage	Years of service	Non-forfeitable percentage
5	25	3	20
6	30	4	40
7	35	5	60
8	40	6	80
9	45	7	100
10	50		
11	60		
12	70		
13	80		
14	90		
15 or more	100		

Vesting upon entry. Under prior law, a plan could require a 3-year waiting period for plan entry, with 100 percent immediate vesting upon entry. The Tax Reform Act of 1986 replaces the 3 year/100 percent alternative with a 2 year/100 percent provision, effective January 1, 1989.

The Tax Reform Act of 1986 is notable for its impact on pension reform. Acceleration in vesting schedules provides the following benefits:

- More workers will be eligible for pensions at retirement.
- Working women who on average change jobs more often than men can increase their probability of ultimately receiving a pension.
- The younger work force will have a more secure retirement.

The 1986 law provides another benefit. Present pension plans cover only about half of the work force. The 1986 law requires private pension plans to cover up to 70 percent of employees, thus benefiting more low-income employees.

Under current law you must be given a statement telling you the amount of vested benefits you have earned if you request such a statement. If you leave your job, you should automatically receive a statement showing your vested benefits regardless of whether you request it or not.

Types of Benefits

The three types of retirement benefits are *normal, early,* and *disability.*

Normal. Most pension plans have designed their benefit programs for retirement at age 65, which is considered the *normal* retirement age. Despite that fact, however, the Federal age discrimination law prohibits an employer from requiring employees to retire before age 70. However, the law forbidding age discrimination does not require an employer to increase pensions for work after 65. Nevertheless, a member of a defined benefit pension plan usually receives a higher retirement allowance for additional time served in the job.

Early. Many pension plans allow employees to take *early* retirement, sometime prior to the plan's normal retirement age. If you do decide to retire *early,* you will receive a smaller monthly retirement allowance than at the usual retirement age of 65. Because the contribution period was shorter, the monthly income at early retirement is reduced by an actuarial formula which takes into account the likelihood that you will receive the pension for more years. Some firms encourage early retirement by paying more than the actuarial equivalent or by offering other incentives, such as a lump-sum payment.

Disability. Some plans provide benefits if an employee is unable to work because of illness or *disability.* Known as disability benefits, plans vary in the definitions of disability as well as in age and service requirements that determine eligibility for these benefits. Each plan specifies eligibility requirements and specifies the amount of disability benefit you will receive if you are disabled.

Survivors' Benefits

Most pension plans that pay monthly benefits are required by law to include a provision for survivors' benefits, called a *joint and survivor annuity.* This provision allows an employee to designate an individual, usually the spouse, to receive benefits if the worker dies. It provides to the survivor a minimum of 50 percent of the benefit payable to the retiree. In order to provide for a survivor, the retiree must accept a lower pension while alive.

The employee no longer has the right to waive the survivor's option without obtaining prior approval of the spouse. As explained earlier in this chapter, under the Retirement Equity Act of 1984 a member of a private pension plan must get the written consent of a spouse before electing not to take a joint and survivor annuity. If this option is not taken, the retiree would receive a higher pension, but the survivor would receive nothing if the retiree dies. The 1984 law also provides that private pension plans must now pay benefits to a surviving spouse if the employee dies after becoming vested, that is, after having worked long enough to earn the right to receive benefits.

Pension plans have a variety of provisions relating to *death benefits.* Death benefit provisions usually are related to an employee's age and years of service with a varying schedule of survivor's benefits depending upon these factors. Some pension plans have no death benefit, but instead pay a lump-sum to a survivor provided by a group life insurance policy.

Funding of Pension Plans

The law now provides that every company with a qualified pension plan must contribute an amount each year that is sufficient to cover the obligations to pay future benefits built up during that year. A plan so structured is known as a *fully funded pension plan.* Prior to the ERISA law many pension plans were *unfunded* or *underfunded.* In these, a company's pension reserves were nonexistent or inadequate to meet future pension benefits. Such pension plans paid benefits directly from the company's operating budget as claims arose. ERISA required unfunded and underfunded pension plans to build up their reserves for past obligations over a period of 30 to 40 years. ERISA also requires that pension funds be invested in safe assets. Most trustees of private pension funds invest in blue-chip company stocks or in fixed-return bonds rather than in more speculative investments.

Other Aspects of Private Group Plans

Other considerations relating to private group plans include insurance of monies in a pension plan as mandated by law; a Summary Plan Description which must be made available to members of the pension plan; and a required statement on how to apply for pension benefits

Insurance for Plan Terminations

ERISA provides an important element of protection in the form of pension plan termination insurance. An important provision of the ERISA law established the Pension Benefit Guarantee Corporation (PBGC), whose purpose is to guarantee to eligible workers that pension benefits will be paid to them even if their employer's plan has insufficient assets to fulfill its commitments. Funding for PBGC is derived from charges levied against company pension plans regulated by ERISA.

PBGC has the power to seize up to 30 percent of a company's net worth if it terminates its defined benefit retirement plan. When a company pension plan is unable to meet its commitments to the beneficiaries, the agency will pay the pensions, up to $750 in monthly retirement benefits per person.

The concept of PBGC is similar to savings bank deposit insurance. However, the number of weak pension plans is much larger than the number of weak savings banks. Potential claims against PBGC, even after counting the agency's ability to take company assets, far exceed the millions in reserves that have been built up since 1974.

Mandatory Summary Plan Description

The 1974 pension reform law requires employers to provide each employee covered by the pension plan with a summary description of the plan as well as changes in the plan in a form that can be readily understood by the average participant. This requirement is very important. It means that you have a legal right to obtain the operating details of your private pension plan from your own company. You can contact the personnel department and ask for the company's pension booklet. A small company may not have such a document. However, if you belong to a union, you can probably find out about your pension by contacting the union representative responsible for this aspect of the company's benefits.

This pension plan summary is referred to as a *Summary Plan Description* or an SPD. It must include information about eligibility requirements for benefits, how you accumulate benefits, how you can lose benefits, whether the plan is covered by plan termination insurance, and how you file a claim for benefits. If there are significant changes in your plan, you are entitled to an updated SPD. Reading your SPD carefully will help you answer the questions in the Self-Study section of this chapter.

Your plan administrator is also required to provide you with a *Summary Annual Report,* which is based on a more comprehensive report that is filed annually with the U.S. Department of Labor. The Summary Annual Report contains information on the financial activities of your plan for that particular year. If you have difficulty obtaining information about your plan, contact the nearest area office of the Labor-Management Services Administration.

Applying for Benefits

Your Summary Plan Description must explain the procedures for filing a claim for your benefits and for appealing a denied claim. The explanation must include such necessary information as whom you should contact, what documents you must provide, and how long you may have to wait for a decision to be made on your claim.

What Is a Good Pension?

A pension is usually thought to be good if, when added to your Social Security benefits, it will provide a monthly income for you of 65 to 80 percent of your preretirement net earnings. A highly-paid employee needs proportionately less in retirement than a lower-paid one. An individual earning $20,000 a year probably spends it all just to survive and probably needs as much in retirement. But a $60,000 executive is probably spending $40,000 with the difference going into taxes, savings, and investments. Such an individual will not need a $60,000 retirement allowance.

SELF-STUDY:
MY PENSION PLAN

The following questions will help you to understand your own pension plan, and are applicable to both private and public pension plans. If you are a member of a private pension plan and do not know the answer to a particular question, contact the individual in your company who can give you the information. If the answer is still not clear, contact the nearest office of the U.S. Department of Labor, Labor-Management Services Administration. If you are a member of a public pension plan, contact your personnel office for answers.

1. Type of Plan

a.   Is your pension plan a
- [ ] defined benefit plan
    - [ ] integrated with Social Security
    - [ ] nonintegrated
- [ ] defined contribution plan
    - [ ] integrated with Social Security
    - [ ] nonintegrated

b.   Is your pension plan financed by
- [ ] employer contributions only
- [ ] employer and employee contributions
- [ ] union dues and assessments

c.   What is your contribution to your pension plan?
$_____ per
- [ ] month
- [ ] week
- [ ] hour, or

What percent of your compensation? _____ percent

2. Credit for Service
a.   How is a year of service earned under your pension plan?
- [ ] by working _____ hours in a 12-consecutive-month period
- [ ] by meeting other requirements. Specify:

_____

_____

b.   The plan year (12-month period for which plan records are kept) end on _____
of each year.   date

c. Does your pension plan credit you for work performed before becoming a participant in the plan?
- ☐ Yes
- ☐ No

d. Does your pension plan credit you for work performed after the plan's normal retirement age?
- ☐ Yes
- ☐ No

e. As of now, _____ , how many years of service have you earned? _____ years
  <small>date</small>

f. What are your plan's *break-in-service* rules?

_____   _____

_____

_____

3. Vesting

a. Which vesting plan applies to you?
- ☐ full and immediate vesting
- ☐ cliff vesting
- ☐ graded vesting
- ☐ other (specify) _____

b. _____ additional years of service are required to be fully vested.

4. Benefits

a. Working beyond the *normal* retirement age
- ☐ will
- ☐ will not

  increase your pension

b. How is your normal retirement benefit computed?

_____

_____

_____

c. What are the requirements for *early* retirement?
  _____ years of age; _____ years of service

d. Assuming your age requirement has been met, how many more years of service are required to be eligible for *early* retirement benefits? _____ additional years of service required

e. How is your *early* retirement benefit computed?

_____

f. Will your Social Security benefit be deducted from your pension benefit?
☐ Yes
☐ No
If yes, what percent of your Social Security benefit? _____ percent

g. Will your retirement benefit be
☐ paid to you monthly for life?
☐ paid to you in a lump-sum?
☐ adjusted periodically for cost-of-living increases?
☐ paid to your survivor in the event of your death?

5. Disability

a. Does your plan provide disability benefits?
☐ Yes
☐ No
How does your plan define *disability?*

_____

_____

c. What are your plan's requirements for eligibility for disability benefits?
_____ years of age
_____ years of service

d. Would disablement for the following conditions make you ineligible for disability retirement benefits?
☐ alcoholism
☐ drug addiction
☐ mental incompetence
☐ self-inflicted injury
☐ other (specify) _____

e. Who makes the decision as to whether your condition meets your plan's definition of disability?
☐ a doctor chosen by you
☐ a doctor chosen by the plan director

f. How is your disability retirement benefit computed?

_____

_____

_____

g. Where do you obtain an application for disability retirement?

_____

To whom must you send it? _____

When? Within _____ months after termination of work

h. If you are qualified for disability benefits, will your benefits be paid to you
☐ for life if your disability continues
☐ until retirement age
☐ until you return to your former job
☐ until you are able to work

6. Survivors' Benefits

a. Does your pension plan offer a joint and survivor option or a similar provision for death benefits?
☐ Yes
☐ No

b. Has the joint and survivor option been waived by your spouse?
☐ Yes
☐ No

c. If death occurs before retirement, your survivor will receive

d. By electing a joint and survivor option, your pension benefit will be reduced _____ percent.

e. If death occurs after retirement, your survivor will receive $ _____ per month
☐ for life
☐ for _____ years
☐ until Social Security payments begin
☐ other (specify) _____

7. Funding of Your Pension Plan

a. Your pension plan is
☐ fully funded
☐ underfunded but building up its reserves
☐ underfunded and not building up its reserves

b. The auditors of your pension fund
☐ have
☐ have not
certified that its reserves are invested in high quality assets.

8. Insurance for Plan Termination

a. Your benefits
☐ are
☐ are not
insured by the Public Benefit Guarantee Corporation (PBGC).

9. Summary Plan Description

a. Your company or union
    ☐ has
    ☐ has not
    given you a Summary Plan Description (SPD).

b. Has your company given you a copy of the latest Summary Annual Report?
    ☐ Yes
    ☐ No

10. Applying for Benefits

a. Will your employer automatically send you a pension application?
    ☐ Yes
    ☐ No

b. Must your application for pension benefits be made on a special form?
    ☐ Yes
    ☐ No

c. The application may be obtained from_____
    within _____ months before retirement.

d. Your application for pension benefits should be sent to

_____

_____

e. The following documents must be presented when
    applying for your pension:_____

_____

_____

f. If your application for benefits is denied, what is the appeal procedure?
    An appeal may be made in writing to _____

_____

    within _____ days.

INDIVIDUAL PRIVATE PENSION PLANS: IRAs, KEOGH PLANS, AND SEP PLANS

More than most countries, the United States is a land of consumers. Of every dollar of income after taxes, the average American spends 95 cents and saves only about 5 cents. While the savings rate in the United States is only 5 percent, in Japan and West Germany it is 15 to 20 percent. Many economists believe that the low savings rate in this country is responsible for restraining investment and slowing down the growth of productivity.

The Economic Recovery Tax Act of 1981 tried to stimulate increased personal savings by allowing every employed person to put away money starting January 1, 1982 in an Individual Retirement Account (IRA) and subtract that contribution from his or her taxable income as long as the individual had earned income and was under age 70½.

These tax-deferred retirement accounts were allowed even though the individuals were covered by a private or public pension plan, by a stock-option plan, a profit-sharing plan, and/or by a private employer tax-deferred plan (Internal Revenue Code, Section 401(k) plan) or a non-profit employer tax-deferred plan (Internal Revenue Code, Section 403(b) plan).

Prior to 1982 under the 1974 ERISA law the only people who could set up IRAs and deduct their contributions were those not covered by a qualified retirement plan. The Tax Reform Act of 1986 reverts to the 1974 law to some extent and allows people who are not covered by an employer's qualified retirement plan to deduct their IRA contributions from taxable income. But it restricts the tax-deductible contributions of high-earning individuals who are participants in a qualified retirement plan.

Self-employed individuals have a special option, known as a Keogh Plan, to make large tax-deductible payments for themselves to a pension plan fund held by an institution/trustee. In certain circumstances, the trustee managing the funds could be the self-employed person. The Tax Reform Act of 1986 keeps intact most of the rules on Keoghs, but the vesting requirements must adhere to the rules of the new law, effective January 1, 1989.

Simplified Employee Pension plans (SEP), authorized by the Revenue Act of 1978, allow non-government employers with 25 or fewer employees, to contribute to SEP-IRAs of their workers and take appropriate tax deductions. The Tax Reform Act of 1986 limits salary deferral of contributions to $7,000, down from $30,000 under the old law.

Individual Retirement Account (IRA)

The Tax Reform Act of 1986 establishes two categories of IRA contributions beginning January 1, 1987:

- A *tax-deductible* IRA contribution, which allows you to defer taxes on the amount deposited and the earnings, identical to the IRA under the 1981 tax act, and
- A *non-tax-deductible* IRA contribution, which allows you to make an after-tax deposit but to defer taxes on all of the earnings.

Under 1986 law, you can still make a full $2,000 IRA contribution if single, $2,250 if married with a non-working spouse, and a $4,000 contribution if married with a working spouse. Two factors determine whether or not your contribution is entirely deductible: your income level and your membership in a pension plan. Either category of IRA contribution lets you save for your retirement as you have in the past and to accumulate tax-deferred earnings in your IRA account, up to April 1st of the year following age 70½.

Answers to the following two questions will help you decide whether you can make a *tax-deductible* or a *non-tax-deductible* contribution to an IRA account.

1. Are you a member of a pension plan?
    If your answer is no, and you are single, you are eligible to make a fully tax-deductible IRA contribution, no matter what your income is. If you are married, neither you nor your spouse can be a member of a pension plan in order to claim the IRA tax deduction. These factors are specified in the 1986 law.
    The 1986 law further specifies that if your answer is yes, that is, you are a member of a pension or profit sharing plan, such as a Keogh plan, an SEP plan, a private employer tax-deferred plan (Internal Revenue Code, Section 401(k) plan), or a non-

profit employer tax-deferred plan (Internal Revenue Code, Section 403(b) plan), then your eligibility to make a tax-deductible IRA contribution depends upon your *adjusted gross income (AGI)*—that is, your yearly income from all sources minus such allowable deductions as alimony, business expenses, moving expenses, and IRA or Keogh deductions.

2. What is your annual income? Your ability to make a deductible IRA contribution depends upon your AGI. The three income levels follow:

    - Family income $40,000 or less; individual income $25,000 or less: you can make the fully deductible $2,000 IRA contribution whether or not you or your spouse are members of a pension plan.
    - Family income $40,000 to $50,000; individual income $25,000 to $35,000: you are eligible to make a partially deductible and a partially non-deductible IRA contribution, even if you are a member of a pension plan. To determine how much is deductible, you may use the following formula to calculate the partial deduction. If, for example, the family income is $44,500, $4,500 is above the income limit. This amount is the basis for calculating the partially deductible and the non-deductible portions of the $2,000 contribution.

        a. $44,500   − $40,000   = $4,500
             (family income)   (income limit)   (amount above
                                                               income limit)

        b. $\dfrac{\$4,500}{\$10,000}$ =   45%   × $2,000   = $900   non-deductible
                                                     (IRA contribution)

        c. $2,000   − $900   non-deductible   = $1,100   fully deductible

        Thus, $1,100 is fully deductible. You may also make a non-deductible contribution of $900 for a total allowable IRA contribution of $2,000.

    - Family income above $50,000; individual income above $35,000: if you choose to make an IRA contribution, it will be non-deductible, unless an individual (or both spouses, in the case of a married couple) are not members of a pension plan.

The following table summarizes the extent of deductibility for a $2,000 IRA contribution:

Deductibility of a $2,000 IRA Contribution

Family Income	Individual Income	Extent of Deduction
A. Covered by a pension plan		
$40,000 and under	$25,000 and under	Fully deductible
Between $40,000–$50,000	Between $25,000–$35,000	Partially deductible
Above $50,000	Above $35,000	Non-deductible
B. Not covered by a pension plan		
$40,000 and under	$25,000 and under	Fully deductible
Between $40,000–$50,000	Between $25,000–$35,000	Fully deductible
Above $50,000	Above $35,000	Fully deductible

Husband and Wife Plan

If only one spouse is employed, it is possible for the working partner to include the non-working spouse in his or her IRA; this is referred to as a *spousal IRA*. The maximum contribution for a *spousal IRA* is $2,250 annually.

How Tax-Deferred Savings Grow

Investing in a tax-deferred IRA compares favorably with a taxable investment of the same size over the same period at the same rate of interest. For instance, assume that an investor in an IRA who is in the 28 percent tax bracket invests $2,000 a year at 7.23 percent interest compounded daily, and makes no withdrawals. And assuming that the amounts and interest rates for a non-IRA investment are the same with deposits and interest figures on an after-tax basis, then after 30 years, the IRA would have grown to $222,000 and the non-IRA investment to $150,000. After deducting taxes from the $222,000, the IRA investment would have yielded $159,840, a difference of $9,840 over the non-IRA investment. The difference would be much greater at higher interest rates.

Distribution of Retirement Funds

You may begin to receive your IRA payments as early as age 59½, but effective January 1, 1985, payments must begin by April 1 of the year following the year you turn age 70½. Furthermore, distributions may be taken over a fixed period not longer than (1) your life expectancy or (2) the joint life and last survivor expectancy of you and any other natural person you name as beneficiary. You may take IRA money as a lump sum or in monthly installments. Funds withdrawn from IRA accounts are taxed as ordinary income.

Under the old rules, payouts had to be made at a rate that would empty the account over the life expectancy of the owner, or the combined life expectancies of the owner and spouse. Effective January 1, 1985, life expectancy can be recalculated as often as every year. Since life expectancy extends to an older age as an individual grows older, the new rule makes it possible to continue payouts indefinitely, providing a continuous source of income to retirees. In effect it makes the IRA nest egg last longer.

Distributions to Beneficiaries

Under the new rules which became effective January 1, 1985, the following applies to distributions to beneficiaries if your death occurs after 1984:

1. Distributions to a beneficiary may be paid over a period not exceeding that beneficiary's life expectancy. However, the distribution must begin within one year of your death.
2. If your beneficiary is your surviving spouse, the surviving spouse may elect to start distribution on a date not later than the date on which you would have reached 70½ had you lived.
3. If no beneficiary is named, your IRA balance will be paid to your estate.
4. If you name more than one beneficiary, payments will be divided equally among them.

5. You can change your beneficiary or beneficiaries at any time. Variations of these rules as well as other rules may be applicable. Check with the institution that holds your IRA account to obtain the specific details relating to distributions.

Independence of an IRA from Social Security

As long as you have attained the age of 59½, you may withdraw funds without penalty from your IRA account whether you continue to work or not. While wages earned after you start to draw Social Security can decrease the Social Security payments you receive, the funds you withdraw from your IRA account have no bearing on the amount of money you receive from Social Security.

IRA Rollover

One special feature of the IRA is the lump-sum distribution. If you should retire from a company and decide to take a lump-sum payout of your earned retirement benefits, these funds can be *rolled over* into an IRA tax-free if done within 60 days. A *rollover* exempts you from Federal taxes on the money until you begin to withdraw the funds between the ages of 59½ and 70½. If you become totally disabled, you may collect your rollover funds at any time, even before age 59½, without the penalties for early withdrawal. In general, an *IRA rollover* account is subject to the same rules as any ordinary IRA.

Frequently Asked Questions

Contrary to the limitations made by the Tax Reform Act of 1986, an IRA can still provide a significantly large nest egg for your retirement years. If you can afford to make an annual IRA contribution, it is recommended that you continue to do so. Although IRA regulations are quite flexible, there are rules you must follow.

When can I withdraw funds from my account? You may begin to withdraw funds from your IRA account at age 59½ or anytime after 59½, but you must begin withdrawal no later than April 1 of the year following the time you reach age 70½. You may collect a lump sum or elect to have it paid in equal monthly, quarterly, or annual installments.

What if I withdraw funds early? To encourage retention of the plan, the Federal government imposes a 10 percent penalty tax on withdrawals prior to age 59½.

What if I am disabled or die prior to retirement? If you become disabled, you may, upon presentation of proof of disability, withdraw money from your IRA account without penalty. The same no-penalty provision applies to your beneficiary if you die before reaching retirement age. The deferred taxes, of course, must be paid when the money is withdrawn.

What if I change jobs? If you leave your present employment for a position with another firm, you simply maintain your IRA account and continue making contributions. Thus, if you change jobs, your IRA continues unaffected by the change.

Must I make a contribution to my IRA every year? You are not required to make a contribution to your IRA plan every year. Your account, however, will continue to earn tax-deferred interest. You may add annually to your retirement account up to the legal maximum amount. These decisions are your own.

The Keogh Plan (for Self-Employed Persons)

Self-employed persons were given the right to establish retirement plans for themselves by the Self-Employment Individual Tax Retirement Act of 1962, known as the Keogh Act (HR-10) after the Congressman who sponsored the law. The law was amended in 1974 by the Employees Retirement Income Security Act (ERISA). A Keogh Plan is designed for self-employed individuals—professionals, such as doctors, dentists, lawyers, and accountants; owners of unincorporated businesses, such as store owners; and members of a partnership.

Unlike IRAs, Keogh plans remain almost unchanged by the Tax Reform Act of 1986, and continue to be an excellent tax-deferred pension plan. One of the few changes that have been made relates to the question: when you retire, how should you take your retirement fund distribution—in a single lump-sum payment or spread out over time? The old law allowed you to moderate the impact of a big income tax liability in the year you withdraw the lump-sum distribution through the use of ten-year averaging. For income tax purposes the ten-year averaging rule treats a lump-sum distribution as if it had been received over ten years, thus greatly reducing the tax liability.

The Tax Reform Act of 1986 replaces the ten-year averaging rule with a five-year averaging rule, effective for lump-sum distributions made on or after January 1, 1987. The five-year averaging provision is available only for a distribution received after age 59½, and can be used only once.

Should you take a lump-sum distribution or spread-out retirement payments? Anyone faced with this question must carefully analyze consumption and investment needs for the years ahead. Cash planning is just as important as tax planning. The answer therefore must be tied to your projection of retirement income and your ability to handle investment decisions. Remember too that a lump-sum distribution can be rolled over into an IRA annuity. (See Annuities, Chapter 4.)

Since 1984 self-employed persons can contribute and exclude from taxation up to 20 percent of their income, up to a maximum annual contribution of $30,000. (Through December 31, 1981, the maximum was $7,500, and through December 31, 1983, $15,000.)

When Benefits Are Paid

The self-employed individual's contributions, plus accumulated interest, become payable on retirement, but not earlier than age 59½ or later than 70½. Distribution will not be made before age 59½ without penalty, except in case of disability or death. Under the plan, the owner's account may be distributed in a lump sum or in payments spread over a specified period. The period cannot exceed, but may be spread over, the individual's life expectancy or the individual's and spouse's joint life expectancy. These periods are determined from published actuarial tables.

Where a Keogh Plan Can Be Established

A Keogh Plan can be established in any financial institution, such as a bank, brokerage firm, or an insurance company.

Self-Employed Part-Time

If you perform part-time or free-lance work, you can open a Keogh account on your part-time or free-lance earnings, even if you also work full-time for a firm that has a qualified pension, profit-sharing, or other retirement plan. For example, lawyers or accountants who work for a corporation but who do legal work or prepare tax returns as a sideline may establish a Keogh account and contribute income based on what they have earned from their sideline work.

Disability or Death Prior to Retirement

Should the self-employed individual die before reaching age 59½, the Plan provides for payment to the designated beneficiary. In case the self-employed person suffers permanent disability before age 59½, the amount is immediately payable to the account holder without penalty.

Simplified Employee Pension Plan (SEP)

The Simplified Employee Pension Plan (SEP) is an expansion of the concept of an IRA and is sometimes referred to as a SEP-IRA plan. Basically it is an IRA created for employees by non-government employers with 25 or fewer employees, and permits contributions from both. The Tax Reform Act of 1986 permits salary deferrals up to $7,000 contributed by both the employer and the employee. Within this maximum, the employee can contribute up to the lesser of $2,000 or 100 percent of earned income. The maximum under the old law that could be contributed by both employee and employer was $30,000 or 15 percent of compensation, whichever was less. The SEP is easier to establish and administer than a regular pension plan and therefore is often used by small businesses.

An employer who makes contributions to a SEP plan must do so for all employees in the company. Contributions to an employee's SEP-IRA are deductible by both employer and employee, thus generating tax savings.

How Your IRA, Keogh, or SEP Plan Grows

The growth of ordinary savings is inhibited by two powerful forces: taxes and inflation. To overcome these obstacles, the IRA, Keogh plan, and SEPs were developed. The principles used in these retirement plans include tax deferral, the magic of compound interest, and the advantage of time.

Advantages of an IRA, a Keogh Plan, or SEP

Significant advantages are available to individual savers who are eligible for an IRA, a Keogh Plan, or an SEP. The Tax Reform Act of 1986 has made some notable changes in the IRA, Keogh, and SEP plans, but in spite of the changes a contribution to one of these plans is an important step in retirement planning. Among the advantages are the following:

- A fully deductible contribution will reduce your current taxable income, thereby reducing your current taxes.
- The interest you earn compounds tax-deferred until withdrawal, enabling your investment to grow spectacularly.
- Most people find it difficult to save money so that deposits to these accounts offer an opportunity for forced savings to be used during their retirement years.
- The penalty tax for early withdrawal discourages removal of these savings for frivolous use.
- The tax-deferred money can be distributed prior to age 59½ in the event of permanent disability or premature death without having to pay the penalty tax.

Is a Tax-Deferred Account for Everyone?

Not necessarily. The answer depends on an individual's age, needs, and financial resources. For example, an individual who anticipates receipt of a large inheritance from relatives may find that investment in a tax-deferral program would tend to *increase* his tax rate after retirement.

Here's another point. The money in an IRA or Keogh is locked in until age 59½. While the money can be withdrawn, the penalty charge is significant, and thus the money is not readily available when you may need it. In some instances it is important to keep your assets liquid because they will be needed in the near future. For example, a young person may be trying to save money for a downpayment on a house, for a potential business opportunity, or for getting married and furnishing an apartment.

A tax-deferred account, like every good investment, has much to offer if you can afford it. However, each person's situation must be analyzed on an individual basis in order to develop the best possible retirement program. Bear in mind that some type of savings plan would be beneficial as a supplement to Social Security and to a private or public pension.

PUBLIC PENSION SYSTEMS

Public pension systems probably began with the British Superannuation Act of 1834. In 1857, New York City established a pension fund for its policemen. Part of the financing for this early plan was derived from the proceeds of sales of confiscated or unclaimed property.

In 1911, Massachusetts was the first state to establish a retirement system, more than a half-century after New York City's pioneering effort. At about the same time, many cities began to introduce pension systems for general municipal employees. Both Philadelphia and Pittsburgh set up pension plans in 1915.

The United States government approved a Retirement Act in 1920 which set up a pension system for Federal civil service employees. Since then, both the number of public pension plans and the membership have grown rapidly. Currently, there are about 7,000 public pension plans covering almost all the employees of the Federal, state and local governments—about 15 million active members. Almost 7 million more members of public pension plans in the United States are receiving benefits or have acquired a vested right to receive retirement or survivor benefits at a subsequent time.

The latest development affecting public pension systems (as well as private pension systems discussed earlier in this chapter) relates to the elimination of sex discrimination in pension benefits. In the case of *Arizona Governing Committee v. Norris,* July 6, 1983, the U.S. Supreme Court handed down a decision requiring that pension benefits be gender-neutral as of August 1, 1983. It ruled that sex-based mortality tables violate Title VII of the 1964 Civil Rights Act. It held that the longer lifespan of women may not be used to justify the payment of lower monthly benefits when they retire. This decision requires revision of pensioner mortality rate tables and is in the process of being implemented by all pension systems. The use of sex-neutral mortality tables for individuals retiring on or after August 1, 1983 will increase annuity payments for some retirees and reduce annuity payments for others. Estimates of the impact indicate that differences will range from less than one percent to about eight percent.

The Federal Civil Service Plans

One of the most favorable features of employment by the Federal government is its retirement system. Since 1920 employees have been covered under the Civil Service Retirement System (CSRS). On June 6, 1986 President Reagan signed into law an act creating the new Federal Employees Retirement System (FERS). The need for a new retirement system for Federal employees began with Public Law 98-21, which provided that Federal employees hired after December 31, 1983 would be covered by Social Security.

A second law, Public Law 98-168, provided for a transition period from January 1, 1984 to January 1, 1986 for employees hired after December 31, 1983. During this period employees were fully covered under CSRS and Social Security benefits. This transition period was extended to December 31, 1986 with the passage of Public Law 99-335, which established FERS.

The new Federal Employees Retirement System is effective January 1, 1987. All new employees hired after December 31, 1983 are automatically covered by FERS. Other Federal employees not covered by FERS have the option to transfer into FERS.

Active members of CSRS and FERS number about 2.7 million, and about 1.8 million retired and disabled civilian Federal employees draw pensions.

Federal Employees Retirement System (FERS)

FERS is a three-tiered retirement plan. The three components are:

- Social Security Benefits
- Basic Benefit Plan
- Savings Plan.

You pay full Social Security taxes and a small contribution to the Basic Benefit Plan. In addition, you are able to make tax-deferred contributions to a savings plan and a portion will be matched by the government.

The three components of FERS work together to give you a strong financial foundation for your retirement years. FERS has the following advantages over CSRS:

- Members can join a tax-deferred savings plan.
- The government matches a portion of a member's savings.
- Members have a choice among three different types of investment funds.
- People who leave the system with at least five years of service qualify for benefits.
- Survivor and disability benefits are available after 18 months of service.

Civil Service Retirement System (CSRS)

Members of CSRS have been brought under Social Security by the 1983 Social Security Amendments. New employees hired on or after January 1, 1984 are automatically covered by FERS and Social Security.

Most workers qualify for retirement at age 55 with 30 years' service including time in the military. The amount of required service drops to 20 years at age 60 and to 5 years at 62.

Pensions are based on salary in the three consecutive highest-paid years and can amount to as much as 80 percent of that figure. A recent tabulation reveals that the average retiree drew about $1,000 a month. Pensions are increased once a year to reflect increases in living costs.

Employees currently employed and covered by CSRS may make an irrevocable election to transfer to FERS between July 1 and December 31, 1987.

Special Groups of Employees

Firefighters, law enforcement officers, and air traffic controllers receive an unreduced benefit at age 50 with 20 years of service, or at any age with 25 years of service. Other groups eligible to join FERS and to receive retirement benefits include military reserve technicians and part-time employees. Members of Congress and congressional employees are also eligible for coverage.

Unfunded Liabilities

A recent Federal pension study indicates that the *unfunded liabilities* of Federal pension systems (the amount of future obligations that are not backed by current assets) is about $1,000 billion. Congress must begin to come to grips with this problem.

Pubic Pension Reform

In February 1980 a proposal was introduced in the Federal House of Representatives which would establish Federal reporting and disclosure requirements and fiduciary standards for public employee pension plans. Known as the Public Employee Retirement Income Security Act (PERISA), the proposal would subject Federal, state, and local government pension plans to many of the same standards required of private pension plans under the terms of ERISA.

PERISA addresses itself to such problems as unfunded liabilities; rules for operation and administration; disclosure of the status of plans to members, taxpayers, and government decision-makers; and prevention of fraud and dishonesty by requiring bonding of the trustees who are responsible for investing a plan's assets.

GLOSSARY

Adjusted Gross Income (AGI). The total of your annual wages, interest, dividends, capital gains (or losses) minus allowable deductions such as alimony, business expenses, moving expenses, IRA or Keogh contributions.

Cliff Vesting. Provides that if an employee has 10 years of service, 5 years starting January 1, 1989, the employee has a non-forfeitable right to 100 percent of the accrued benefit derived from employer contributions, with no vesting before then.

Contributory Pension Plan. Both the employer and the employee share the cost of the contribution in some prescribed proportion. (See Noncontributory Pension Plan.)

Defined Benefit Plan. A pension plan in which your monthly retirement allowance is tied to both years of credited service and salary. The employee usually contributes to the plan but the employer is responsible for contributing enough into the pension fund to buy an annuity that will provide the defined benefit. (See Defined Contribution Plan.)

Defined Contribution Plan. A pension plan in which the employer and/or employee contributes a fixed amount each year to a fund invested by the plan's administrator to earn income. At retirement the money credited to your account is used to purchase an annuity that will provide a monthly pension. You receive only as much annuity income as the accumulation in your account will buy. (See Defined Benefit Plan.)

Disability Benefits. Some plans provide benefits if an employee is unable to work because of illness or disability. Plans vary in their definitions of "disability" as well as age and service requirements which determine eligibility for these benefits.

Early Retirement Benefits. Retirement at an age before 65 will provide a smaller monthly retirement allowance. In *early* retirement you have contributed less money and are likely to receive a pension for more years than at the usual retirement age of 65.

Employee Retirement Income Security Act (ERISA). A Federal pension reform act, approved in 1974, that establishes rules for private employers engaged in interstate commerce regarding eligibility for pensions, funding, vesting, financing, survivors' benefits, and disclosure to participants.

Fully Funded Pension Plan. Exists when funds contributed during each year are sufficient to cover the obligations to pay future benefits built up during that year. (See Unfunded Pension Plan and Underfunded Pension Plan.)

Graded Vesting. Provides 25 percent vesting after five years of service with an additional five percent for each additional year up to 10 years, plus an additional 10 percent for each year thereafter, or 100 percent vesting after 15 years of service. The Tax Reform Act of 1986 requires that companies vest workers 20 percent after three years, then 20 percent per year until they are fully vested after seven years, starting January 1, 1989.

Individual Retirement Account (IRA). A personal retirement fund that can be established by an individual, regardless of whether he or she is participating in other retirement programs, by making tax-deductible contributions up to $2,000 per year.

Individual Retirement Account Rollover. A lump-sum payout of your earned retirement benefits from an employer can be *rolled over* into an Individual Retirement Account tax-free if done within 60 days. This is referred to as an *IRA rollover.*

Integrated Pension Plan. A pension plan tied in with Social Security so that a participant's monthly pension amount is reduced by a percentage of the monthly Social Security benefit the participant is to receive.

Joint and Survivor Annuity. A covered employee designates an individual, usually the spouse, to receive benefits if the worker dies. It provides to the survivor a minimum of 50 percent of the benefit payable to the retiree. To pay for this coverage the retiree must accept a lower pension while alive.

Keogh Plan. A retirement plan for self-employed individuals under the Self-Employment Individual Retirement Act of 1962.

Noncontributory Pension Plan. A pension plan financed entirely by the employer. The majority of corporate pension plans are noncontributory.

Normal Retirement Benefits. Most pension plans have designed their benefit programs for retirement at age 65, the *normal* retirement age. While some employees work beyond 65, the Federal law forbidding age discrimination does not require an employer to increase pensions for work after 65.

PBGC. See Pension Benefit Guarantee Corporation.

Pension. A benefit, usually monthly, paid to an individual who has retired from active work.

Pension Benefit Guarantee Corporation (PBGC). An agency established by the Employee Retirement Income Security Act (ERISA) of 1974 which guarantees benefits to private pension plan members even when a plan's assets are insufficient to fulfill the commitments.

Qualified Pension Plan. One which meets a set of specified criteria, developed by the Internal Revenue Service, that enables the employer to deduct contributions to the plan from taxable income as a business expense.

Simplified Employee Pension (SEP). A retirement plan, authorized by the Revenue Act of 1978, that allows employers to contribute to IRAs of their workers and take appropriate tax deductions.

Summary Plan Description (SPD). A summary description of a pension plan that the Employee Retirement Income Security Act of 1974 requires be given to each employee covered by the plan. It must include information on eligibility requirements for benefits, accumulation of benefits, loss of benefits, termination insurance, and the method for filing a claim for benefits.

Survivors' Benefits. Pension plans are required by law to include a provision for survivors' benefits. (See Joint and Survivor Annuity.)

Underfunded Pension Plan. Exists when a company's pension reserves to meet future pension benefits are inadequate. (See Fully Funded Pension Plan and Unfunded Pension Plan.)

Unfunded Pension Plan. Exists when a company does not have pension reserves to meet future pension benefits. (See Fully Funded Pension Plan and Underfunded Pension Plan.)

Vesting. The absolute right of an employee to receive money from a retirement plan even if he or she resigns or is fired. Employees' contributions *vest* immediately and can be withdrawn when the employee leaves the job. The rights of employees to employer contributions are generally subject to limitations, including service time requirements and amount limits. (See Cliff Vesting; Graded Vesting.)

Chapter 4
Savings, Investments, Life Insurance, and Annuities

Up to this point we have reviewed the two major sources of retirement income, which include Social Security (Chapter 2) and pensions (Chapter 3). This chapter is concerned with other sources of retirement income, including savings, investments, life insurance, annuities, and miscellaneous sources. These three areas of income—Social Security, pensions, and other sources—are the mainstays of retirement income. Those of you who expect to draw income from all three areas will enjoy a financially secure retirement. In fact, your retirement income from these three sources will probably exceed your working-life income, primarily because such a large proportion of it is tax-exempt (in particular, Social Security income).

This chapter will give you the background you need to understand the role of savings and investments as well as life insurance and annuities. Careful and thorough use of the self-study sections will help you set your financial house in order and keep it that way. A mastery of the material in this chapter will assist you in planning a more secure and relaxed retirement.

SAVINGS

For many people saving money appears to be an unattainable goal. Nevertheless, savings and investments are essential not only to the individual but also to the growth and sustenance of the American economy.

The Lifetime Nest Egg

The average American accumulates a small, personal nest egg for retirement through the process of making monthly payments on the mortgage and through the purchase of ordinary life insurance. The monthly mortgage payments build up equity in the family home, and ordinary life insurance premiums help cash value grow. In addition, the average family tries to save its unspent cash income, averaging over the long-term between 5 and 7 percent of disposable income per year. These savings are usually deposited in savings banks, savings and loan associations, and commercial banks. Up to the latter part of 1982, these funds were deposited into *passbook savings accounts,* but since that time bank *money market deposit accounts* (MMDA) have become available.

Passbook Savings Accounts vs. Money Market Deposit Accounts

Passbook Savings Accounts pay a relatively low interest rate, about 5.25 or 5.5 percent, while bank *money market deposit accounts* are yielding between 7 and 10 percent, but also require a minimum balance. Until January 1, 1985, the required minimum balance was $2,500. On January 1, 1985, the required minimum balance dropped to $1,000. If the balance falls below a bank's specified minimum, the account pays the passbook savings rate. Money in the passbook savings account or in the money market deposit account is safe, insured by the U.S. Federal Deposit Insurance Corporation or the U.S. Federal Savings and Loan Insurance Corporation up to $100,000 per account, and it is liquid, available for withdrawal whenever the need for cash arises. The yield on money market deposit accounts is favorable, and some of these accounts offer check-writing privileges. Some banks allow you to write three checks a month and also set minimum amounts, such as $250 or more per check. Cash withdrawals are unlimited, but seven days' notice may be required.

If your savings are earning only 5.25 or 5.5 percent in a passbook savings account, it makes sense to transfer your funds into a higher-yielding bank money market deposit account. A higher rate of interest may be offered by Certificates of Deposit, U.S. Treasury Bills and Notes, and Money Market Mutual Funds, discussed in the following section under *Investments*, and should be considered in your retirement financial plan.

Negotiable Order of Withdrawal (NOW) Accounts

A new era in banking services began in 1981 when all commercial banks, savings and loan associations, mutual savings banks, and credit unions were authorized to offer *Negotiable Order of Withdrawal (NOW)* accounts. These are checking accounts that earn interest, or they may be viewed as savings accounts on which you can write checks. Balance requirements and interest rates may vary from bank to bank. As set up in one particular bank, for example, ordinary NOW accounts require no minimum balance and pay 5.25 percent on balances over $500. If your balance were $600, you would earn 5.25 percent on $100. However, if you maintain a $1,000 balance, the bank would pay 5.25 percent on the entire amount.

Super NOW Accounts

In late 1982 and early 1983 banks began to offer *Super NOW accounts*, which are savings accounts with check-writing privileges. Generally, Super Now accounts pay higher interest rates than ordinary NOW accounts but also require higher minimum balances. In one type of Super NOW account, the bank pays about one percent less than the bank's money market deposit account and requires a minimum balance of $2,500. As of January 1, 1985 a bank may reduce the required minimum balance to $1,000. If, for example, the bank's money market account were paying 8.80 percent, the Super NOW account would pay about 7.80 percent. Some banks apply a penalty fee if the account falls below the minimum balance. Each bank sets a variety of rules and regulations that govern NOW, Super NOW, and money market deposit accounts. Before opening one or more of these accounts, you should comparison shop among the financial institutions.

Emergency Savings Fund

Every retiree or retired couple should have an *emergency savings fund* to provide a cushion in case of unforeseeable emergencies. The importance of an emergency reserve is to provide protection for you against the unexpected, enabling you to be prepared for whatever may occur. The amount set aside should equal the retirement cost of living for an individual retiree or a retired couple for a period of about three to six months. A retired couple, for example, whose living expenses are $1,000 a month, should have between $6,000 and $12,000 in an emergency savings fund. This type of emergency fund is necessary even though your Social Security and pension income is certain and will continue.

At least $5,000 of your emergency savings fund should be deposited in a bank money market deposit account, because it offers safety, liquidity, and yield. The balance should be deposited in U.S. Treasury paper, Certificates of Deposit, or tax-exempt bonds, depending on individual circumstances. Moreover, decisions on where to invest surplus funds depend on economic conditions, such as interest rates and the extent of inflation. Decisions of this type should be made with the advice and guidance of a reliable financial counselor.

SELF-STUDY: MY EMERGENCY SAVINGS FUND

Your financial retirement plan should include an emergency savings fund equal to three to six months of your annual cost of living. Calculate the status of your emergency savings fund and set a goal for achieving the required amount as follows:

For single retiree or couple:

Annual cost of living in 19____	$_____
Emergency savings fund should be	$_____
Actual savings are	$_____
Surplus or shortage is	$_____

If you are short, divide the shortage by the amount you can afford to save each week to determine the number of weeks required to reach your goal. For example:

$$\frac{\$3,000 \text{ shortage}}{\text{Can save } \$30 \text{ a week}} = 100 \text{ weeks, or about 2 years.}$$

Consumption of Savings

A significant source of retirement income is the savings and investments which you accumulated over your working life. If you withdraw a portion of your capital every month during your retirement to live on, how long would your nest egg last? The answer depends on the interest rate the money is earning and the amount you withdraw monthly, which is then aggregated to yield an annual total.

The following table prepared by the U.S. League of Savings Associations answers this question. Regardless of the amount of capital you consume, if the interest rate paid by the institution equals the percent of principal you withdraw, the fund could last indefinitely. For example, if you have $10,000 invested, earning 8 percent interest, and you withdraw 12 percent a year, your $10,000 will last about 14 years. On the other hand, if you have $10,000 invested, earning 8 percent interest, and you withdraw 8 percent a year, your capital will last indefinitely because you are withdrawing only the interest earned.

Table 4.1

Number of Years Your Money Could Last at Various Interest Rates and Percentages of Principal Withdrawn Annually*

Interest rate paid	Approximate number of years at percent of principal withdrawn annually										
	5%	6%	7%	8%	9%	10%	11%	12%	13%	14%	15%
5%	∞	37	26	20	16	14	12	11	10	9	8
6%		∞	34	24	19	16	13	12	10	9	9
7%			∞	31	22	18	15	13	11	10	9
8%				∞	29	21	17	14	12	11	10
9%					∞	27	20	16	13	12	10
10%						∞	26	19	15	13	11
11%							∞	24	18	14	12
12%								∞	23	17	14
13%									∞	22	16
14%										∞	21
15%											∞

*Assumptions made in this table are the following:

1. Withdrawals are made at the end of each month.
2. There are no premature withdrawals or penalties.
3. Interest is compounded continuously under the 365/360 formula which provides the highest return possible under current banking regulations.

Note: The symbol ∞ means "*infinity.*"

Source: Table 4.1 is reprinted with the permission of the U.S. League of Savings Associations.

INVESTMENTS

Some people who are planning their retirement have been making investments in the course of their working lives and have acquired a general picture of the intricacies of the subject. Others have been unable to save and invest and are thus novices in the field. However, at the point of retirement many public pension systems permit lump-sum distributions of excess reserves or rollover of tax deferred annuity funds and many private pension plans allow you to take a lump-sum distribution at retirement. This situation requires you to make some investment decisions, and it is essential for you to understand some of the alternatives.

A lump-sum distribution at retirement can be worthwhile if you know how to invest the money prudently. For example, one retiree who chose a lump-sum settlement from a retirement plan invested wisely in a safe, high-yield money market fund. Another retiree invested part of his settlement in several highly speculative stocks and the rest in a regular savings account paying 5.5 percent interest. He would have done better to leave his money in the pension fund.

You have many investment alternatives in handling your lump-sum distribution even though interest rates fluctuate. You can invest your money as the first retiree did, in a safe fund that will protect your capital and that pays an interest rate which may be higher than that paid by your pension fund. The second retiree invested in highly speculative stocks that may decline in value resulting in capital losses, with the rest in a regular savings account paying a low rate of interest. Another consideration may be your health. If your health is poor and you do not expect to live out your normal lifespan, you should consider taking a lump-sum distribution at retirement so that you may own and control your capital and transmit it to your heirs or to your favorite charity. On the other hand, lump-sum distributions should be taken by people who can handle money responsibly and who perhaps can afford whatever risk may be entailed. If you do not fit this description, leave your money in the pension fund. Then, you will not be disturbed by the problems associated with overseeing your investments, although you will have to be satisfied with a more modest standard of living.

The following sections will provide you with a brief introduction to the various investment alternatives which are available to you, and will analyze each in terms of safety and yield.

Stocks.

The term *stocks* actually refers to two types, known as *common stocks* and *preferred stocks.* These are described below.

Common Stocks

Some common stocks should be included in the portfolios of most investors. Common stocks are the most popular form of investment in the United States. Over 25 million Americans own stock directly, and many more are indirect holders through their interest in pension funds and other intermediaries, such as insurance companies. The 1970s were not good years for the stock market, but the 1980s may be better.

When you buy shares of common stocks, you become a part owner of the enterprise that issued the stock, and you expect to participate in the profits of the firm, if there are any. *Common stocks* may be defined as those shares in a corporation which give their respective owners the right to control the enterprise and to share in the profits, known as *dividends,* after expenses and prior claims have been paid. The amount of the dividend to be paid to the common stockholders and the time of payment are within the discretion of the Board of Directors of the corporation.

Traditionally, common stocks have been considered a means of protection against inflation, rising in value as prices increase. However, average stock prices declined over the past decade, while consumer prices more than doubled. Therefore, common stocks have not provided inflation protection. But, stockholders have received dividends and can continue to count on them to supplement Social Security and their pension.

Investing in common stocks is not for amateurs. Investment advice can often be contradictory, and the future is unpredictable. An investment advisor should be consulted before investing even a small portion of your funds in the stock market.

Preferred Stocks

Preferred stocks are shares in a corporation that are entitled to receive fixed and stated dividends before earnings are distributed to the common stockholders. However, the fixed return is not guaranteed. The company's Board of Directors has the authority to pay or not pay the preferred stockholders' dividend, depending on the amount of profits earned in a given year. If the dividend is not paid, the company cannot pay dividends to common stockholders either.

Preferred stock is "preferred" not only in payment of dividends, but also in case the corporation is to be dissolved. In such a situation, the claims of preferred shareholders come before those of common stockholders, but after those of bondowners.

Preferred stocks are not necessarily better than other types of investments.

Cumulative Preferred. *Cumulative preferred stocks* are entitled to receive dividends which the corporation, for one reason or another, has failed to pay in previous years. The dividends on this type of security accumulate until paid. Unpaid dividends on cumulative preferred stock must be paid before dividends on common stock are resumed.

Convertible Preferred. Some preferred stock is *convertible,* carrying the right of exchange for common stock. Preferred stockholders may or may not have voting power in the corporation. Shares of preferred stock have a *par value,* that is, the value amount printed on the face of the certificate, such as $25, $50, or $100 per share.

Callable Preferred. Many issues of preferred stock are *callable,* enabling a company to call in its preferred stock and to redeem it for at least the par value of each share. Yields on preferred stock correlate closely with bond yields, paying interest four times a year.

Bonds

Bonds are written promises to repay a loan on a specified date, called the date of maturity, while paying the bondholder a specified amount of interest at regular intervals, which is usually twice a year. On the date of maturity, the borrower, either a company or a governmental unit, will return the investor's capital. Referred to as fixed-income assets, bonds are usually issued in units of $1,000 or more and bear a fixed interest rate, known as the *coupon rate.* The value of the bond fluctuates in the bond market inversely with interest rates so that when interest rates are high, bond prices are low, and when interest rates are low, bond prices are high. Maturity dates may extend from ten to thirty or more years into the future.

Conservative investors usually hold a relatively high proportion of bonds. Conventional wisdom holds that bonds are the principal investment for individuals who are approaching retirement age or who are at retirement age. This view is generally correct. Bonds are considered more conservative investments than common stocks because the interest return is fixed over the life of the bond, and in case of bankruptcy or liquidation of a firm, the bondholders have the first lien against the assets of the corporation. Preferred stockholders have the second lien, and the common stockholders divide up what is left.

When you own a bond, you know exactly how much you will receive when interest is paid, and if you hold the bond until the date of maturity, you will get back your initial investment in full. If you sell your bond before maturity, you can earn a gain or take a loss, depending upon the bond's market price at the time of the sale.

Corporate Bonds

Corporations issue a wide variety of bonds. For example, *mortgage bonds* are secured by a mortgage on a specific piece of property, usually of a durable nature such as land, buildings, or machinery. *Debenture bonds* are not backed by any specific piece of property but by the general credit of the corporation. *Convertible bonds* give their holders the right, within a particular time and under certain stated terms, to change them into stock.

Bonds are bought and sold by brokers and securities dealers for the public. It is not necessary to keep a bond until it matures—you can sell a bond you hold or buy one previously held by someone else. In the process of trading you can earn a capital gain or incur a loss when you sell.

The investor must be able to assess the financial soundness of a particular bond before buying it. A bond with a higher degree of risk must pay a higher interest yield to compensate the investor for assuming the higher risk. Individual investors do not have the expertise for rating bonds. They rely on independent bond-rating services. The two largest are Moody's Investors Service and Standard and Poor's Corporation. The best quality corporate bond with the smallest degree of risk is rated Aaa by Moody's or AAA by Standard & Poor's (known as triple-A bonds). The scale used by Moody's continues Aa1, Aa2, Aa3, A1, A2, A3, Baa1, Baa2, and Baa3. The last three ratings designate medium grade, but still investment grade. Below investment grade ratings are Ba1, Ba2, Ba3, B1, B2, B3, Caa, Ca, and C. If you want to buy a bond, tell your broker that you want an issue rated Aaa, Aa1, Aa2, or Aa3, but preferably Aaa.

Government Bonds

A large variety of government bonds is available for sale to investors. These include U.S. Treasury Bonds; U.S. Savings Bonds; U.S. Agency Securities, such as those issued by the Government National Mortgage Association, the Federal National Mortgage Association, the Federal Home Loan Bank System, and the Federal Farm Credit System; and municipal bonds, which are issued by states, counties, and municipalities, and their various agencies.

The states cannot tax the interest earned on U.S. government bonds because of a Supreme Court decision when Chief Justice John Marshall stated in McCulloch v. Maryland, 1819, that a state or local tax on a Federal instrumentality is invalid. However, U.S. government bonds are not exempt from Federal income tax. On the other hand, the Federal government may not tax the interest earned by owners of municipal bonds, instrumentalities of state, county, or local governments, because of the general constitutional principle of mutual independence of the Federal and state governments. These bonds are also tax-exempt in the states and municipalities in which they were issued.

However, you are liable for taxes on the interest you earn on bonds issued by states other than the one in which you live. For example, if you live in New York and receive interest on a bond issued by the State of Colorado, you must report the income in your New York State tax return. But if you live in New York and own a bond issued by the State of New York, you will not have to pay Federal, state, or city taxes on the interest.

A recently-enacted Federal law states that in calculating their gross income, retirees must include half of their Social Security income and all of their income from tax-exempt bonds. If their gross income exceeds $25,000 for a single individual or $32,000 for a couple filing a joint return, then taxes must be paid on half of the Social Security, although not on the tax-exempt bonds. Legislation has been introduced in Congress to modify or eliminate this requirement.

U.S. Treasury Bonds. U.S. Treasury bonds are obligations of the U.S. Government with maturities of ten or more years. The older U.S. Treasury bonds are bearer bonds, that is, the owner's name does not appear on the certificate and is not registered on the books of the issuer. Postdated interest coupons, representing ownership, are attached to the bond. They are clipped as they become due and presented at a bank for deposit or in exchange for cash. Interest paid on these older bonds ranges from 3.5 to 4.5 percent. They sell currently at deep discounts from par value.

As of January 1983, all new Treasury bonds are issued in registered form only which means that the owner's name is inscribed on the certificate and is recorded on the Treasury's books. Ownership of these bonds may be registered in the name of one person, in the names of two or more individuals, or in the name or names of minors. In the early 1980s, Treasury bonds were paying 12 to 14 percent. New issues in 1985 paid 10 to 11.5 percent, depending upon the term of maturity. Interest on registered securities is paid automatically by U.S. Treasury check every six months from the issue date. The return on U.S. Treasury bonds is about one percentage point less than the return on triple-A corporate bonds. This is to be expected because corporate bonds do involve somewhat more risk than U.S. Treasury bonds and the interest on corporate bonds is fully taxable.

U.S. Treasury bonds are issued in the following denominations: $1,000, $5,000, $10,000, $100,000 and $1,000,000. Fifteen-year bonds are issued in January, July and October. Longer term bonds are issued during quarterly financings: every three months on the 15th of February, May, August, and November.

To get detailed information about purchasing a U.S. Treasury bond, contact the Federal Reserve Bank nearest you. The Federal Reserve Bank's twelve regional offices are located in Atlanta, Boston, Chicago, Cleveland, Dallas, Kansas City, Minneapolis, New York City, Philadelphia, Richmond, St. Louis, and San Francisco. The Federal Reserve Banks also sell U.S. Treasury bills and notes, which are described in this chapter under Instruments of the Money Market.

U.S. Treasury bonds are a sound investment for the investor seeking maximum safety of capital and a steady high rate of interest. When interest rates begin to fall, the astute investor will seek to lock in a high rate of interest by buying for the long term. You must carefully follow interest rate movements to determine the ideal time to buy U.S. Treasury bonds. You will find this information in the financial pages of your daily newspaper or by contacting the nearest branch of the Federal Reserve Bank.

U.S. Savings Bonds. The U.S. government sold two types of savings bonds prior to January 1980: Series E and Series H. Starting January 1980 the Series E and H bonds were replaced with two new series, EE and HH.

Series EE Savings Bonds. The Series EE savings bond is an appreciation-type security whose maturity is set at 12 years. As of November 1, 1986, the minimum guaranteed rate was set at 6.5 percent compounded semiannually. If the bond is held for at least 5 years, it pays interest equal to 85 percent of the average yield on Treasury securities with five years remaining to their maturity, or 6.5 percent, whichever is more. For the period November 1, 1985—April 30, 1986 the rate is 8.36 percent. The variable rate is adjusted every six months, November 1 and May 1.

Series EE bonds are available in eight denominations: $50, $75, $100, $200, $500, $1,000, $5,000, and $10,000. They sell at 50 percent discount from face value so that, for example, a $100 bond costs $50. If a bond is not redeemed at maturity, it continues to earn interest. The bonds are sold at banks and other financial institutions or through convenient payroll deduction plans. There is no sales charge or commission.

The advantages are numerous. Savings bonds are safe, with principal and interest guaranteed by the United States government. If lost, stolen, or destroyed, they will be replaced by the Treasury Department. EE bonds may be redeemed six months from the date of issue at most banks. They can be purchased conveniently through a Payroll Savings Plan. Moreover, interest on EE bonds is subject to Federal income tax but not to state or local income taxes. Reporting of interest, for Federal income tax purposes, may be deferred until the EE bonds are cashed.

Series HH Savings Bonds. Series HH bonds are issued in four denominations: $500, $1,000, $5,000, and $10,000, and sell at full face value. Interest on Series HH bonds issued on or after November 1, 1986 is paid semiannually by U.S. Treasury check at a rate of 6.5 percent per annum. HH bonds reach maturity 12 years after purchase.

A major advantage of Series HH savings bonds is the semiannual interest check. Current income is a significant objective in financial planning for retirement. The interest earned on E and EE bonds accumulates but is tax-deferred until the bonds are cashed. When E and EE bonds mature or at the time you retire, you can exchange the redemption value of your E and EE bonds for the Series HH bonds. This further postpones taxes on the accumulated interest until you cash in the HHs. The semiannual interest, however, is subject to Federal income tax, but not to state or local income taxes. Such interest must be reported for Federal income tax purposes for the year in which interest is paid. By exchanging your E and EE bonds for HH bonds you keep your principal intact, have a steady income for at least 10 years, and, when the HH bonds are cashed, the tax will be at your post-retirement rate. The amomunt of E or EE bonds you can exchange for HH bonds in a year is unlimited, but EEs must be six months old before they can be exchanged. The exchange can take place only at a Federal Reserve Bank or one of its branches, or at the Bureau of the Public Debt.

The E, EE, H, and HH bonds are subject to other taxes, such as estate, inheritance, and gift taxes, whether Federal or state, but they are exempt from all other taxation imposed on principal or interest by any state or local taxing authority.

U.S. Agency Securities. Some of the U.S. government agencies that raise funds through public offerings include the Government National Mortgage Association, the Federal National Mortgage Association, and the Federal Home Loan Mortgage Corporation. The bonds sold by these agencies are referred to in the investment world by nicknames—Ginnie Maes, Fannie Maes, and Freddie Macs. Ginnie Maes are backed by Government-insured Federal Housing Administration (FHA) and Veterans Administration (VA) mortgages that add a safety feature for individual investors. Fannie Maes and Freddie Macs, backed by conventional mortgages (uninsured), are of particular interest to institutional investors, and not to individual investors.

These bonds can be purchased only through a commercial bank or a stock brokerage firm, requiring payment of a commission. They cannot be purchased directly from the issuing agency. Holders of these obligations receive interest payments by check. The interest is subject to Federal income tax, but is exempt from state and local income taxes.

These agencies buy mortgages from financial institutions that have actually made the loans. They then package similar mortgages into pools amounting to millions of dollars. The agency securities backed by these mortgages are sold to investors who receive a return that reflects the interest paid by the individual homeowners. The agency bonds are called *pass-through* securities because the homeowner's payments of interest and principal are passed through to investors who buy shares in one or more pools of mortgages.

Ginnie Maes. The Government National Mortgage Association (GNMA) is a branch of the U.S. Department of Housing and Urban Development. It is the leading issuer of pass-through certificates, with over $225 billion worth outstanding, representing more than 80,000 separate pools of mortgages. The Ginnie Mae offers the highest interest rate of any government security, is generally sold in maturities of 30 years, in a minimum denomination of $25,000. To encourage purchases by small investors many mutual funds that specialize in these securities sell units of Ginnie Maes for as little as $1,000 each.

Most Government securities pay interest semiannually. Ginnie Maes, on the other hand, make payments monthly, including interest and part of the principal. Retirees usually prefer monthly payments. The investors, however, must understand that part of the monthly check is principal. If they spend it, they discover later that their principal has diminished. It is important that they spend each month only the interest, setting aside the principal for further investment. The payback of principal occurs because homeowners try to repay their mortgages more quickly, or refinance existing mortgages at lower rates.

The advantage of buying into a Ginnie Mae mutual fund or unit investment trust is that the monthly principal and/or interest paid back to you can be reinvested when the fund or trust is instructed to do so.

Municipal Bonds

Bonds issued by States, counties, and cities are called *municipals*. They offer tax advantages which make them attractive to people in higher income tax brackets. A New York City resident, for example, who owns a New York City bond or a New York State bond pays no taxes to the Federal, New York State, or New York City governments on the interest earned. The decision to buy or not to buy a municipal depends upon the stated interest rate, or coupon rate, and your tax bracket. For example, if you can earn 15 percent on an investment that is not tax-free and you're in the 50 percent income tax bracket, you get to keep only 7.5 percent. If a municipal pays a rate higher than 7.5 percent, you're ahead.

Municipals, like taxable bonds, must be considered in terms of their safety. If a municipality is about to go bankrupt, the investment would not be sound. It is important to ascertain the bond rating of the municipal. Choose the high-grade bonds, those rated triple A. The *risk-return* relationship pertains to municipals just as it does to stocks. That is, the higher the risk, the higher the interest return. The State or city will pay you a higher rate to make the offering attractive if there is an element of risk involved.

There are two principal varieties of municipal bonds. *General obligation bonds* pledge the faith and credit of the government that issues them, meaning that the taxing authority of the issuer will insure payment of interest and principal. The repayment of *Revenue bonds* is tied to a particular source of revenue, such as a bridge, a tunnel, an airport, or a specific tax, such as a sales tax. Always check the bond rating before buying.

Instruments of the Money Market

The *money market* is the collective name for transactions involving the borrowing and lending of money for a short term by the government, banks, large corporations, securities dealers, and individual investors. In investment circles, "short term" is considered to be one year or less. When individuals or businesses have more cash on hand than they currently need, they often find the money market an attractive place to temporarily invest their funds to earn interest. At the same time, the government or other businesses may require funds for a short term and are willing to pay interest for the use of the money.

Some of the short-term instruments traded in the money market include the following: U.S. Treasury bills, certificates of deposit, commercial paper, banker's acceptances, and repurchase agreements. Most of these instruments can be purchased by individuals through the banking system, but many require a minimum purchase amount ranging from $10,000 to $25,000. A much smaller amount is required to purchase a small portion of a portfolio of money market instruments through a money market mutual fund, to be discussed later.

The short-term credit instruments traded in the money market have two very important characteristics: a very high degree of safety and a high degree of liquidity, which means the ability to get your cash back quickly without loss. Interest yields on these instruments have recently been among the highest available. This is so because short-term investments are more responsive to current market conditions, such as interest rate changes, than long-term investments.

U.S. Treasury Bills

The United States Government sells securities which are of the highest quality. In today's uncertain market for investors, the ultimate safe haven for short-term funds is the *U.S. Treasury bill*, or *T-bill*. These short-term securities, which mature in 3, 6, or 12 months, are backed by the full faith and credit of the U.S. Government. They pay an attractive yield that is not subject to state and local income taxes, only to Federal income taxes that are payable in the year the T-bill matures, not the year in which you receive the income or discount. They are almost as liquid as cash since they may be sold at any time without interest penalty.

T-bills are unique in that they do not pay interest after the government has had the use of your money, as in the case of certificates of deposit, savings accounts or most bonds. Instead, the T-bill gives you your yield shortly after you buy it because you buy the bills at a discount from face value. For example, you send the Treasury $10,000, the minimum amount required to buy a T-bill. If the actual cost of a 91-day, or three-month bill, were $9,640, when the Federal Reserve Bank receives your $10,000, they send you a check for $360. At the end of 91 days you would either receive the full $10,000, or you could roll it over into a new bill and again get a discount. You pay no commission or redemption fee.

Since you receive the discount well in advance of the maturity of the bill, the true yield on an annual basis works out to be higher than the discount. The difference could be a percentage point or more.

There are several ways to buy Treasury bills. You can buy a T-bill through your bank or broker, paying a fee of $25 to $50 per T-bill. Or, you can buy them by mail or in person at any Federal Reserve Bank or branch. To buy a T-bill, you must fill out an application, known as a tender or bid, that requires only your name, address, Social Security number, signature, date, whether you want to reinvest at maturity at whatever rate then prevails, and whether you are submitting a competitive or noncompetitive bid. Purchasers under one million dollars buy on a noncompetitive basis. This means the buyer will receive a price or discount equal to the average bid of all the big-money bidders.

To buy a $10,000 bill, you need to send a bank cashier's check or a certified personal check, payable to the Federal Reserve Bank, with the completed form. Above $10,000, you can invest in $5,000 increments. You receive a receipt as evidence of ownership. Engraved certificates are no longer given, which is an advantage since they could be stolen or counterfeited.

Interest rates for three-and six-month T-bills are set by the Treasury at weekly auctions, held every Monday. Auctions for 52-week T-bills are held by the Treasury every four weeks on Thursday. If you buy by mail, the envelope containing the application and check must be postmarked no later than midnight of the day preceding the auction. If it is late, it will automatically be held until the next week's auction. If you buy in person, you must hand in the application and check not later than 1:00 P.M. of the day of the auction for that week's rate. If you arrive later or arrive on any other day, it will be held for the following week's auction.

Whether to buy the short-term or relatively long-term bills depends on your individual situation and a guess as to the future course of interest rates. In a period of declining rates, it would be prudent to nail down current higher yields by buying longer-term bills. But in periods of uncertainty, many investors stick to the short-term bills.

U.S. Treasury Notes. The United States Government borrows billions of dollars by selling notes; these are IOUs backed by the full faith and credit of the U.S. Government. Treasury Notes have maturities of two to ten years, and are issued in denominations of $1,000, $5,000, $10,000, $100,000, and $1,000,000. The minimum investment for two-year to four-year notes is $5,000, and four-year to ten-year notes, $1,000.

After you have sent in a completed application form and certified check, payable to the Federal Reserve Bank, you will receive a certificate. The interest earned is sent to you automatically by the U.S. Treasury every six months from the issue date.

During recent years the Treasury generally has observed the following financing schedule:

a. Two-year notes are issued at the end of each month.

b. Four-year notes are issued in March, June, September, and December.

c. Five-year notes are issued in January, July, and October.

d. Several securities are issued during the quarterly financings, usually including a three-to-five year note and a seven-to-ten year note. These are issued every three months on the 15th of February, May, August, and November.

Treasury Notes may be considered as a money market instrument even though they run longer than one year, because they can be traded when they are closer to maturity. T-notes may be purchased through your bank or broker, at a commission, or through the Federal Reserve Bank, without payment of a commission.

Certificates of Deposit

A *Certificate of Deposit* (CD) is a type of savings deposit available to anyone who deposits a specified sum of money for a set period of time. Banks have been offering six-month Certificates of Deposit since 1978, requiring a minimum deposit of $10,000 and paying an interest rate .25 percent higher than the six-month Treasury bill rate. As of October 1, 1983 deregulation became effective. This means that the Federal government no longer tells banks what types of CDs they can offer. Banks can now set their own interest rates, terms, and minimum deposits. Most banks now accept $500 minimum deposits, and many accept as low as $100. The interest rate paid is competitive. Your entire investment in CDs, as in any savings account, is insured up to $100,000 by the Federal Deposit Insurance Corporation or the Federal Savings and Loan Insurance Corporation. The word *term* means how long you keep your money deposited in a particular account. As of October 1, 1983, banks are free to offer high rates with any term they want, starting with 32 days and lasting up to five years, accepting terms for any number of days in between. For example, if you have to pay a particular bill in exactly one year, two months, and three days, you can open a 429-day CD.

CDs of $100,000 or larger have negotiable interest rates paid on the investment. Individuals or institutions purchasing these CDs usually shop around for the highest interest rates available.

Since all bank interest is fully taxable, the interest you earn on your CD is also fully taxable. In addition, if you withdraw any of the principal before maturity for whatever reason, you must pay a penalty. The minimum loss is 31 days' interest on accounts that are due in one year or less. If you have not earned sufficient interest to pay the penalty, it is deducted from your principal. CDs were started in order to induce savers to keep money in banks counteracting the rapid shift of savings to money market funds. CDs are safe and yield reasonable returns.

Commercial Paper

Corporations will pay an investor for the short term use of cash. A corporate IOU is issued to raise funds for limited periods, usually 30 days or less. The investor receives no collateral for this loan, which is usually in denominations of $100,000 or more. The interest paid is above that of the T-bill, frequently about 5 percent above. Higher yields correlate with higher risk. Be sure to check ratings of commercial paper. The highest ratings are F-1 (Fitch Investors Service), Prime-1 (Moody's), and A-1 (Standard & Poor's). Commercial paper is sold directly by issuers; and by dealers, brokers, and investment bankers. This is not for amateurs.

Banker's Acceptances

Import and export transactions frequently involve a loan known as a *banker's acceptance*. The process calls for the seller to draw a draft that is payable by the buyer within a stipulated period of time. The bank then enters the picture by guaranteeing payment at maturity, *accepting* the draft. This means that the draft can be sold in the open market. It can be purchased by a money-market fund at a discount and redeemed at maturity for the full amount.

Repurchase Agreements

Repos is a shortened name given to repurchase agreements. The bank, anxious to borrow money for a short period of time, sells Treasury bills to a money market fund with the provision that the bank buy them back the next day, or within the period of time agreed upon. However, the bank buys them back, at a higher price or at a specific interest rate. Repos actually are loans with Treasury securities as collateral.

Mutual Funds

A *mutual fund*, a popular form of investment today, is a company which collects the funds of hundreds or thousands of small investors through the sale of stock and then uses these funds for investment purposes. The investment philosophy of a fund and the types of investments it makes are spelled out in its prospectus. Over 2,000 mutual funds currently operate in the United States.

Investment Objectives

Mutual funds may be classified according to their investment objectives as follows:

- *Growth funds*—the most popular form of mutual fund, investing primarily in common stocks, and seeking long-term capital appreciation;
- *Growth and income funds*—stress growth plus income, investing in quality stocks for long-term capital appreciation, but also investing in bonds to assure regular interest income;
- *Balanced funds*—stress income over growth, investing in quality bonds to provide steady, high income, but also investing in quality stocks;
- *Income funds*—stress current income, investing in quality bonds to maintain a high level of current income to its shareholders. These funds are an attractive objective for investors in moderate-to-low income tax brackets, particularly retired investors;
- *Specialty funds*—invest in such areas as money market instruments, municipal bonds, Ginnie Maes, gold, Eurodollars, foreign stocks, commodities, options, energy securities, and so forth.

Structure of Mutual Funds

In addition to investment objectives, mutual funds may be classified by their share-issuance policy (whether they are closed-or open-end funds) and whether they are load or no-load funds. A *closed-end company* is one in which a fixed number of shares of stock have been issued and those shares are traded at the prevailing market prices listed on one or more of the major stock exchanges. New shares are issued infrequently. In contrast, an *open-end company* continuously sells new shares of stock and purchases the shares from those desiring redemption, buying and selling its shares at a fixed price, and using whatever funds it has for its investment.

A *load fund* is a mutual fund which charges a commission, or *load,* ranging between 7.5 and 8.5 percent, charged against the shares you buy or sell. The 8.5 percent is the maximum charge set by the U.S. Securities and Exchange Commission (SEC). A *no-load-fund* charges no sales fee, has no sales force, and waits for investors to buy its shares. Both load and no-load funds charge a management fee, which amounts to one percent or less of the interest earned on the money you have invested in the fund. The newer funds do not charge a sales fee, and the management fee is about .67 basis points or .67 of one percent.

Advantages of Investing in a Mutual Fund

The advantages of investing in a mutual fund are as follows:

- You need only a small deposit. The required minimum varies from about $1,000 to $5,000.
- Your money is professionally managed.
- The management fee is very small.

Types of Mutual Funds

Four types of mutual funds are described below.

Stock Mutual Funds. For inexperienced investors or for those with little time to study financial developments, *stock mutual funds* offer an alternative to individual stocks. If you are approaching retirement age or are retired, and desire to invest in the stock market, the stock mutual fund will enable you to minimize risk by investing in dozens of different stocks instead of just two or three stocks, as the moderate-income investor usually does. It also offers professional investment management, which a small investor cannot otherwise receive.

Some stock mutual funds are known as *growth funds* because they concentrate on purchasing stock for capital gains. Some of these funds are more aggressive than others. There are *growth and income funds* that seek to balance their stock purchases between those bringing capital gains and those earning high income for their investors. These funds avoid stocks that pay no dividends. Some growth and income funds also invest in bonds.

Corporate Bond Mutual Funds. A *corporate bond mutual fund* offers diversification through its holding of debt of several corporations instead of just one or two. This frees the investor of the worry of default. Factors you should consider in buying into a corporate bond mutual fund are the sales charge or load, noting that a no-load fund is preferable; the management fee, which should be under one percent; the balance in the fund's portfolio, which should have a reasonable balance between risk and yield.

Municipal Bond Mutual Funds. You can buy municipal bonds singly just as you can corporate bonds, or you can buy into a *municipal bond mutual fund* which holds a large pool of municipal bonds, offering you diversification and a reduction in the degree of concern over default. Interest earned on a single municipal bond or from a municipal bond mutual fund is exempt from Federal income taxes. You should consider buying into a municipal bond fund which holds issues of your own home state so that the interest earned will be exempt from state income taxes as well, and from a local income tax if one is imposed. If you have a choice, choose the no-load fund over the load fund. Depending upon your income tax bracket, the municipal bond fund is worth considering as an investment.

Money Market Mutual Funds. Because yields on cash in savings banks and savings and loan associations have been held down by interest-rate ceilings, *money market mutual funds* have become very popular. Money market funds invest in high-yielding, safe, and liquid money market instruments including U.S. Treasury bills and notes, certificates of deposit, commercial paper, banker's acceptances, and repurchase agreements. A *tax-free money market fund* makes investments that earn interest exempt from Federal and from some state income taxes. The advantages of money market funds are relatively high yield, diversification, low risk, withdrawal of funds without penalty, ability to write checks against your fund holdings in amounts of $500 or more, no sales or redemption charges, and low management fees. Possible disadvantages are that money market funds do not have Federal deposit insurance as do certificates of deposit offered by banks; yields are not fixed or guaranteed, changing daily; and some funds invest in lower-grade commercial paper that carry some degree of risk. The pros outweigh the cons, however. When short-term interest rates are high, money market funds offer a safe, attractive investment.

As financial intermediaries that combine the funds of many shareholders and invest the pooled money in a portfolio of short-term assets, money market mutual funds have minimum deposit requirements ranging from $100 to $5,000 and pay yields that change daily. Funds can be withdrawn at any time and checks can be written on your account; although many funds set a minimum of $250 for each check.

Unit Investment Trusts (Unit Trusts). Brokerage firms have set up *unit investment trusts* or *unit trusts* which package offerings of corporate bonds, municipal bonds, and pools of Ginnie Maes and Fannie Maes. When you buy into a unit trust, you get an interest, called a unit, in a fixed portfolio of securities. As a group, unit trusts offer the investor the following benefits:

- *Marketability.* Your units can be sold on any business day at the bid price with no sales or redemption charge.
- *Diversification.* An owner of units holds a proportionate share of a professionally selected portfolio of bonds from a variety of sources with different yields and maturities.

- *Convenience.* Unit owners enjoy the convenience of having the officials of the *unit trust* handle such services as coupon clipping, reinvestment of interest, safekeeping of securities, monitoring of callable bonds, and providing year-end statements.
- *Professional supervision.* Although there is no management fee, professionals continuously look after the securities in each trust until redemption or call.

The interest earned by unit trusts holding Ginnie Maes, Fannie Maes, or corporate bonds is taxable, while interest earned by portfolios of government securities is tax-free in at least one jurisdiction. An investor in a unit trust gets a fixed dollar return that will not change over the long term. This is attractive for people approaching retirement or already retired because it provides a steady, guaranteed income.

Your House and/or Other Real Estate

The house you own is an investment in real estate, and home prices have risen over the decades of the 1960s and 1970s. In 1960 the average house sold for about $17,500, in 1970 about $30,000 and in 1980 about $65,000. Home ownership has been a sound investment in terms of capital gains. The deductions you enjoy on your income taxes include the interest you pay on your mortgage loan as well as your property tax payments. In addition, after you reach the age of 55, you can enjoy a capital gain of up to $125,000 tax free, if you sell your home, another advantage of home ownership.

In addition to their homes, many older people and retirees have made moderate investments in other real estate and mortgages to gain extra retirement income. The favorite options for real estae investment selected by retirees are the following: buy a two-family house, live in one unit and rent out the other; buy a house as an investment, rent it out at a rental which will cover mortgage payments and maintenance, and reap the appreciation in value; buy a house or a condominium a number of years in advance of retirement, and rent it out until retirement when you move in, thus hedging against price increases. Or, on a more ambitious level, buy a small apartment house or commercial building, with ownership partly financed by a mortgage.

A person approaching retirement may invest directly in real estate by buying first and second mortgages. Although they yield comparatively high returns, first and second mortgages tie up capital for long periods. Such an investment involves some risk and a problem of yield. Whether the higher yield will balance the greater risk depends on the proximity of retirement as well as the adequacy of the security behind the mortgage.

Real Estate Investment Trust (REIT)

During the late 1960s and early 1970s, buying stock in a *Real Estate Investment Trust* (REIT) was considered an ideal way to participate in real estate if you didn't want to buy property or make a mortgage loan on your own. Professionally managed, REITs made investments in big commercial properties and shopping centers. The investor was able to pull out anytime by selling his shares, and some of the dividends qualified as a long-term capital gain, providing a significant tax advantage. The commercial real estate market collapse of 1973–1974 resulted in a collapse of the REIT stock price index from its 1972 base of 100, to 17 by the end of 1974. The recovery of REITs has been slow and uneven; the REIT track record is poor. An investment in a REIT is highly speculative and is not recommended for a retiree or a near-retiree.

Gold, Silver, and Collectibles

In the past few years, many investors have put their money into tangibles such as gold and silver and a variety of collectibles, including diamonds and other precious stones, art, antique furniture, stamps, coins, rare books, antique cars, or Tiffany glass. Investors turn to gold to counteract double-digit inflation, to diversify an investment portfolio, or simply to enjoy the security of owning this precious metal as insurance for the day when all paper assets will be worthless. Some investors buy gold coins or gold bars. Others invest in gold commodity futures, gold-mining stocks, or shares in a gold mutual fund, which probably invests in a combination of bullion, coins, and mining stocks. Silver prices follow precisely the movements of gold prices. Investors in collectibles do so in the hope that the item or items will increase in value, yielding a profit to the investor.

In 1971 gold was selling at $35 an ounce and in early 1980 at $800 an ounce, an all-time high. In 1979 silver prices increased sevenfold in twelve months. Since then, gold and silver prices have fallen sharply and may continue to decline. Like most investments in collectibles, gold and silver offer no return and few tax advantages, while at the same time you must pay purchase and redemption charges, sales taxes, and insurance and storage fees. Prices are volatile, and you must rely on the opinion of an expert to assure you that you're getting what you paid for.

How much does the average person know about the cut, color, clarity, or carat of a diamond? Or the difference between an imitation and a genuine diamond? If you collect as a hobby, you can spend many happy hours enjoying your collection. However, if you are seeking a profit, you should choose other alternatives.

INVESTMENT TIPS

The interest or dividend return you can earn on an investment is directly related to the amount of risk you are prepared to assume. An axiom of investing is that the greater the risk you are prepared to take, the greater the return you can expect. Very high risk investments will yield very high returns if you select a winner. But risk always involves the element of potential loss, and if you select a loser, you may lose all or most of what you have invested.

Each individual has a specific level of risk tolerance. To determine your own risk tolerance, take the "risk quotient" test in the Self-Study section. It is incumbent upon a financial counselor to determine a client's risk tolerance before suggesting particular investments. As an investor, it is your responsibility to stay in the risk zone that leaves you comfortable with your selection. High risk investments should not be undertaken by those who are concerned about the safety of the principal. Such investments should be undertaken only by wealthy individuals who have a high "risk quotient" and who will not suffer too much by significant losses.

As a prospective retiree, you begin to think about maximizing retirement income and keeping taxes as low as possible. In addition, you want to have the feeling of security that comes from knowing your monthly income is certain and uninterrupted. Therefore, you should take a conservative approach in your investments, seeking those that offer safety, liquidity, and good yields with minimum risk. Figure 4.1, The Investment Pyramid, indicates conceptually the structure of a portfolio for the average small investor. The foundation of the pyramid represents minimum risk investments in which most of your portfolio should be stored. A much smaller proportion should go into moderate risk investments, depending upon your risk tolerance. None of your money should be in high risk or very high risk investments.

Figure 4.1

The Investment Pyramid

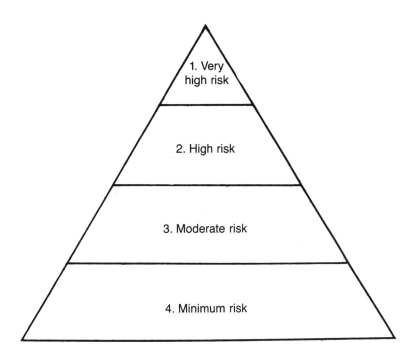

Table 4.2 classifies investments according to the levels of risk depicted in the investment pyramid. The items listed in group four of Table 4.2 are the financial instruments that are worry-free, that are easily convertible into cash if you should need it, and that pay close to top interest rates: bank money market deposit accounts, money market mutual funds, certificates of deposit (CDs), U.S. Treasury issues and any of the other forms of investment included in group four. The average small investor should not risk capital in very high risk or high risk investments, which are the forms of investment included in groups one and two of Table 4.2.

A suggested investment strategy for the average small investor is offered in Table 4.3. The percentage distribution may be modified to suit your individual needs, and some may wish to invest in a few of the offerings in group three of Table 4.2 if your risk tolerance is higher. This does not mean that in financial planning for your retirement you must divest yourself completely of your stock holdings, but simply that you change your portfolio mix, putting a higher percentage of your assets into minimum risk invest-ments, such as those suggested in Table 4.3

Table 4.2

Investments Classified by Level of Risk

1. **Very High Risk Investments—a sophisticated form of gambling**
   Commodities futures
   Options: puts and calls
   Collectibles
   Oil and gas drilling ventures
   Raw land
   Gold, silver, and other precious metals
   Penny stocks
   Foreign stocks
   Margin accounts

2. **High Risk Investments—containing elements of speculation**
   Common stocks of low quality
   New issues of stocks and bonds
   Speculative grade bonds with the following ratings:
      Standard and Poor's ratings: BB, B, CCC, CC, D
      Moody's ratings: Ba, B, Caa, Ca, C

3. **Moderate Risk Investments—offering regular income and potential long-term growth**
   "Blue Chip" common stocks and preferred stocks
   Investment grade corporate and municipal bonds with the following ratings:
      Standard & Poor's ratings: AAA, AA, A, BBB
      Moody's ratings: Aaa, Aa, A, Baa
   Variable annuities
   Investment real estate other than your home
   Stock and bond mutual funds whose goals are income and long-term growth

4. **Minimum Risk Investments—offering safety, liquidity, and good yield**
   Bank money market deposit accounts
   Money market mutual funds
   Insured Certificates of Deposit
   U.S. Treasury paper: bills and notes
   Tax-exempt bond mutual funds
   Individual tax-exempt municipal bonds rated AAA
   U.S. Government Savings Bonds
   Federal agency bonds: GNMA, FNMA
   (Other minimum risk investments include the equity in your home, fixed annuities, and cash value life insurance)

This suggested portfolio is not necessarily appropriate during a period of high inflation. Different types of investments perform better at different stages of the business cycle. However, when you retire, you should not be concerned with shifting investments around over the course of a business cycle. Furthermore, doing so will not guarantee that your savings and investments will stay ahead of inflation. In a period of high inflation, you may wish to shift half of your municipal bond fund investments into a money market deposit account or a money market mutual fund where interest rates reflect inflationary conditions. A long period of high inflation is detrimental to savings and investments, benefiting only the debtor who is able to pay off long-term debt with cheap money. A long period of high inflation will eventually erode your nest egg. If it is any consolation, your Social Security benefits will keep pace with inflation.

Table 4.3

An Investment Strategy for the Average Small Investor with Limited Resources

Type of Investment	Percent of total investment
1. Bank money market deposit account Any bank: accounts are insured up to $100,000 each	25%
(Interest is fully taxable by the Federal government and by State and local governments.)	
2. U.S. Treasury paper (guaranteed by the U.S. government) a. U.S. Treasury Bills (T-Bills) b. U.S. Treasury Notes	25%
(Interest is fully taxable by the Federal government, but exempt from State and local income taxes.)	
3. Tax Exempt Municipal Bond Funds (a tax shelter) a. A Tax Exempt Bond Fund holding the bonds of your home state or its municipalities	50%
(Interest is exempt from Federal government income taxes and from your home state and local income taxes)	
b. Intermediate Tax Exempt Bond Funds holding municipal bonds of jurisdictions outside your home state to gain diversification	
(Interest is exempt from Federal government income taxes but taxable by your home state and local government)	

SELF-STUDY:
AN ANALYSIS OF MY INVESTMENT PORTFOLIO

1. **How do you calculate your "Risk Quotient" (RQ)?** To determine your investment risk tolerance, answer the questions in the chart below. Circle the number for each item that most closely describes you and enter it in the score column.

Calculation of "Risk Quotient"

Item						Score
Your age	21-30	31-40	41-50	51-60	Over 60	
	4	5	7	5	1	
Total family income	$10,000-20,000	$20,001-30,000	$30,001-50,000	$50,001-75,000	Over $75,000	
	1	2	4	6	8	
Savings	$2,000-5,000	$5,001-15,000	$15,001-40,000	$40,001-75,000	Over $75,000	
	1	3	5	8	10	
Your home (Equity)	$20,000-60,000	$60,001-100,000	$100,001-150,000	$150,001-200,000	Over $200,000	
	1	2	3	4	5	
Life insurance	$10,000-20,000	$20,001-50,000	$50,001-100,000	$100,001-200,000	Over $200,000	
	1	2	3	4	5	
Dependents	Only yourself	One additional	2-3	4-5	More than 5	
	10	6	4	2	1	
Investment income used for living costs	Never	Seldom	Occasion-ally	Often	Always	
	10	8	5	3	1	
Employ-ment and income security	Very stable		Fairly stable		Unstable	
	10		5		1	
Major medical or disability income insurance	Have both		Have one		Have neither	
	10		4		1	
Attitude toward risk	Enjoy risk-taking		Will take occasional risks		Avoid risks	
	10		5		1	
Investment principal earmarked for major goals	Yes: for education, and retirement		No: but need for overall security		Could afford to lose my principal	
	1		4		15	
					Total	

2. **How should you invest based on your "RQ"?** After calculating your "risk quotient" score, you know approximately the risk level that you can handle. A suggested portfolio mix is offered below for each risk level. The percentages are approximate and tend to be conservative, reflecting the author's interpretation of investment markets. Depending on the outlook for inflation, it is suggested that no more than 50 percent of your portfolio should be placed in "very high risk" investments even if your "RQ" score falls between 81 and 100. See Table 4.2 for a listing of specific investments arranged by risk level.

Suggested Portfolio Mixes for Various Risk Levels

| | Percent of your portfolio | | | |
Your "risk quotient" score	Very high risk investments	High risk investments	Moderate risk investments	Minimum risk investments
81 to 100	35%	30%	25%	10%
61 to 80	20%	30%	25%	25%
31 to 60	0	5%	15%	80%
11 to 30	0	0	10%	90%

3. Using the following worksheet, enter the current dollar value of each of your assets. Then, compute the percentage of your portfolio in each type of investment. This will enable you to determine whether the proportions conform with your needs or desires.

Current Value and Percentage Distribution of Assets as of: _____ (date)

Assets	Current dollar value	Percent of total
Savings bank accounts	_____	_____
Certificates of Deposit	_____	_____
Stocks:		
Common stocks	_____	
Preferred stocks	_____	
Total stocks	_____	_____
Bonds:		
Corporate bonds	_____	
Government bonds	_____	
Total Bonds	_____	_____
Mutual Funds:		
Money market funds	_____	
Stock mutual funds	_____	
Bond mutual funds	_____	
Total Mutual Funds	_____	_____
Equity in your home*	_____	_____

Other real estate:
  Residential and
  commercial   _____
  Unimproved land   _____
  Mortgage investments _____
  Real Estate
  Investment Trust   _____
  Total Other
  Real Estate   _____   _____
Precious metals:
  Gold   _____
  Silver   _____
  Total Precious Metals   _____   _____
Other:
  Itemize: _____   _____

_____   _____
Total Other   _____   _____

                                                                 100.0%
                 Grand Total   _____   _____

_____

*Estimated current property value minus mortgage balance

LIFE INSURANCE

How much life insurance you need or whether you need it at all is affected by your age and, even more important, by the number of your dependents. This type of protection, an important element in your retirement financial plan, changes dramatically over time.

The Need for Life Insurance

In the course of your working years, life insurance serves two functions: first, to provide financial protection for survivors in case of the breadwinner's death; and, second, to assist the insured in building a nest egg in the form of savings, hopefully for retirement. You have probably purchased at least one *cash value life insurance policy,* requiring premium payments for a set number of years or until an established age or perhaps for life. These permanent, or cash value life insurance policies contain a savings component. In contrast is *term insurance,* which contains no savings component and expires after a specified number of years, so that a higher premium may be charged at your older age. The premium of a term policy is significantly less than that for a cash value life policy, but term insurance is a good buy and would pay your survivors the face value of the policy if you die.

With a permanent or cash value life insurance policy, you pay a fixed premium as you grow older; it builds up a cash value at a gradually increasing rate; you have the right to cash it in for its accumulated value or to borrow against it; and, if you die, your survivors receive the face value of the policy.

Another form of cash value life insurance is *single premium life,* in which the insured makes a single premium payment and no further payments are due. Perhaps along the way you may also have purchased an *endowment policy* for a particular purpose such as a child's education. The endowment policy is a type of cash value life insurance in which savings accumulate more rapidly than in other types of similar insurance. Another type of insurance you may have purchased is a *specialized policy,* such as mortgage insurance, which would pay off the remaining loan on your house if you die.

The Changing Role of Life Insurance

As your retirement time approaches, you must make certain decisions about your insurance: How much financial protection is still needed for your dependents? Do you still need insurance as the means of saving money? Is this an opportune time to cash in some policies and then to use the proceeds for other investments or for financing other projects?

During our working years, advertisements and insurance agents tell us that every breadwinner with a young family should carry life insurance. This concept has assumed the strength of a golden rule in financial planning. As the years have passed, however, the breadwinner's children have grown to adulthood, retirement is imminent and the financial condition of the breadwinner and spouse has improved significantly from what it was when the policy was bought. As a result, the near-retiree is almost certain to be faced with premium payments no longer needed or wanted and with funds available from old policies which can be converted into investments offering lifetime income.

If your children are self-supporting, your mortgage paid off, other income-producing investments made, and your survivors' rights under Social Security and your pension plan achieved, you may discover that you need only a relatively small insurance policy to cover final medical and burial expenses.

On the other hand, situations may exist that would be served well by the ownership of life insurance. When a prospective retiree has a physically handicapped or mentally retarded child or a spouse without adequate retirement income, a life insurance policy can provide a lump sum payment to a beneficiary. This sum, if properly invested, could yield a safe, regular monthly income to a dependent. For higher income individuals life insurance can serve another need during the retirement years. At the death of the breadwinner or spouse, life insurance proceeds can pay Federal and state inheritance taxes that may become due, thus preventing an uneconomical and unwanted forced sale of estate assets to pay these taxes. Thus, life insurance can help to preserve the estate for the heirs.

Reviewing Your Insurance Needs

Cash value life insurance policies usually include a table in the document which indicates the amount of cash the insurance company would pay if the policy were surrendered at various times. This is a lesser amount than the face value or the amount paid in case of death. It is the amount of money you have paid into the company as part of your annual premium which is essentially a savings element, together with the interest which has been earned over the years.

If you have been paying premiums on a cash value policy for 20 to 25 years, the cash value is usually about half the face value of the policy. This sum can be withdrawn and invested in some way which would yield a higher interest rate than that paid by the insurance company.

The alternative is to convert the cash value into an annuity contract. Although you can buy the annuity from the company that issued the life policy, you are not obligated to do so and may be able to get a better return from another company. The company from which you intend to buy the annuity should arrange withdrawal of the cash value and the surrender of the policy in such a way, referred to as a *rollover,* that you would avoid the income tax that could be imposed on a straight withdrawal of the cash value.

Investigating the many alternatives open to you is a major facet of retirement planning. The best time for a searching review of your insurance program is when your retirement is within sight. You may wish to seek the help of a trusted financial advisor or an insurance agent to review and evaluate the alternatives available to you.

ANNUITIES

A problem faced by many people at retirement is what to do with a lump sum distribution from a retirement plan. One choice is to roll it over into one or more IRA instruments within 60 days after receiving it. This will provide a guaranteed lifetime income with minimum tax liability.

How Annuities Work

In your financial plan for retirement, an *annuity* can work for you in the following way: it will guarantee you a lifetime income, eliminating the fear that you will outlive your savings. Assume that you are planning to retire at age 65 with a $10,000 nest egg. If you keep the money in a bank paying 5 to 6 percent interest, it will produce an income of about $40 to $50 a month. And, if you begin to draw on the principal every month in order to raise your level of living, you run the risk of using up your money before you die.

The annuity was invented to handle this type of problem. When a person buys an annuity, the individual exchanges a sum of money for the company's promise to pay an agreed amount periodically, beginning immediately or at a designated age and continuing until death. An annuity is a form of life insurance policy in reverse. With life insurance your survivors get paid if you die. With an annuity you get paid if you live. In calculating its charge for an annuity, an insurance company uses actuarial tables, just as it does in setting the premium on a life insurance policy. The actuarial table gives "average" life expectancy. Some annuitants will live longer than others. Those who die sooner receive fewer payments. The unexpended funds are used to pay those who live to a ripe old age. While this may not seem fair to the ones who die early, it insures that everyone can get an equal guarantee of complete income protection for life.

Therefore, an annuity is a guaranteed income plan usually purchased from a life insurance company to provide retirement income, most often bought during the working years and paid back to the individual (the annuitant) during retirement. When you buy an annuity, you are lending money to an insurance company which you will get back later with interest. The company lends out your money at higher interest rates.

Types of Annuity Plans

Annuities incorporate a variety of distinctive features. The money you pay to the issuing company may be paid in three different ways.

- A *single premium annuity* is purchased with a single large payment using the proceeds you may have received as a lump-sum settlement from a pension fund or an insurance policy.

- A *fixed premium annuity* is purchased by making a series of fixed, equal payments on a monthly or annual basis.
- A *variable premium annuity* is purchased by installment payments, the size of which may be changed at your discretion.

An *immediate annuity* is one whose payments may start immediately, and is usually related to the single premium annuity. You can also arrange for payments to start at an age specified in the annuity contract. This is called a *deferred annuity.*

Other arrangements for payout of the money you will receive relate to the time span for payment. A *straight life annuity* guarantees a stipulated monthly income for one person for life. It pays no death benefits to your survivors, nor does it have a cash surrender value. A $10,000 annuity for a 65-year-old woman would yield monthly payments between $70 and $90. The figures for a 65-year-old man would be higher because the average man has a shorter life span than the average woman of the same age. The use of separate actuarial tables for men and women has been ruled discriminatory and unconstitutional by the U.S. Supreme Court. As the new unisex mortality tables come into use, annuity figures for both men and women will be the same. In a *life with a term certain* payout, one person is guaranteed lifetime income with a guarantee period, such as *10 years certain* or *20 years certain.* If you die before the end of the certain term, a designated beneficiary receives the same monthly income for the remainder of the period. Under the option, known as the *cash refund annuity,* a lump-sum payment is made to your designated beneficiary. Under the *joint and survivor annuity,* lifetime income is guaranteed for two persons. The cost depends on the age and sex of each person. You will note in Table 4.4 that a man of 65 has a life expectancy of 13.9 years and a 65-year old woman, 18.3 years. Costs of an annuity for a woman are higher because of her average longer life expectancy. Unisex mortality tables eliminate the cost differences.

Table 4.4
Life Expectancy for Men and Women, Ages 55–65

Age	Average number of years remaining	
	Men	Women
55	20.6	26.2
56	19.9	25.3
57	19.1	24.5
58	18.4	23.7
59	17.7	22.9
60	17.0	22.1
61	16.4	21.3
62	15.7	20.6
63	15.1	19.8
64	14.5	19.1
65	13.9	18.3

Source: U.S. Department of Health and Human Services

A variation of the *life with a term certain* payout is the *installment-refund annuity.* Lifetime payments are guaranteed under this plan. However, if you should die before the total of the payments equals the purchase price, payments would continue to your beneficiary until the amount paid out is equal to the purchase price.

A recent development is the *wraparound annuity.* What distinguishes the wraparound from other deferred annuities is your control over the investment of the funds in the account. You can decide to invest your money in a money market fund or any other type of mutual fund, or you can invest in stocks or bonds, and you can switch back and forth to take advantage of changes in market conditions.

A distinction is made between *fixed dollar annuities* and *variable annuities.* In a *fixed dollar annuity* your funds are invested in a portfolio of bonds, paying a set amount of interest. Your annuity therefore is set to pay you a fixed monthly amount which remains unchanged over the years. In a *variable annuity,* you buy a certain number of "units" whose value will fluctuate each month because the company invests your payments in the stock market and stock prices fluctuate daily. Your monthly annuity will depend on the value of the "units" you own that month, and your monthly check will fluctuate.

In a *tax deferred annuity,* payments to your account are made with pre-tax dollars which become tax sheltered, and also you pay no taxes on the interest as it accumulates. When you eventually withdraw the money after you retire, you pay income taxes, but at that point you are presumably in a lower tax bracket. In this sense it is similar to an IRA or a Keogh Plan. Employees of public school systems and nonprofit organizations usually arrange to have a payroll deduction before taxes to build up contributions in a tax deferred annuity.

Advantages of Annuities

Annuities as a source of retirement income have both advantages and disadvantages. Among the advantages of an annuity are the following:

1. It is the safest way to guarantee a fixed monthly income for life.
2. It is structured in such a way that you will never outlive your capital because it will pay you as long as you live.
3. It requires no medical examination, a practice which may benefit the company, since you would probably collect fewer payments if you were not very healthy.
4. It frees you from the responsibility of money management and the headache of having to make investment decisions.
5. It offers a tax benefit in that some part of each annuity payout qualifies as *return on capital* which is tax-free.

Disadvantages of Annuities

Some of the disadvantages of annuities as a source of retirement income are significant. These include the following:

1. Because the monthly payment is fixed for the rest of your life, most offer no protection against inflation, which takes its toll every year to a greater or lesser degree.
2. The money you invest is tied up forever, because an annuity contract is irrevocable by either side once payments to you have begun.

3. If you should need a large sum of money in an emergency situation, you cannot borrow against your annuity once payments have begun.
4. Sales charges and management fees can be very large and thus can make quite a dent in your potential return.

Who Should Buy An Annuity?

Who, then, is likely to buy an annuity? One prospective customer is a person with a large sum of money who would like to avoid the responsibility of money management and who needs maximum income but wants absolute safety in terms of guaranteed monthly payment. Or, perhaps, a couple who has sold the family home at a good profit and is satisfied to have a fixed monthly income for life under a *joint and survivor annuity*. In any case, shop around and compare contracts. Watch out for disclaimers and qualifiers in the contract, and make sure your net monthly income is clearly stated.

MISCELLANEOUS SOURCES OF RETIREMENT INCOME

Up to this point, savings, investments, life insurance, and annuities have been considered as sources of retirement income. A number of additional sources of retirement income are available. An analysis of each of these follows:

Employment: Full-Time or Part-Time

A major source of retirement income is employment, either full-time or part-time. Many retirees find that they are unable to make ends meet through Social Security alone or supplemented by a small pension or other income. Others who are able to live comfortably on the income they have may find retirement life unsatisfying or unsuitable for their particular psychological and emotional needs. Such retirees will be in the job market again, seeking either full-time or part-time employment. Chapter 10 looks at second careers.

Reverse Mortgages

For many retirees, their main assets often are the homes in which they live. Through the *reverse mortgage,* these retirees can cash in on the increased value of their homes and then continue to live in them. It works in the following way: If you bought a $20,000 home in 1950 that is now worth $70,000, you could arrange to borrow up to 80 percent of that, or $56,000. The money could be taken out in a lump-sum and invested in an annuity, or in monthly installments to be paid to you by the bank over a specified period, for example, ten years. At the end of that time, you must repay the loan of $56,000 plus interest. If your house appreciated in value over that period, you could *roll over* the mortgage and take out a new one for the increased value of your home, and thus continue to receive monthly checks. Or, you could sell the house and pay off the mortgage. Or, if you died before the loan matured, your estate could sell the house to satisfy the debt. The problem is that the couple may outlive their capital. The concept of a reverse mortgage was approved in 1978 by the Federal Home Loan Bank Board, which regulates federally chartered savings and loan associations.

Workers' Compensation

All fifty states provide *Workers' Compensation,* a form of disability benefits paid to workers for job-related injuries, accidents, and illnesses. It is the oldest form of social insurance in the United States, dating back to 1908 when Congress set up a program under the Federal Employees Compensation Act to cover specified federal employees in hazardous occupations. Most people today are covered by state programs.

Typical benefits for a fully disabled person range from 60 to 65 percent of a worker's take-home pay. The worker may also receive Social Security benefits at the same time, provided that the combination does not exceed 80 percent of pre-disability monthly earnings.

Veterans' Benefits

Veterans of American wars are entitled to a variety of benefits distributed by the Veterans Administration, including low-cost life insurance, VA hospital and medical care, VA guaranteed home loans, allowances for education and training, disability, and death and pension benefits. Pension benefits can provide a significant amount of retirement income for an eligible veteran and family. The amount of the pension varies in accordance with a veteran's disability, financial need, income, number of dependents, and net worth. If you are a veteran and think you are eligible, you may write, phone, or visit your nearest VA regional office.

Rents and Royalties

Additional sources of retirement income are *rents* and *royalties*. *Rents* may be derived from the ownership of residential or commercial properties which yield monthly income in the form of rent, usually paid by a tenant to an owner or landlord. A *royalty* is a form of compensation paid to the owner of a right, such as a patent, oil, or mineral right, for the use of it, or compensation from a work paid to its author or composer.

Hobby Income

Hobbies and crafts are often turned into sources of retirement income. How much can be earned depends on the market in your area and on the supply and demand factors. Pottery making, furniture making and/or finishing, photography, writing poetry or short stories, mosaic art, and macramé can be translated into a source of retirement income. You can work full-time or part-time depending on your own interest. Some communities have nonprofit shops which display and sell items made by senior citizens and retirees. After deducting overhead costs for operation of such an outlet, the balance of the selling price goes to the maker of a handcrafted article.

Inheritances

Individuals who are in their forties, fifties or sixties today may have parents living who are in their sixties, seventies, or eighties. It is probably reasonable to expect that the younger generation will receive inheritances from the older generation. An inheritance may be nominal or it may be significant. A larger inheritance, when it becomes available, often makes the difference between marginal and comfortable financial status at retirement.

Non-Cost Services

Equivalent to extra income is money not spent. Retirees have good reason to pinch pennies on services which annually consume up to 25 or 30 percent of after-tax income.

Savings can be achieved when people do more things for themselves, such as home and car repairs, painting, and furniture repair and refinishing. Do-it-yourself books are available at most home centers and libraries.

Another way to save money on services is through the age-old barter system, that is, swapping skills with friends and neighbors. An individual with carpentry or woodworking skills can exchange these for electrical or plumbing skills.

Public Welfare

Social assistance, or public welfare, refers to the availability of benefits which are conditional on proof of need. Today this includes the Federal Supplemental Security Income or SSI program, (discussed in Chapter 2), the Medicaid program (discussed in Chapter 9), and food stamps. The Supplemental Security Income (SSI) program, approved by Congress in 1972, effective January 1, 1974, provides a guaranteed annual minimum income for the needy aged, blind, and disabled. Medicaid provides health care benefits for the needy, and food stamps can be exchanged for food items in the supermarket. These are sources of retirement income for some.

SELF-STUDY: MY MISCELLANEOUS INCOME

Estimate your miscellaneous sources of retirement income in the following table.

Source of retirement income	Estimated monthly income
Employment	$_____
Reverse mortgage	_____
Workers' Compensation	_____
Veterans' pension	_____
Rents	_____
Royalties	_____
Hobby income	_____
Other (itemize):	
_____	_____
_____	_____
_____	_____
Total	$_____

GLOSSARY

Annuity. Guarantees a fixed income over a specific period of time to the insured or the insured's beneficiary, of a specified payment for life or for a period of years. (See Cash Refund Annuity, Deferred Annuity, Fixed Dollar Annuity, Fixed Premium Annuity, Immediate Pay Annuity, Installment Refund Annuity, Joint and Survivor Annuity, Life Annuity With a Term Certain, Single Premium Annuity, Straight Life Annuity, Tax Deferred Annuity, Variable Annuity, Variable Premium Annuity, Wraparound Annuity.)

Balanced Mutual Fund. Balances its investment holdings among common stock, preferred stock, and bonds.

Banker's Acceptance. In international trade a seller draws a draft that is payable by the buyer within a stipulated period of time. By accepting the draft, a bank guarantees payment at maturity, thus enabling the draft to be sold in the open market.

Basis Point. One graduation on a 100-point scale representing one percent. For example, the difference between 10.50% and 10.85% is 35 basis points.

Bear. One who believes that the stock market will decline. (See Bull.)

Bearer Bond. Does not have the owner's name registered on the books of the issuer or on the certificate. Interest and principal, when due, are payable to the holder. (See Coupon Bond, Registered Bond.)

Blue Chip Stock. A stock in a company known nationally for the quality and wide acceptance of its product or services, and for its ability to earn large profits and to pay dividends regularly.

Bond. A written promise, basically an IOU or promissory note, to repay a loan on a specified date while paying the bondholder a specified amount of interest at regular intervals, usually twice a year. (See Bearer Bond, Callable, Convertible, Coupon Bond, Debenture Bond, General Mortgage Bond, Registered Bond.)

Bull. One who believes that the stock market will rise. (See Bear.)

Callable. A *bond* or *preferred stock*, which may be redeemed by the issuing corporation under specified conditions before maturity. (See Convertible.)

Call Option. A right to buy a fixed number of shares of stock at a specified price within a limited period of time. The purchaser hopes that the stock's price will go up by an amount sufficient to provide a profit when the option is sold. If the stock price remains the same or goes down, the investment in the *call option* is lost. (See Put Option.)

Capital Gain. The profit received from the sale of a capital asset.

Capital Loss. The loss resulting from the sale or exchange of a capital asset.

Cash Refund Annuity. Pays income to the insured for life, but if the insured dies before the payments equal the amount the insured put into the annuity less specified administrative charges, the balance is paid to the insured's beneficiary or beneficiaries in a lump sum. (See Installment Refund Annuity, Joint and Survivor Annuity.)

Cash Value. The amount available in cash if a person voluntarily terminates a whole life insurance policy or an endowment policy before it becomes payable. If the insured has been paying the premiums on a cash value policy for 20 to 25 years, the *cash value* is usually about half the face value of the policy.

Certificate of Accrual on Treasury Securities (CATS). Securities which represent ownership of interest or principal payments on U.S. Treasury notes or bonds, which in turn are direct obligations of the U.S. Government. CATS are taxable zero coupon securities that are extremely liquid. (See Zero Coupon Bond.)

Certificate of Deposit (CD). A type of savings deposit available to anyone who deposits a specified sum of money for a set period of time. Since the deregulation of banking, effective October 1, 1983, each bank can set its own rates, terms, and minimum deposits. A CD usually carries a penalty for early withdrawal.

Closed-End Mutual Fund. Issues a limited number of shares, traded at prevailing market price and listed on one or more of the major stock exchanges. New shares are issued infrequently. (See Open-End Mutual Fund.)

Collectible. An item purchased for its value or enjoyment. Investors may purchase a collectible in the expectation that its value will increase and thus yield a profit when it is ultimately sold. Items include jewelry, diamonds, rare books, paintings, other art works, stamps, antiques, Oriental rugs, and so forth.

Commercial Paper. A corporate promissory note, usually in denominations of $100,000 or more, used to raise funds for limited periods, usually 60 days or less. Higher risk loans pay higher interest rates.

Common Stock. Securities which represent an ownership interest in a corporation and the right to share in profits, known as *dividends,* after the company pays its expenses and prior claims. Owners of *common stock* have the potential of earning not only dividends but also capital appreciation. (See Preferred Stock.)

Common Stock Mutual Fund. The most popular form of mutual fund; funds are invested primarily in common stocks.

Compounding. The process of earning interest on the interest already earned on an investment. When interest is left to accumulate, *compound interest* is earned.

Convertible. A *bond* or *preferred stock* which may be exchanged by the owner for common stock or another security, usually of the same company, in accordance with the terms of the issue. (See Callable.)

Coupon Bond. Postdated interest coupons are attached to the bond, and are clipped as they become due. The coupon or coupons are presented at a bank for deposit or exchange for cash. The bank collects from the issuing corporation or government. (See Bearer Bond, Registered Bond.)

Cumulative Preferred Stock. A security which has a provision that if one or more dividends are omitted, the omitted dividends must be paid before dividends may be paid on the company's common stock. (See Participating Preferred Stock, Callable, Convertible.)

Debenture Bond. Backed by the general credit of the corporation and not by any specified piece of property.

Deferred Annuity. Begins to pay out after several years. (See Immediate-Pay Annuity.)

Dividend. The payment to the holder of *common stock* or *preferred stock* by a corporation. On common stock, the *dividend* varies with the fortunes of the company and may be omitted if business is bad. On preferred stock, the *dividend* is usually a fixed amount. (See Common Stock, Preferred Stock, Interest.)

Emergency Savings Fund. A cash reserve that will serve as a cushion in case of an unexpected emergency, in an amount equal to the cost of living for from six months to a year, depending on individual needs.

Endowment Insurance Policy. A cash value life insurance policy that assesses premiums over a specified period of time. At the end of that time, the *cash value* equals the *face value* and is redeemed. Used for a child's education or for retirement income.

Equity. The net investment in a business enterprise or in a home that represents ownership and/or that portion of borrowed funds or a mortgage which the owner has amortized.

Fannie Maes. The nickname for bonds issued by the Federal National Mortgage Association (FNMA), a private corporation created by Congress, to serve as a secondary mortgage market. *Fannie Mae* bonds may be purchased through a bond broker or by buying into a mutual fund which specializes in these securities. (See Ginnie Maes, Unit Trust.)

Fixed Dollar Annuity. Pays a fixed monthly amount that remains unchanged over the years because the funds in the annuity account are invested in a portfolio of bonds that pay a set amount of interest. (See Variable Annuity.)

Fixed Premium Annuity. An annuity purchased by making a fixed payment each month or each year. (See Single Premium Annuity, Variable Premium Annuity.)

Futures Contract. A contract to buy or sell a given commodity on a future date for a specified price. The market that handles *futures contracts*, known as the *futures market*, trades in agricultural products such as wheat, soybeans, pork bellies, metals, and also financial instruments. Businesses utilize futures as a hedge against price changes. Speculators buy and sell futures to profit from price changes.

General Mortgage Bond. Secured by a blanket mortgage on a company's property. Some *mortgage bonds* are secured by a specific piece of property, such as land, buildings, or machinery.

General Obligation Bond. A *municipal bond* whose payment of interest and repayment of principal are backed by the full faith and credit of the issuing government. (See Revenue Bond.)

Ginnie Maes. The nickname for bonds issued by the Government National Mortgage Association (GNMA), a subsidiary organization of the U.S. Department of Housing and Urban Development, which guarantees funds invested in the mortgage market by institutional investors, such as pension funds. *Ginnie Mae* bonds may be purchased through a bond broker or by buying into a mutual fund that specializes in these securities. (See Fannie Maes, Unit Trust.)

Immediate Pay Annuity. An annuity which begins to pay immediately. (See Deferred Annuity.)

Income Mutual Fund. Seeks to return a higher level of dividends than other types by investing in high-yielding common stocks, preferred stocks, and bonds.

Installment Refund Annuity. Pays income to the insured for life, but if the insured dies before the payment equals the amount the insured put into the annuity less specified administrative charges, the balance is paid to the insured's beneficiary or beneficiaries in regular payments until they reach that amount. (See Cash Refund Annuity, Joint and Survivor Annuity.)

Interest. Payments a borrower pays a lender for the use of money. A corporation pays *interest* on its bonds to its bondholders. Banks pay *interest* to depositors. (See Bond, Dividend.)

Joint and Survivor Annuity. Guarantees income to two or more people, generally a husband and wife, so that the surviving spouse can receive the same monthly income or some percentage portion of the monthly income as long as the survivor lives. (See Cash Refund Annuity, Installment Refund Annuity.)

Life Annuity With a Term Certain. Payout to one person is guaranteed for life with a guarantee period, such as *10 years certain* or *20 years certain.* If the insured dies before the end of the *certain term,* a designated beneficiary receives the same monthly income for the remainder of the period. (See Straight Life Annuity.)

Life Insurance. Income protection for one's dependents against the hardships they would suffer from the loss of the insured's income if the insured died prematurely. (See Annuity.)

Limited Payment Life Insurance. Similar to a *whole* or *straight life insurance* policy except that premium payments end after a specified number of years, such as 10, 20, or 30 years, or at a specified age. The insured is still covered for life insurance after the premium payments are completed.

Load Mutual Fund. Maintains a sales force and charges a commission or *load* for the shares one buys. In most cases, no commission is charged when shares are sold. About two-thirds of mutual funds are *load mutual funds.* (See No-Load Mutual Fund.)

Margin Account. An investor maintains a deposit of money in a brokerage account. When a stock is bought, only part of the purchase price is cash; the rest is borrowed from the broker. *Buying on margin* is done in the hope of a price advance, enabling the trader to repay the loan and make a profit. If the market declines, however, the broker may request an additional deposit in the margin account. If it is not forthcoming, the stock is sold to liquidate the loan, and the trader suffers a loss.

Money Market. The collective name for transactions involving the borrowing and lending of money for a short term by the government, banks, large corporations, securities dealers, and individual investors. Short term is considered to be one year or less.

Money Market Deposit Account (MMDA). Savings deposited in a savings bank, savings and loan association, or commercial bank that are invested in money market instruments, earning a relatively high rate of interest, and insured by the U.S. Federal Deposit Insurance Corporation or the U.S. Federal Savings and Loan Insurance Corporation. (See Money Market Instruments, Money Market Mutual Fund.)

Money Market Instruments. Short-term paper traded in the *money market,* such as, *U.S. Treasury bills, certificates of deposit, commercial paper, banker's acceptances,* and *repurchase agreements.*

Money Market Mutual Fund. A *mutual fund* whose investments are in high-yield *money market instruments.* Its purpose is to make this type of investment, which is normally purchased by institutions in large denominations of $100,000 or more, available to individuals of moderate means who can buy into the fund with as little as $1,000.

Moody's Investors Service. A well-known stock and bond rating service. The highest rating is Aaa (Triple A) and the lowest is C. (See Standard & Poor's Corporation.)

Municipal Bonds. Debt securities issued by States, counties, and cities that pay interest income, usually exempt from Federal income taxes, and exempt from the income tax of the State that issued the bonds. Bonds issued by counties or other subdivisions within a state are exempt from the income tax of the home state as well as from Federal income taxes. (See General Obligation Bond, Revenue Bond.)

Mutual Fund. A company that collects the funds of hundreds or thousands of small investors through the sale of stock and then uses the funds for a variety of investments. A *mutual fund* is classified according to its investment objective. (See Balanced Mutual Fund, Common Stock Mutual Fund, Income Mutual Fund, Specialized Mutual Fund.)

National Association of Securities Dealers Automated Quotations (NASDAQ). An automated information network which provides brokers and dealers with price quotations on securities traded *over-the-counter*, namely, stocks of companies without sufficient shares, stockholders, or earnings to qualify for listing on a major exchange.

Negotiable Order of Withdrawal Account (NOW account). Checking accounts that earn interest, or viewed another way, savings accounts on which checks can be written. Savings banks, savings and loan associations, commercial banks, and credit unions were permitted to offer *NOW accounts* starting in 1981. Ordinary *NOW accounts* require no minimum balance and pay the same interest as *passbook savings accounts.* (See Super NOW Account.)

No-Load Mutual Fund. Has no sales force, charges no commission or sales fee, and waits for investors to buy its shares. About one-third of *mutual funds* are *no-load.* (See Load Mutual Fund.)

Open-End Mutual Fund. Continuously sells new shares of stock and purchases the shares of those desiring redemption, buying and selling its shares at a fixed price and using whatever funds it has for investment. (See Closed-End Mutual Fund.)

Options. (See Call Option, Put Option.)

Par Value. As applied to stocks and bonds, the face value printed on the stock certificate or on the bond instrument. Par value is assigned at the time of original issue. Many stocks are issued with no par value.

Participating Preferred Stock. A company's stock which is entitled to its stated dividend and also to additional dividends on a specified basis after payment of dividends on the company's common stock. (See Callable, Convertible, Cumulative Preferred Stock.)

Passbook Savings Account. Unspent cash income that is deposited in a savings bank, a savings and loan association, or a commercial bank. The account pays a relatively low interest rate, about 5¼ or 5½ percent, and is insured by the U.S. Federal Deposit Insurance Corporation or the U.S. Federal Savings and Loan Insurance Corporation for up to $100,000 per account.

Penny Stocks. Issues selling at less than $1 a share. These low-priced issues are often highly speculative.

Preferred Stock. Securities entitled to receive fixed and stated *dividends* before earnings are distributed to the common stockholders. *Preferred stock* represents an ownership interest in a corporation, usually having the right to vote when preferred dividends are in default for a specified period. In case of bankruptcy or liquidation, *preferred stock* holders have priority over common stockholders in the division of the company's assets, but only after bondholders have been paid. (See Callable, Common Stock, Convertible, Cumulative Preferred Stock, Participating Preferred Stock.)

Price/Earnings Ratio (P/E Ratio). One of the methods for gauging the value of a stock. A stock's current market price divided by the most recent earnings-per-share figure.

Put Option. A right to sell a fixed number of shares of stock at a specified price within a limited period of time. The purchaser hopes that the stock's price will go down by an amount sufficient to provide a profit when the option is sold. If the stock price remains the same or goes up, the investment in the *put option* is lost. (See Call Option.)

Real Estate Investment Trust (REIT). Similar to a *mutual fund.* Small investors buy shares in a REIT that invests in real estate, including shopping centers and large commercial properties. Return on investment is liberal, but because of the nature of the real estate market, a REIT is highly speculative.

Registered Bond. Registered on the books of the issuing company or governmental unit in the name of the owner whose name also appears on the bond. A *registered bond* can be transferred only when endorsed by the registered owner. (See Bearer Bond, Coupon Bond.)

Repurchase Agreement. Known as a *repo.* A bank in need of money for a short period of time, usually one or more days, borrows money from a *money market fund*, using U.S. Treasury securities as collateral. The bank sells Treasury paper to the *money market fund* with the provision that it will buy the paper back within the specified period of time.

Revenue Bond. A *municipal bond* whose payment of interest and repayment of principal are backed by the income earned by the facility, such as an airport, bridge, or tunnel, built with the money raised by the bond issue. (See General Obligation Bond.)

Reverse Mortgage. Enables retirees to cash in on the increased value of their homes by borrowing against the increased value, taking money out in a lump-sum and investing in an *annuity*, yielding regular monthly income. The concept of a *reverse mortgage* was approved in 1978 by the Federal Home Loan Bank Board, which regulates Federally chartered savings and loan associations.

Savings Bond. A security sold by the U.S. Government that offers fixed income with minimum risk and minimum investment. The bonds are sold at a discount and the interest accumulates over a designated time period.

Single Premium Annuity. An annuity purchased with a single lump-sum payment. (See Fixed Premium Annuity, Variable Premium Annuity.)

Specialized Mutual Fund. Concentrates its investments in one or two fields, such as gold, Eurodollars, money market instruments, commodities, options, foreign stocks, energy securities, and so forth.

Specialized Policy. Covers a particular situation, such as mortgage insurance, which would pay the unpaid balance of the mortgage on the insured's house if the insured should die before completing the mortgage payments.

Standard & Poor's Corporation. A well-known stock and bond rating service. The highest rating is AAA (Triple A), and the lowest, D. (See Moody's Investors Service.)

Straight Life Annuity. Guarantees a stipulated monthly income for one person for life, but ends with that person's death, making no payments to beneficiaries or survivors. It has no cash surrender value. May be appropriate for individuals who have no dependents and want maximum income. (See Life Annuity With A Term Certain.)

Super NOW Account. The Super Negotiable Order of Withdrawal Account (Super Now Account), started in late 1982, pays an interest rate that is higher than the NOW account but somewhat less than a Money Market Deposit Account, requires a minimum balance, but offers checking privileges. If an account falls below the minimum balance, the bank applies a penalty fee. These accounts are insured up to $100,000 each and place no limit on the amount of the check written as long as the required minimum balance is maintained. (See Negotiable Order of Withdrawal Account (NOW Account).)

Tax Deferred Annuity. Payments to an annuity account are made with pre-tax dollars, which become tax-sheltered. The insured pays no income taxes on the amount deposited in the annuity account or on the interest earned by the principal. When the insured eventually begins to withdraw the money after retirement, he or she pays income taxes on the amounts withdrawn, but at that point is presumably in a lower tax bracket.

Term Life Insurance. Covers the insured for a specified number of years, usually one, five, or ten years, paying the beneficiaries the face amount of the policy if the insured dies within the specified period. The premium is less than a whole life or endowment policy because it accumulates no cash value and represents the cost of pure insurance plus a charge for administration. It is renewable at the end of each *term* until age 65 or 70.

Unit Trust. A *mutual fund* in which units of ownership are purchased in a fixed and diversified portfolio of securities, including corporate bonds, municipal bonds, and preferred stock, which provide a steady, guaranteed income.

Universal Life Insurance. A new form of life insurance that enables the policy holder to vary both the amount of premium payment and the amount of death benefit to fit the changing needs of a growing family. Cash values can grow at competitive interest rates, giving the insured some control over the speed of cash buildup.

U.S. Treasury Bill. Known as *T-bills,* these short-term securities, maturing in 3, 6, or 12 months, are backed by the full faith and credit of the U.S. Government. The *T-bill* pays an attractive yield that is exempt from State and local income taxes, subject only to Federal income taxes. It is sold at a discount from its $10,000 face value.

U.S. Treasury Bond. A security that matures in ten or more years, selling at face value, and paying a fixed rate of interest twice a year throughout ownership. Backed by the full faith and credit of the U.S. Government, the interest is exempt from State and local income taxes, subject only to Federal income taxes.

U.S. Treasury Note. A security that matures in two to ten years. The minimum investment for a two to four-year note is $5,000 and for a four-year up to a ten-year note, $1,000. Backed by the full faith and credit of the U.S. Government, the interest is exempt from State and local income taxes, subject only to Federal income taxes.

Variable Annuity. The monthly payment fluctuates because the funds in the annuity account are invested in a portfolio of stocks, and stock prices fluctuate daily. If average stock prices rise, the insured receives a higher annuity, and vice versa. (See Fixed Dollar Annuity.)

Variable Life Insurance. A new form of life insurance that has a fixed premium similar to a whole life insurance contract but which enables the insured to direct the investment of the cash accumulation among a variety of mutual funds and other types of investments, while providing a guaranteed minimum death benefit.

Variable Premium Annuity. An annuity purchased by monthly or annual installment payments, the size of which may be changed at the insured's discretion. (See Fixed Premium Annuity, Single Premium Annuity.)

Whole, or Straight, Life Insurance. As long as the insured pays the premiums, he or she is insured for life. It includes a savings feature, or *cash value,* against which the insured can borrow, paying interest on the loan. The insured can withdraw the *cash value* completely if he or she terminates the life insurance. When he or she dies, the beneficiaries collect the face value of the policy.

Workers' Compensation. A form of disability insurance benefits paid to workers for job-related injuries, accidents, and illnesses. It is a source of retirement income for individuals with job-related disabilities.

Wraparound Annuity. Enables the owner of the annuity to control the investment of the funds in the account. The owner can invest in stocks or bonds or in a money market mutual fund or any other type of mutual fund, and can switch from one form of investment to another to take advantage of changing market conditions. (See Fixed Dollar Annuity, Tax Deferred Annuity, Variable Annuity.)

Zero Coupon Bond. Sells at a discount, pays interest only at maturity, and promises a large capital (interest) accumulation by maturity. For example, an 8-year *zero coupon bond,* priced at $302, with a yield of 15 percent, would pay $1,000 after 8 years, a tripling of the original investment. The IRS requires that taxes be paid on the annual interest earned by a corporate *zero coupon bond* even though not collected. Buying a "home state" municipal *zero coupon bond* eliminates the tax problem. Types of *zero coupon bonds* include CDs, Corporates, Municipals, Treasuries, and more. (See Certificates of Accrual on Treasury Securities (CATS).)

Chapter 5
Budgeting, Credit, Inflation, Taxes, and Tax Shelters

In retirement planning it is essential to know your financial goals. The first step is to calculate your net worth, which requires that you list your assets and liabilities. Knowing your financial situation at a given point will enable you to plan ahead and to decide where you would like to be financially one year from now, five years from now and on into retirement. The tool for accomplishing this is a budget. This chapter analyzes the budgeting process in detail.

The chapter then examines the role of credit in retirement, describing some of the basics of credit, the illegality of age discrimination, borrowing against your assets, and the use of credit cards.

Inflation is a problem faced by everyone. However, the impact of inflation is particularly devastating on fixed-income retirees. The alternatives for dealing with the problem are limited, but the problem must be dealt with. The section on coping with inflation discusses some suggestions for the retiree.

Finally, this chapter considers the question of taxes and tax shelters in retirement, the impact of the Tax Reform Act of 1986 on older Americans, and why tax shelters are important in the retirement plan.

DEVELOPING A RETIREMENT BUDGET

A budget, which is essentially a spending plan to help you manage your money effectively, is a step in the right direction. Most people can benefit by spending their income more wisely, especially in a period of inflation. Whether you have had experience with a budget or not, it is essential that you plan a budget before you retire. This will enable you to estimate how much money you will need in relation to how much income you expect to have. Most retirees must face the fact that they will have to adjust their spending to fit a reduced income. Fortunately, many expenses will diminish or disappear entirely. For example, savings will accrue in income taxes and in job-related expenses which in retirement are non-existent, such as transportation to and from the job, clothing, meals away from home, and the ability to perform certain services for yourself which previously had to be paid for. However, other expenses may increase or arise for the first time, such as hobby and recreational expenses and certain medical costs.

HOW MUCH RETIREMENT INCOME IS ENOUGH?

A middle-income retiring couple will need between 60 and 80 percent of their preretirement income to live on approximately the same level as they did while employed. If you're single and earning in the middle-income range, you'll need 55 to 75 percent of preretirement income to maintain your present standard of living. Singles and couples in the higher income ranges will need lower percentages of their preretirement incomes because, in general, the higher the income, the greater the reduction in post-retirement living expenses. Table 5.1 indicates retirement income targets at various levels of gross annual income.

Table 5.1

Required Retirement Income Targets

Current Gross Annual Income	Percentage Replacement Required*	Retirement Income Target
$30,000	80%	$24,000
40,000	75%	30,000
50,000	75%	37,500
60,000	70%	42,000
70,000	65%	45,500
80,000 or more	60%	48,000

*These percentages are flexible and can vary depending upon individual circumstances.

HOW MUCH OF A "NEST EGG" DO YOU NEED ?

Often the problem is that many retirees cannot meet their retirement income target. Social Security benefits alone, which provide about 20 to 25 percent of retirement income, are inadequate for a comfortable retirement. Other sources of income, including pensions (Chapter 3), savings and investments, cash value of life insurance, annuities, and miscellaneous sources (Chapter 4), are necessary to supplement Social Security benefits to provide a comfortable income for retirement. For example, a couple with a current gross annual income of $50,000 would require about $37,500, 75 percent of $50,000, to live comfortably after retirement. To illustrate with some hypothetical figures that will vary widely in individual circumstances, a $37,500 retirement income target may be achieved as follows: assume Social Security benefits of $9,000 and a company pension of $17,500, for a total of $26,500. This leaves a shortfall of $11,000 which must be generated by savings and investments. Assuming an average return of 7 percent, the "nest egg" required in this illustration is about $150,000 to $160,000.

By financial planning and budgeting long enough in advance of retirement you can be certain that your post-retirement income will provide you with the level of living you desire. If you conclude that it will not, you will have the time to develop additional sources of income, or to adjust to the idea of living on less by reducing expenditures.

A Typical Retirement Expense Budget

Table 5.2 presents a typical retirement expense budget for a retired couple. The expenditure figures are allocated after the payment of personal income taxes. Each figure may vary by plus or minus 5 percent since a budget for expenses is a very personal matter. No two people think precisely the same in these matters. However, the percentage distribution among the groups can be useful as a bench-mark in evaluating your own expenditure pattern, whether your annual retirement income is $15,000, $25,000, or higher. The percentages are derived from actual annual budgets for retired couples and represent an approximate distribution.

Table 5.2

Annual Expenses of an Average Retired Couple

Budget Item	Percent*
Housing	30%
Food	22%
Medical and dental care	10%
Transportation	8%
Clothing and personal care	5%
Gifts and contributions	5%
Recreation, reading, other	20%
Total	100%

*Percentages are approximate, but may be useful as a benchmark in evaluating your own expenditure pattern.

The housing or shelter item includes rental costs or homeowner costs, whichever applies. Rental costs include contract rent, estimated costs of fuel and utilities where these are not part of the rent, and insurance on household contents. Homeowner costs are based on the assumption that retired couples own their homes and need make no payments for mortgage principal or interest.

The food item includes food-at-home costs, about 90 percent of the food total, as well as a number of meals away from home and an allowance for meals for guests, both of which vary.

Transportation includes costs of ownership and operation of an auto by auto owners and public transportation for nonowners of autos.

The medical care component provides for out-of-pocket costs for Medicare and allows for items not covered by Medicare, such as dental care, eyeglasses, most out-of-hospital prescription and nonprescription drugs, and a checkup visit to a physician.

The clothing percentage includes new clothing as well as cleaning and repairs. Personal care includes personal grooming costs such as barber shop and beauty shop services as well as costs of cosmetics and perfumes. The other expenses are self-explanatory.

The Budgeting Process

The budgeting process can be summarized in the following six steps.

1. ***Calculate Your Net Worth.*** Before attempting to develop and implement a budget, it is important to know how you stand financially. Every business prepares a financial statement, known as a balance sheet, at least once a year to get a clear picture of its assets, liabilities, and net worth at a given moment in time. An understanding of your assets (the financial and material possessions you own), your liabilities (your debts or the amounts you owe), and your net worth (your assets minus your liabilities), tell you your financial position so that you can plan for the future more intelligently. Your net worth position, if it is adequate, can provide a cushion for emergencies which you can draw upon if any special need arises. An adequate net worth position can also provide you with an inflation cushion which may help you someday to restore your budget to balance. Worksheet 5.1 in the Self-Study section will enable you to compute your net worth, an essential step in financial planning for retirement.

   A net worth statement should be drawn up at least once a year. This provides you with the opportunity to study your financial position, to determine whether you are better off or worse off than the previous year, and to set goals and take steps that will help you to improve your position. Your net worth changes every year in the same way that your income and spending patterns change.

2. ***Record Your Current Expenses.*** Before you can begin to draw up a budget, it is necessary to have an accurate record of your current spending pattern. You will be surprised at how much this will tell you, particularly if you have never previously kept such data. You may have a formal written budget, or you may be functioning with a time-tested allocation of your money even though you have never written it down. In any case, you must start by analyzing precisely how you are spending your money now.

   You must keep an exact record of every expenditure you make for every day of the month. No amount expended, no matter how small, may be omitted. You should keep such records for at least a year before you can use the figures for any projection. A year is a reasonable yardstick since month-to-month expenses vary for such items as clothing, insurance, and even entertainment. Such a set of data will reveal much about your personal habits, likes, and dislikes. And certainly such a record will answer the question heard so often, "Where does all my money go?" Worksheets 5.2 and 5.3 in the Self-Study section provide the format for collecting this information.

3. ***Estimate Your Retirement Spending Pattern.*** Once you have data on your current spending pattern (Worksheet 5.3), you can enter the monthly averages and the year's total for each expense item in columns (2) and (3) of Worksheet 5.4 in the Self-Study section. This will enable you to estimate your first year's retirement spending pattern in columns (4) and (5) of Worksheet 5.4. Some of your expenses, particularly those which are job-related, will cease or almost cease when you retire. For example, the cost of your lunches at work or the cost of coffee-breaks will stop. However, there will be a counterbalancing increase in "at home" food costs. Other expenses will continue but be lower after retirement. For example, your clothing costs will probably be lower, since retirees generally dress more casually. Your Federal income taxes will be lower because you will probably be in a lower tax bracket. However, this is

not always true since some fortunate individuals enjoy a retirement income which is about equal to preretirement income.

Starting at age 65, all individuals enjoy some income tax benefits, such as an extra income tax exemption. Remember too that your Social Security income is not taxable by the Federal, state, or city government. Your housing cost may be less if you have paid off your mortgage by the time you retire. Some of your expenses may be higher after retirement, such as health insurance to supplement Medicare gaps. Also, you will probably find an increase in expenditures for hobbies, recreation, and travel.

4. Estimate Your Income After Retirement. Assuming that you have decided whether to work or not after retirement, you should now be able to estimate your retirement income. (See Worksheet 5.5 in the Self-Study section.) If you plan to work part-time or full-time, estimate your take-home pay both monthly and for the year. Some or all of your income tax expense may be taken care of by withholding before you arrive at take-home pay. Will your spouse continue to work after you retire? Until when?

If you will be receiving a pension, estimate the amount you will receive. Enter also your Social Security benefits, anticipated or actual, computed as closely as you can, and any other income you expect to receive including annuities, royalties, interest, dividends, veterans' benefits, rents from real estate, profit-sharing plans, or other income you will be receiving. Record all these figures on Worksheet 5.5.

5. Reconcile Your Income and Expenses. Worksheet 5.6 is a summary table which you can use for balancing your estimated retirement income and expenses. If your income is greater than your expenses, you will have a surplus. What an ideal situation! However, if your income is smaller than your expenses, then you end up with a deficit, which will require some adjustments, such as the following: (1) increase your income; (2) reduce your expenses; (3) consume available capital. If you consume some of your capital by selling securities or real estate or withdrawing money from your emergency savings fund or your money market fund, your future income will be reduced and further adjustments in your calculations will have to be made. Possible solutions for a deficit in your anticipated retirement budget should be recorded on Worksheet 5.7.

6. Review and Adjust Budget Items. At the end of every two or three months, you can check your expenditure pattern to note whether you are in line with your averages or are overspending and building up a deficit. A two-or three-month period is adequate to spot where the problems lie. You may find, for example, that meals outside the home and the phone bills are larger than anticipated based upon your projected expenditures. If, for whatever reason, you find that you cannot reduce those expenditures, then in order to keep your budget in balance, you will have to cut back on other expenditure items.

In some instances, you may find it necessary to reexamine your priorities. If you were building up your savings for a vacation and a new refrigerator, you may decide that you cannot save for both at the same time. If your savings schedule is not on target, you may wish to use such devices as automatic payroll deductions, if still employed, or monthly transfers from your checking account to your savings account.

Tips on Budgeting

Try not to become bogged down in nickel-and-dime details. Round your budget entries to the nearest dollar. Remember that the budget is a tool which, if used correctly, can give the typical household a realistic focus on income and outgo and on how you handle your money. The budget plan should reflect your retirement goals as well as your goals for the current year, and it must be flexible enough so that you can adapt to changing circumstances.

Every household, especially a retiree's, needs a financial plan which incorporates specific savings programs for achieving specific goals. Your budget is a very personal tool. It should reflect your own needs and goals and should be developed from your own experience. Do not permit the needs and goals of others to influence your budget. Your current income as well as your projected retirement income should be reflected in your budget. The expectations of others, either family or friends, should play no role in the budget decisions which you make. A budget will help you to think about and plan for the future. At the same time it will help you to live within your means. A budget can make your retirement years secure and satisfying.

Good money management habits can be developed with time and effort. Once you have mastered the technique, you will find that you can live free of money problems.

SELF-STUDY:
PLANNING MY BUDGET

1. On Worksheet 5.1 record the value of all your assets and all your liabilities as of a particular date. You have listed your assets in the previous chapter. Since our income tax year is January 1—December 31, a suggested date is December 31. If you repeat the analysis each year as of December 31, you will have a series which you can study to note changes in your financial condition. Note that total assets minus total liabilities equals your net worth, an important figure to know in personal money management.

Worksheet 5.1

Assets, Liabilities, and Net Worth of

Name:_____ As of _____
(date)

Assets	Amount
Cash on hand	$_____
Checking accounts	$_____
Savings accounts	$_____
Certificates of deposit	$_____
Credit union accounts	$_____
Life insurance, cash value	$_____
Annuities, current value	$_____
Profit-sharing plans, cash value	$_____
Pension reserves, cash value	$_____
U.S. Treasury paper	$_____
Common stocks, today's value	$_____
Preferred stocks, today's value	$_____
Bonds, today's value	$_____
Mutual fund shares, today's value	$_____

Assets	Amount
Money owed to you	$_____
Your home, market value	$_____
Your vacation cottage, market value	$_____
Other real estate	$_____
Automobile (his), Blue Book value	$_____
Automobile (hers), Blue Book value	$_____
Home appliances	$_____
Furniture	$_____
Recreation and hobby items	$_____
Collections (art, stamps, coins)	$_____
Antiques	$_____
Furs	$_____
Jewelry	$_____
Other assets: list them (include IRA, Keogh, etc.)	
_____	$_____
_____	$_____
_____	$_____
Total assets	$_____

Liabilities

Mortgage(s), balance(s) due	$_____
Automobile(s) loan(s), balance(s) due	$_____
Installment debts, balance due	$_____

Liabilities	Amount
Charge accounts, balance due	$_____
Personal loans, balance due	$_____
Other debts owed: list them	
_____	$_____
_____	$_____
_____	$_____
Total liabilities	$_____
Net worth	
Total assets	$_____
minus Total liabilities	$_____
equals Net worth	$_____

2. On Worksheet 5.2 record your daily expenses. To get your budget started, you must have figures which represent your current experience. Therefore, you will have to collect expenditure data for every day of every month. You can purchase large worksheet paper in a stationery store to list all the days of each month from the 1st to the 30th or 31st day with the expense items as indicated in the first column. Record each daily expenditure to get an accurate total for each month.

    After a month has elapsed, aggregate your total for each expense item, and transfer the total to Worksheet 5.3. Use large worksheet paper to record the totals for each month. After you have twelve months of data, aggregate the twelve months to obtain a total for the year for each expense item. Finally, to calculate the monthly average expenditure for each expense item, divide the total for the year by 12, and enter these results in the last column.

Sample Worksheet 5.2

Daily Expense Record

Expense	Date						29	30	31	Total
	1	2	3	4	5					
Food: Total										

Expense	Date						29	30	31	Total
	1	2	3	4	5					
Housing: Total										
Rent or mortgage payment										
Property or local taxes										
Heat										
Electricity										
Gas										
Telephone										
Water										
Home insurance										
Maintenance										
Transportation: Total										
Car										
Gasoline and oil										
Auto insurance										
Maintenance										
Public transportation										
Clothing: Total										
New clothing										
Dry cleaning										
Laundry										
Clothing repair										
Personal care: Total										
Barber service										
Beauty shop										
Cosmetics and perfumes										
Other										

Expense	Date 1	2	3	4	5			29	30	31	Total
Medical care: Total											
Medical											
Dental											
Drugs											
Hospital/Health insurance											
Miscellaneous											
Other expenses: Total											
Loan/installment payment											
Life insurance											
Recreation											
Vacation											
Gifts											
Contributions											
Dues											
Miscellaneous											
Social Security taxes											
Personal income taxes											
Savings											
Total expenditures											

Sample Worksheet 5.3

Monthly Expense Record

Expense	Jan	Feb	Mar	Apr			Nov	Dec	Total	Monthly average
Food: Total										
Housing: Total										
Rent or mortgage payment										
Property or local taxes										
Heat										
Electricity										
Gas										
Telephone										
Water										
Home insurance										
Maintenance										
Transportation: Total										
Car										
Gasoline and oil										
Auto insurance										
Maintenance										

Expense	Jan	Feb	Mar	Apr			Nov	Dec	Total	Monthly average
Public transportation										
Clothing: Total										
New clothing										
Dry cleaning										
Laundry										
Clothing repair										
Personal care: Total										
Barber service										
Beauty shop										
Cosmetics and perfumes										
Other										
Medical care: Total										
Medical										
Dental										
Drugs										
Hospital/ Health insurance										
Miscellaneous										

Expense	Month						Nov	Dec	Total	Monthly average
	Jan	Feb	Mar	Apr						
Other expenses: Total										
Loan/ installment payments										
Life insurance										
Recreation										
Vacation										
Gifts										
Contribu- tions										
Dues										
Miscellan- eous										
Social Security taxes										
Personal income taxes										
Savings										
Total expenditures										

3. On sample Worksheet 5.4 record the last two columns of data from sample Worksheet 5.3. These monthly averages and the year's total for each expense item should be entered in columns (2) and (3) of Worksheet 5.4. Now you are in a position to estimate your first year's retirement spending pattern in columns (4) and (5). Column (4) is an estimate for your first

year of retirement, and column (5) is the monthly average, which is derived by dividing the year's total by 12. How do the figures compare with your current spending pattern?

Sample Worksheet 5.4

Estimating Your First Year's Retirement Expenses

Expense (1)	Current spending pattern		Estimated retirement spending pattern	
	Monthly average (2)	Year 19___ (3)	First year (4)	Monthly average (5)
Food: Total	————	————	————	————
Housing: Total	————	————	————	————
Rent or mortgage payment	————	————	————	————
Property or local taxes	————	————	————	————
Heat	————	————	————	————
Electricity	————	————	————	————
Gas	————	————	————	————
Telephone	————	————	————	————
Water	————	————	————	————
Home insurance	————	————	————	————
Maintenance	————	————	————	————
Transportation: Total	————	————	————	————
Car	————	————	————	————
Gasoline and oil	————	————	————	————
Auto insurance	————	————	————	————
Maintenance	————	————	————	————
Public transportation	————	————	————	————
Clothing: Total	————	————	————	————
New clothing	————	————	————	————
Dry cleaning	————	————	————	————
Laundry	————	————	————	————
Clothing repair	————	————	————	————

Expense (1)	Current spending pattern		Estimated retirement spending pattern	
	Monthly average (2)	Year 19___ (3)	First year (4)	Monthly average (5)
Personal care: Total	_____	_____	_____	_____
Barber service	_____	_____	_____	_____
Beauty shop	_____	_____	_____	_____
Cosmetics and perfumes	_____	_____	_____	_____
Other	_____	_____	_____	_____
Medical care: Total	_____	_____	_____	_____
Medical	_____	_____	_____	_____
Dental	_____	_____	_____	_____
Drugs	_____	_____	_____	_____
Hospital/Health insurance	_____	_____	_____	_____
Miscellaneous	_____	_____	_____	_____
Other expenses: Total	_____	_____	_____	_____
Loan/installment payments	_____	_____	_____	_____
Life insurance	_____	_____	_____	_____
Recreation	_____	_____	_____	_____
Vacation	_____	_____	_____	_____
Gifts	_____	_____	_____	_____
Contributions	_____	_____	_____	_____
Dues	_____	_____	_____	_____
Miscellaneous	_____	_____	_____	_____
Social Security taxes	_____	_____	_____	_____
Personal income taxes	_____	_____	_____	_____
Savings	_____	_____	_____	_____
Total expenditures	_____	_____	_____	_____

4. On Worksheet 5.5 estimate your first year's retirement income. This will require some estimating since Social Security and pension payments do not become final until you are approaching your retirement date. However, you can obtain estimates from your Social Security office and your pension system.

Worksheet 5.5

Estimating Your Retirement Income

	Amount	
Income	Monthly	Yearly
Take-home pay (if still employed)		
Husband	$_____	$_____
Wife	_____	_____
Pension		
Husband	_____	_____
Wife	_____	_____
Social Security benefits		
Husband	_____	_____
Wife	_____	_____
Other income		
Annuities	_____	_____
Royalties	_____	_____
Interest	_____	_____
Dividends	_____	_____
Veterans' benefits	_____	_____
Rents	_____	_____
Profit-sharing plans	_____	_____
Other income		
_____ (Specify)	_____	_____
_____ (Specify)	_____	_____
Total income	$_____	$_____

5. On Worksheet 5.6 enter your total estimated retirement income from Worksheet 5.5, and your total estimated first year's expenses from Worksheet 5.4. Will you have a surplus or a

deficit? If you have a deficit, use Worksheet 5.7 to record your possible solutions to bring your budget into balance.

Worksheet 5.6

Surplus or Deficit in First Year's Retirement Budget

Income	Amount	
	Monthly	First Year
Total income	$_____	$_____
Total expenses	$_____	$_____
Surplus or deficit	$_____	$_____

Worksheet 5.7

Alternative Solutions for a Deficit

1. Increase income

	Gross income	Costs
Full or part-time employment	$_____	$_____
Other:_____	$_____	$_____

2. Reduce expenses

Item to be reduced	Means of reducing	Amount of reduction
_____	_____	$_____
_____	_____	$_____
_____	_____	$_____
_____	_____	$_____

3. Consume capital

Item to be consumed	Amount available	Resulting future reduction in income
_____	$_____	$_____
_____	$_____	$_____
_____	$_____	$_____
_____	$_____	$_____

6. On Worksheet 5.8 you can keep track of your actual expenditures for each budget item on a monthly basis and compare your outlays against your monthly projection. The projections are derived from Worksheet 5.4 where you calculated the monthly average for each expense item in column (5).

   On Worksheet 5.9 you can compare your projected and actual monthly income and determine whether you are in a surplus or deficit position. This is the goal of the budgeting process.

   You can use Worksheet 5.2, Daily Expense Record, to obtain your actual monthly data.

Worksheet 5.8

Your Retirement Expense Budget for the Month of _____ 19_____

Expense	Projected	Actual
Food: Total	$_____	_____
Housing: Total	_____	_____
Rent or mortgage payment	_____	_____
Property or local taxes	_____	_____
Heat	_____	_____
Electricity	_____	_____
Gas	_____	_____
Telephone	_____	_____
Water	_____	_____
Home insurance	_____	_____
Maintenance	_____	_____
Transportation: Total	_____	_____
Car	_____	_____
Gasoline and oil	_____	_____
Auto insurance	_____	_____
Maintenance	_____	_____
Public transportation	_____	_____

Expense	Projected	Actual
Clothing: Total		
New clothing		
Dry cleaning		
Laundry		
Clothing repair		
Personal care: Total		
Barber service		
Beauty shop		
Cosmetics and perfumes		
Other		
Medical care: Total		
Medical		
Dental		
Drugs		
Hospital/Health insurance		
Miscellaneous		
Other expenses: Total		
Loan/installment payments		
Life insurance		
Recreation		
Vacation		
Gifts		
Contributions		
Dues		
Miscellaneous		
Personal income taxes		
Total expenditures	$	$

Worksheet 5.9

Your Retirement Income and Surplus or Deficit for the Month of _____19____

Income	Projected	Actual
Take-home pay (if employed)		
Husband	$_____	_____
Wife	_____	_____
Pension		
Husband	_____	_____
Wife	_____	_____
Social Security benefits		
Husband	_____	_____
Wife	_____	_____
Other income		
Annuities	_____	_____
Royalties	_____	_____
Interest	_____	_____
Dividends	_____	_____
Veterans' benefits	_____	_____
Rents	_____	_____
Profit-sharing plans	_____	_____
Other income		
_____ (Specify)	_____	_____
_____ (Specify)	_____	_____
Total income	$_____	$_____
Total income	$_____	$_____
Total expenses (from Worksheet 5.8)	$_____	$_____
Income minus expenses (surplus or deficit)	$_____	$_____

USING CREDIT IN RETIREMENT

The advice Polonius gave to his son, "Neither a borrower nor a lender be," was eminently sound. That advice remains paramount today. However, there are times when the exigencies of life make it necessary to seek credit. If you must borrow, you must also remember that credit costs something: you must not only pay back what you have borrowed, but also pay interest and other charges. If you are planning to borrow, you must first find out how much it will cost, and then decide whether you can afford it.

Credit costs can vary significantly. Under the terms of the Federal Truth in Lending law, the creditor must tell you, in writing and before you sign any agreement, the *finance charge* and the *annual percentage rate* (APR). The *finance charge* is the total dollar amount you must pay when you borrow a specified amount of money. It includes interest costs, service charges, insurance premiums, and possibly appraisal fees. The *annual percentage rate* (APR) is the percentage cost of credit on an annual basis.

All creditors, including banks, stores, car dealers, credit-card companies and finance companies, must give you these two pieces of information before you sign a credit contract. These two facts about a loan will enable you to compare credit costs to be sure that you are getting the best deal. Shop around; do not accept the first offer.

Creditors look for the three Cs to evaluate a borrower: *Capacity*—can you repay the debt?; *Character*—will you repay the debt?; and *Collateral*—is the creditor fully protected if you fail to repay? Some creditors use a *credit-scoring* or statistical system to predict whether you're a good credit risk. They rate you on a scale and then make a decision either to make or deny the loan.

Age Discrimination Is Illegal

The Federal Equal Credit Opportunity Act says that age, sex, marital status, race, color, religion, national origin, or the fact that you are poor or on welfare or Social Security may not be used to discriminate against you in any part of a credit transaction. While this law does not guarantee that you will get credit, it clearly states that a creditor may not use any of those grounds as an excuse to refuse you a loan if you qualify, or to lend you money on terms different from those granted another person with similar income, expenses, credit history, and collateral.

Prior to this law many older persons had complained about being denied credit based on their age. Many retirees also found that their credit was suddenly cut off or reduced. The Federal Equal Credit Opportunity Act changed this because under this law, a creditor may ask your age but may not deny you credit for that reason. Creditors may use a *credit-scoring system* and *score* your age, but, if you are 62 or older, you must be given at least as many points for age as any person under 62.

An older individual applying for a mortgage loan may have some difficulty, such as a 65-or 70-year old person seeking a 25-or 30-year mortgage. The law permits a creditor to require specific information related to age in this situation, including when you plan to retire or how long you will continue to be earning your current salary. On the other hand, an older individual who is prepared to make a large downpayment on a house might qualify for a relatively small mortgage loan, assuming that the home is a sound investment. Remember that the lending institution owns a mortgaged home until the very last monthly payment of principal and interest is made.

Borrowing Against What You Own

In the previous chapter reverse mortgages were discussed as a potential source of retirement income. Essentially the reverse mortgage takes advantage of the increase in the value of your home over the years. Borrowing against the value of the home you own is handled traditionally by *refinancing* your original mortgage. The lending institution is often pleased at the opportunity of taking back the old low-rate mortgage and issuing a new first mortgage at a higher rate. It may even offer you a few percentage points less than the going rate of mortgage interest or possibly even forgive part of the indebtedness. Another possibility is taking out a *second mortgage* on your home, but interest rates can be two or three percentage points higher than the current mortgage rates, and the repayment period is usually limited to between 5 and 15 years. Monthly mortgage payments would be quite high.

Other possibilities for borrowing against your assets include loans using your negotiable securities, such as stocks and bonds, or your savings in a passbook account, certificates of deposit, or credit union shares as collateral. Interest rates charged when your own savings are used as collateral are uniformly low, usually a point or two above the interest you collect on your account.

Most banks, credit unions, and consumer finance companies will accept cars, boats, and planes as collateral for loans. However, interest rates are at about the level charged on installment loans, and repayment periods are short.

For individuals approaching retirement or already retired, if the size of the loan you seek is modest, your best bet is a credit union. If you need a larger loan, the lowest rates are generally charged by commercial banks.

Use of Credit Cards

If financial planning for retirement is to be effective, it is essential that individuals in their working years learn the meaning of discipline in credit and money management. Our society is geared to the philosophy of "buy now, pay later." This inflationary psychology has led people to believe that if they bought now and paid later, they would pay their bills with cheaper dollars. Unfortunately, the dollars are not always available when the bills come due. In addition, our personal bankruptcy law, which was liberalized in 1979, encourages people to go deeper into debt. If they are then unable to extricate themselves, they go to a bankruptcy attorney to see what can be done.

The wisest way to use your credit cards is to pay off the full amount of your balance due every month. There's no denying that credit card shopping is convenient, and, in addition, it's a free loan because charges to your account are often a month behind. However, only about one-third of credit card users pay their outstanding balances every month.

The maximum percentage of a family's take-home pay that should be used for credit payments should range between 10 and 15 percent. The mortgage payment should not be greater than 25 to 30 percent of take-home pay. When credit card debt begins to exceed 15 percent, you're reaching the danger point, and you must begin immediately to take remedial steps. The best prescription is to cut your credit cards up and discard them. The next step is to set up a strict budget which should incorporate a schedule for paying off your creditors. This is the only way you can develop an effective financial plan for retirement. Effective personal money management is an essential ingredient for avoiding the many problems associated with excessive debt.

The Tax Reform Act of 1986 phases out the deductibility of interest paid as finance charges for the use of credit cards, car loans, student loans, and other consumer loans. The phase-out is accomplished over a four-year period: in 1987 only 65 percent of such interest is deductible, 40 percent in 1988, 20 percent in 1989, and 10 percent in 1990. For 1991 and thereafter such interest is no longer deductible.

SELF-STUDY:
THE STATE OF MY CREDIT

Take the following test to determine whether your outstanding credit card and/or installment loans are within reasonable limits.

Credit cards	Outstanding balance	Monthly payment
_____	$_____	$_____
_____	_____	_____
_____	_____	_____
_____	_____	_____
_____	_____	_____
_____	_____	_____
_____	_____	_____
Total monthly debt repayment		$_____
Loans		
_____	$_____	$_____
_____	_____	_____

Loans	Outstanding balance	Monthly payment
Total monthly debt repayment		$_____
Grand total monthly debt repayment		$_____

Substitute totals in the following:

$$\frac{\text{Grand total monthly debt repayment}}{\text{Take-home pay for one month}} = \text{Percent of your monthly income owed to creditors}$$

If the percent of monthly income owed to creditors is greater than 15 percent, you must begin immediately to take the remedial steps discussed previously.

COPING WITH INFLATION

Inflation means that the general level of prices for goods and services is rising. People understand this very well. They know that the cost of a shopping trip to the supermarket will be higher than the previous visit. In 1942, bread cost 9¢ a pound, and coffee was 28¢ a pound. Today a loaf of bread costs approximately one dollar and a pound of coffee, approximately three dollars. In 1942 you could buy a Cadillac for $3,000; today the price is close to $18,000. Not only have these costs risen, but it is more expensive to go to the movies or a theater, to take a vacation, to buy heating oil, to purchase clothing, furniture, and household appliances, and to obtain medical and other services.

Increases in living costs have been particularly serious since 1973. Four categories of necessities—food, shelter, energy, and medical care—make up about 60 percent of the total market basket of expenditures incurred by typical urban families. Since 1973 the costs of goods and services in these categories have increased sharply and at an accelerating rate, hitting retirees particularly hard because they are so dependent on these necessities.

In the 1960s the average annual rate of inflation was 2.1 percent; in the 1970s, 6.2 percent, and for the first half of the 80s, 5.9 percent. (See Table 5.3.) A 5.9 percent annual average rate of inflation means the loss in real income of an equivalent amount. A retiree with a $10,000 income loses 5.9 percent or $590. Or, to put it another way, the $10,000 now buys the equivalent of $9,410 of goods and services. Continuing inflation eats away at fixed incomes, making it more and more difficult to make ends meet.

A nest-egg savings account also shrinks in value when the rate of inflation exceeds the interest rate, which is currently 5.25 percent in a commercial bank and 5.5 percent in a passbook savings account. This hurts retirees and those approaching retirement.

Table 5.3

Annual Rate of Inflation, 1960–1986

Year	Percentage increase	Year	Percentage increase	Year	Percentage increase
1960	1.5%	1970	5.5%	1980	12.5%
1961	0.7	1971	3.4	1981	8.7
1962	1.2	1972	3.4	1982	3.9
1963	1.6	1973	8.8	1983	3.3
1964	1.2	1974	12.2	1984	3.5
1965	1.9	1975	7.0	1985	3.6
1966	3.4	1976	4.8	1986	0.7
1967	3.0	1977	6.8		
1968	4.7	1978	9.0		
1969	6.1	1979	13.4		
Average 1960s	2.1%	Average 1970s	6.2%	Average 1980–1986	5.2%

Source: U.S. Department of Labor, Bureau of Labor Statistics, as measured by the Consumer Price Index for Urban Wage Earners and Clerical Workers, U.S. City Average, All items, December to December, 1967 = 100. (CPI - W)

Impact on Retirees

As prices rise, retirees find that they must spend more for necessities, and that they are now unable to purchase the same items they were able to buy previously with the same amount of money. This is the typical inflation experience. If you are living on a budget, the problem becomes obvious immediately because your spending pattern is based on costs that apply to an earlier period. When prices are increasing rapidly, your working budget will tell you this quickly. The situation requires some revisions so that your budget correctly reflects the changing economic picture. In a non-inflationary situation, it was suggested that your budget be revised annually, but in an inflationary period it is necessary to make adjustments on a monthly basis. Retirees living on fixed incomes react to price increases immediately.

Even if you have not been operating with a budget, you are also aware of inflation whether you're retired or still in the work force. Your money simply evaporates more rapidly. This of course may be caused by carefree spending and overuse of your credit cards. If this is the case, you must decide to curb your spending. An inflationary situation will alert you to this need more quickly.

In an inflationary period, many older workers' dreams of retirement become unaffordable. They find it difficult to make ends meet while fully employed and become seriously concerned when they contemplate trying to live on a lower retirement income. The tendency is to stay at work longer and to postpone the retirement date in the hope that conditions will return to a more normal situation.

It is obvious therefore that high rates of inflation have a detrimental financial impact on fixed-income retirees. The argument that retirees are well off is not always valid.

Measures Against Inflation

The options available to people living on limited or fixed incomes are few. The three alternatives are: to consume capital; to increase income; and/or to reduce expenses. Consuming your capital is hardly a long-term solution to the problem of coping with inflation unless you are sure that your capital supply will not be consumed in your lifetime. The average person does not have a very large nest egg to begin with. But even for those who have managed to accumulate some savings and investments, consuming capital is not the suggested solution to the problem.

One of the soundest ways to avoid letting your nest egg wither after retirement is to increase your income, if you're able to do so, by adding a fresh flow of new, inflated earnings. Continuing to earn an income after retirement does not mean you have to keep on doing what you're doing today. You may consider working part-time, possibly through one of the new job-sharing or flexitime systems that some companies are adopting to make part-time employment more attractive. You may wish to set up your own business or expand a hobby or pastime you now enjoy into a money-making proposition.

The third alternative, to reduce expenses, simply means studying each of the major budgetary items—food, clothing, shelter, health care, and the other expense items—and cutting the amount you spend on them. This means you must sharpen your shopping skills. You must learn to time your purchases to sales, to use discount stores, to avoid impulse buying, to carefully examine your purchases for quality, and to make your clothing last longer by following the instructions on the care labels. Energy costs and medical costs, important in everyone's budget but especially in the budgets of retirees, will probably continue to exceed the inflation rate in the 1980s. You will have to adopt cost-saving energy tactics, including installing insulation, updating your heating system to make it more efficient, and possibly lowering the thermostat setting. Solutions for the control of the inflation of medical costs are not readily available. Perhaps the expansion of Health Maintenance Organizations, known as HMOs, can be of some assistance.

If you are unable to cope with inflation, you can seek professional assistance. Financial counseling is available through credit unions, some banks, and other institutions. You can check with your local senior citizens center.

TAXES

The Tax Reform Act of 1986, signed by President Reagan on October 22, 1986, is a sweeping overhaul of our income tax law, ushering in a new era in income taxation. Most significantly for all citizens the law restores equity and fairness in our tax structure by shifting some of the impact of the income tax from individuals to corporations.

For individuals, the 1986 law consolidates the rate structure and lowers tax rates. Moreover, the Tax Reform Act increases the personal exemption for individuals, spouses, and dependents, and also increases the standard deduction. To make up for the reduction in tax rates, the increases in the personal exemption, and the standard deduction, the Act expands the tax base of the individual income tax by making more of your income subject to tax. This is accomplished by repealing or restricting previously allowed deductions and credits and by increasing corporate taxes. Theoretically, the new law thus achieves its goal of being revenue-neutral, collecting the same amount of taxes under the new law as under the old law.

Basic Rate Structure

For 1988 and later years the Act replaces the former 14-bracket rate structure, which had rates ranging from 11 to 50 percent with a two-bracket structure of 15 and 28 percent. An estimated fifty percent of taxpayers will fall into the new 15 percent bracket. However, for 1988 and later years the 1986 law imposes a 5 percent surcharge on taxable income between $71,900 and $149,250 for joint returns and between $43,150 and $89,560 for single filers, bringing the effective marginal rate to 33 percent for these higher-income individuals and families. On incomes above $149,150 for joint returns and above $89,560 for single filers, the tax rate drops back to 28 percent. The move to these lower rates involves a transition in 1987 when five brackets ranging from 11 to 38.5 percent prevail.

Personal Exemption

The Tax Reform Act also provides a sizable increase in each taxpayer's personal exemption—that is, in the amount you subtract from your taxable income for yourself and your dependents. The new law increases the personal exemption for individuals, spouses, and dependents from its 1986 level of $1,080 to $1,900 for 1987, $1,950 for 1988, and $2,000 for 1989. The 1989 amount will be adjusted for inflation starting in 1990.

Individuals who are 65 or over or blind can take an extra $600 standard deduction for each individual if married and filing jointly, or $750 if single. For those both elderly and blind, two extra standard deductions are allowed. These amounts will be indexed for inflation beginning in 1989.

Standard Deduction

Beginning in 1987, the new law increases the standard deduction (previously referred to as the zero bracket amount or ZBA); that is, the maximum amount of income that an individual can earn which is not subject to income tax. If your taxable income, after you take your personal exemption, doesn't exceed the standard deduction, you need not file. For 1987 and 1988 the standard deductions are as follows:

Standard Deduction

Filing status	1987	1988
Joint returns	$3,760	$5,000
Heads of households	2,540	4,400
Single individuals	2,540	3,000
Married individuals filing separately	1,880	2,500

Broadening the Base

The 1986 Tax Reform Act lowers tax rates, but at the same time makes more of your income subject to tax, a change that is known as base-broadening. It is estimated that about 15 percent of all taxpayers will have a tax increase. The law repeals the following deductions: the two-earner married couple deduction, political contributions, residential energy-saving credits, State and local sales tax deductions, interest paid on personal-use or credit card loans, the $100/$200 exclusion of dividend income, and charitable contributions for taxpayers who don't itemize. Moreover, the law restricts contributions to IRAs, Simplified Employee Pension plans, and Tax Deferred Annuity plans.

The Act continues to allow deductions for mortgage interest on the taxpayer's principal and second homes; State and local personal and property taxes; State and local income taxes; and up to $125,000 of your one-time profit capital gains on the sale of your principal residence if you're 55 or older.

Deductions that the 1986 law changes include medical expenses, but only if they exceed 7.5 percent of adjusted gross income, up from 5 percent in the previous law; and employee business expenses and miscellaneous expenses only if they exceed 2 percent of adjusted gross income. These expenses were fully deductible under the previous law. Under the 1986 law, 80 percent of business, entertainment and business travel meals will be deductible to the extent they are not reimbursed by the employer.

IMPACT OF THE TAX REFORM ACT ON OLDER AMERICANS

The changes introduced by the Tax Reform Act of 1986 will remove millions of low-income families from the tax rolls, including about 750,000 elderly. This is accomplished by having low marginal rates in a two-bracket structure, and a higher personal exemption and standard deduction.

Profit on the Sale of a Home

Under present law, up to $125,000 of profit from the sale of your home is exempt from taxes. This tax benefit can make your retirement years more financially secure and adds new flexibility to your retirement planning.

To be eligible, you must be 55 or older when you sell your principal residence. The exclusion from taxes applies only to a principal residence that you have owned and lived in for at least three of the five years preceding the sale. If you are married, only one spouse must meet the age, ownership, and residency tests. Furthermore, you can take the exclusion only once in your lifetime. For purposes of this limitation married couples are treated as one. If one spouse used the exclusion before marriage, the other spouse forfeits the right to this tax break.

The $125,000 limit is not cumulative. If you exclude from taxation $65,000 of the profit on the sale of one home, for example, the other $60,000 is forfeited. You cannot carry an unused portion forward to be applied against the gain on the sale of another home.

If you realize a $150,000 gain, for example, you can escape the tax on the first $125,000, and postpone tax on the rest if you buy a new home that costs at least $25,000. The gain you roll over into the new home will not be taxed until such time as you give up home ownership: that is, sell a house for the last time and do not reinvest your equity in another more costly house. You elect the exclusion by filing Form 2119, Sale or Exchange of Personal Residence.

Income Tax Assistance

Many of the almost 29 million Americans who are 65 or older run into problems in fulfilling the annual chore of filing an income tax return with the Federal government. Some of the basic difficulties faced by these people include which forms to use, how to fill them out, whether or not to itemize deductions, and whether to file jointly with a spouse or separately. If you have a problem, the Internal Revenue Service is available to help you, even to the extent of computing your taxes so that you pay the smallest amount. Call or visit your nearest Internal Revenue office.

You may wish to obtain a free copy of Internal Revenue Publication Number 17, *Your Federal Income Tax*, from the I.R.S. You can also get free tax advice nationwide from volunteer tax counselors trained by the Internal Revenue Service to counsel retirees. Write to AARP-NRTA, Tax-Aide Program, Department RG, 1909 K Street, N.W., Washington, D.C. 20049, for the location of the counselor nearest you.

You may wish to obtain the assistance of a professional accountant or tax attorney, but you must be prepared to pay the required fee.

If you wish to obtain the details of a particular state's income tax laws or any one of its other taxes, contact the Public Information Division of the Department of Revenue or Taxation in the particular state's capital.

Tax Shelters for Retirement Planning

A *tax shelter* is an investment that legally enables you to defer taxes or ultimately to diminish taxes. These goals can be accomplished by investing soundly in assets that you leave untouched for a long period of time. This seasoning process in conjunction with compounding of interest will steadily increase the size of your investment.

If you are an average small investor, you can benefit from a tax shelter investment by putting your money into one or more of the following:

IRA and Keogh Plans

The Tax Reform Act of 1986 made changes in Individual Retirement Accounts (IRAs) and Keogh plans for self-employed people, discussed in Chapter 3. However, these retirement plans still allow money to grow, and taxes are deferred until you withdraw it. The tax-deferred feature enables your investment to grow faster than an ordinary investment.

Home Ownership

When you own your home, your mortgage interest and property taxes are deductible, two deduction items not available to renters. Moreover, you have the one-time exclusion of a $125,000 capital gain when you sell your home if you are 55 or older.

Pensions

The money contributed by your employer is tax-free. You will not pay taxes on it until you retire.

Tax-Deferred Annuities

The money you invest in a tax-deferred annuity is not taxed when you put it in and is tax-free while it is accumulating. When you begin to receive payments, you pay the taxes due.

Municipal Bonds

These are one of the best tax shelters, particularly for those in the 28/33 percent tax brackets. The interest earned is not taxable by the Federal government and is tax-exempt from the state income tax in the state in which the bond was issued.

U.S. Government Savings Bonds

Series EE and HH U.S. savings bonds, which were discussed in Chapter 4, offer the advantage of tax deferral. You pay taxes on the interest you have earned when you cash them in.

Other Tax Shelters

Tax shelters, not designed for the average small investor because of their high risk and the possible loss of all the money put into the venture, include oil and gas drilling, cattle raising, mineral excavation, and real estate developments. The Tax Reform Act of 1986 severely restricts the tax write-offs that have long been a major appeal for investors in these types of activities. These tax shelters are now less attractive to investors willing to assume such a risk.

The Rollover as a Tax Shelter

People who receive a lump-sum settlement from an employee retirement plan or a profit-sharing plan will owe no Federal tax on any portion of the settlement that is reinvested in another employee retirement plan or an Individual Retirement Account (IRA) administered by a lending institution or an insurance company. You must act within 60 days of receiving your distribution in order to retain for yourself that all-important tax-deferment benefit. Unless you make the *rollover* within the 60-day period, the money you receive in the lump-sum settlement becomes taxable as income. This rollover option applies also to money accumulated in a tax-deferred annuity. As an extension of the tax shelter principle, it is a worthwhile benefit because it allows you to defer taxes.

GLOSSARY

Adjusted Gross Income (AGI). The total of your annual wages, interest, dividends, capital gains (or losses) minus allowable deductions such as alimony, business expenses, moving expenses, IRA or Keogh contributions.

Annual Percentage Rate (APR). The *finance charge* over a full year expressed as a percentage, reflecting all the costs of the loan. (See Finance Charge.)

Assets. All money, investments, and other property owned by an individual, a family, or a business. (See Liabilities, Net Worth.)

Blue Book. A publication of the National Automobile Dealers Association (NADA) that lists the average price paid for used cars at a specified time.

Budget. A spending plan designed to help you manage your income efficiently.

Capital. Money or its equivalent in property and securities.

Consumer Credit Protection Act. A Federal act that includes the Fair Credit Billing, Equal Credit Opportunity, Fair Credit Reporting, Consumer Leasing Acts, and the Truth in Lending Act.

Consumer Price Index (CPI). An index, prepared by the U.S. Department of Labor, Bureau of Labor Statistics, reflecting monthly changes in the relative cost of a specific *market basket* of goods and services as measured against a base year.

Cosigner. Someone who agrees to accept responsibility for a loan if the original borrower defaults.

Credit. Loans to individuals, businesses, or governments from the savings of individuals and businesses. (See Interest.)

Credit Card. A type of credit activated by the presentation of a plastic card, allowing the cardholder to purchase items on credit from any business that accepts the card.

Credit Life Insurance. Life insurance covering the repayment of a loan should the borrower die.

Credit Scoring. An objective method for evaluating whether an individual is a good credit risk. (See Three Cs of Credit.)

Credit Union. A depository institution formed as a cooperative by individuals who are required by law to meet specific credit union requirements.

Deficit. The amount by which expenditures exceed income. (See Surplus.)

Deflation. A decrease in the general level of prices for goods and services. (See Inflation.)

Economic Recovery Tax Act of 1981 (ERTA). Federal law which reduced income taxes for everyone, and modified estate and gift taxes significantly.

Finance Charge. The total dollar amount you must pay when you borrow a specified amount of money. It includes interest cost, service charges, insurance premiums, and possibly appraisal fees. (See Annual Percentage Rate.)

Financial Independence. The ability to enjoy your usual standard of living with income from one or more income sources other than income from your personal services or work.

Inflation. An increase in the general level of prices for goods and services. (See Deflation.)

Interest. Annual cost of borrowed money. (See Finance Charge, Annual Percentage Rate.)

Liabilities. All forms of indebtedness for which an individual, a family, or a business is legally liable. (See Assets, Net Worth.)

Net Worth. Monetary value of an individual, a family, or a business. It is equal to total assets minus total liabilities. (See Assets, Liabilities.)

Second Mortgage. A loan that uses as security a piece of property that is already security for a first mortgage.

Standard Deduction. The amount all of us may deduct when we file an income tax return. It is the threshold, or floor, for determining whether or not you can itemize.

Surplus. The amount by which income exceeds expenditures. (See Deficit.)

Tax. A contribution exacted of individuals, businesses, and other organizations by the government, according to law, for the government's general support and for the maintenance of public services.

Tax Equity and Fiscal Responsibility Act of 1982 (TEFRA). Federal law which made adjustments in some taxes and deductions to restore some degree of equity.

Tax Shelter. An investment that legally enables you to defer taxes or ultimately to diminish taxes.

Three Cs of Credit. In evaluating a borrower, creditors use *Three Cs: Capacity*, sufficient income to enable a borrower to repay the loan; *Character*, traits making up an individual's nature that would make the borrower want to repay the loan; and *Collateral*, sufficient assets of the borrower to fully protect repayment of the loan.

Zero Bracket Amount (ZBA). The maximum amount of income that an individual can earn which is not subject to income tax. In the Tax Reform Act of 1986 ZBA is replaced by a standard deduction. (See Standard Deduction.)

Chapter 6
Estate Planning: Wills, Trusts, Probate, Estate and Gift Taxes

ESTATE PLANNING

Estate planning is the process of analyzing your assets and liabilities, managing them effectively during your lifetime, and disposing of them at your death so as to best serve the needs of your beneficiaries. It takes a lifetime to create an estate, and yet at death many estates are reduced by as much as 20 to 50 percent because of taxes and settlement costs resulting from poor planning. To minimize estate shrinkage and to transfer as great a portion of your assets as possible to your heirs requires careful planning.

Many people think that estate planning is an area reserved only for wealthy individuals. This is not true. The typical middle-class family owns a home, furniture and furnishings, and an automobile, possibly two, as well as savings, some investments, life insurance, and hobby items worth a great deal. When you add it all up, the total is usually surprising. This is the package to be analyzed in estate planning.

The purpose of this chapter is to introduce basic concepts in estate planning in order to help you achieve your long-term goals and to assure security and well-being for your family. The material is up-to-date, including the sweeping changes in this field made by the Economic Recovery Tax Act of 1981. This legislation makes estate planning all the more necessary and urgent.

Objectives of Estate Planning

Estate planning has three principal objectives:

1. The primary objective is to make certain that your property is distributed according to your wishes and the needs of your beneficiaries. An effective estate plan will provide for the individuals you care about, leaving them what you want them to have.

2. To minimize Federal and state estate and inheritance taxes, which are levied on an individual's estate at death.

3. To keep settlement costs to a minimum. The goal is to lower the nontax costs associated with dying, such as legal and accounting fees.

Most people cringe at the thought of planning for death, and therefore procrastinate and postpone this effort. However, the head of a household as well as the other spouse should have an estate plan. Anyone who fails to undertake estate planning will impose upon his or her heirs a host of unnecessary costs and problems.

In general, people usually think of family members as beneficiaries. However, the concept is much broader, also including friends, charities, educational institutions, and other objects of your bounty.

It is recommended that an individual seek professional advice and that a lawyer be called upon to handle the details of an estate plan whether they seem simple or complex. While a lawyer specializing in this area is essential, advice can also be obtained from trust companies in banks as well as from life insurance salespeople, whose possible bias must always be kept in mind.

Tools of Estate Planning

The essential tools of estate planning are *wills, trusts, gifts, life insurance*, and *agreements related to business interests*. Of these, the most important is a *will*, which will distribute your assets in accordance with your wishes. The will appoints an *executor* who will be responsible for distributing your assets as well as a *guardian*, who will be responsible for the care of minor children, if any.

The second tool is a *trust*. A trust is a written agreement which provides for the professional management of assets, usually under the direction of a *trustee*. It is a very flexible tool which can reduce taxes as well as probate fees.

The third tool consists of *gifts*. Gifts can be given to your children, grandchildren, relatives, or charities while you are still living, or they can be given after your death through a charitable foundation or trust. A charitable foundation can be created during your lifetime or through your will.

Life insurance is the fourth tool. A life insurance policy can provide income for the family, or can be used to fund a trust or a business agreement. If your assets are invested, a life insurance policy can provide liquidity.

Agreements related to business interests are an important area of concern in estate planning. Suppose the owner of a business wishes to transfer the portion of his or her ownership to designated heirs, with the surviving owners retaining control of the business. A legal agreement can solve this problem, and can be arranged in the estate plan.

Steps in Estate Planning

The basic steps you must take to prepare an effective estate plan are explained below.

1. ***Inventory your assets and their value.*** The first step in estate planning is to identify each of your assets and to estimate the value of each. You can take these directly from the net worth statement which you prepared in Chapter 5, Worksheet 5.1. This inventory of your assets should be compiled in cooperation with your spouse, and with your children, if they are old enough. A full and accurate inventory is helpful to your attorney in implementing your wishes wisely.

2. ***Identify your heirs and their needs.*** The major concern of most married men is their wives. Children grow up, get married, and pursue their own careers. At that

point, a wife who has had a short-term career may have only a modest pension and a wife who has not pursued her own career may be out of touch with the job market and, because of her age and lack of employable skills, may have a problem in obtaining paid employment. Therefore, your first responsibility is to take care of the needs of your spouse. Usually the home is owned jointly and full control of the home passes to the surviving spouse. However, if there is any question about prudent management of the balance of your assets, both of you should discuss this important matter together. The best interests of children, grandchildren and other heirs must also be considered in this discussion. Together you must reach a decision on whether or not to place these assets in a *trust* to be managed by a *trustee*. Trusts will be discussed later.

3. ***Estimate cash requirements of the testator.*** The *testator*, or maker of a will, must estimate cash requirements to cover the costs of the last illness and funeral expenses. In addition, several other obligations must be paid in cash shortly after the death of the estate owner. These are estate and inheritance taxes, if any; debts of the decedent, such as outstanding loans and unpaid bills; property taxes, if any; and legal fees for administering the estate. These obligations must be paid in full before any property can be distributed to the beneficiaries.

   If sufficient cash or near-cash assets are not available to satisfy these obligations as they fall due, the nonliquid assets of the estate must be sold to pay them. These estimated costs should be available in the form of cash, highly marketable stocks or bonds, savings accounts, or life insurance.

4. ***Select appropriate estate planning tools.*** The fourth step in estate planning is to decide which tools you will need to achieve your objectives. This step requires the services of a lawyer, who must make the required decisions as to the most appropriate tools for your particular situation. You and your spouse will certainly need wills. Need for the other tools varies from one situation to another. These tools in combination will help you to meet your goals concerning distribution, property management, tax planning, and any other objective you may have.

5. ***Consult with a specialist in estate planning.*** Theoretically, estate planning can be done by the individual on his or her own. You can probably save money. However, if you do it yourself, you run the risk of making a costly error. Outside experts may save you more money than they cost you. Professionals will help you plan your estate while you are living, and after your death, will administer the estate to insure that your wishes are achieved. It is recommended, therefore, that you seek professional advice.

   A lawyer who is a specialist in estate planning should be called upon to handle the details of an estate plan whether they seem simple or complex. A competent lawyer can be obtained by recommendation of a friend or by contacting your local bar association. Good rapport between you and your lawyer is essential. It is important to discuss fees before any work is initiated. You should be given a firm estimate of total costs in advance. If you do not feel comfortable with the lawyer you have chosen, find someone else. You have the right to look elsewhere.

SELF-STUDY: DATA FOR MY ESTATE PLAN

1. Refer to your net worth statement, which you prepared in Chapter 5, Worksheet 5.1. Review this inventory to be sure that the list of assets is complete and that the values are up-to-date.

2. List your heirs, including spouse, children, grandchildren, relatives, charities, and other beneficiaries you wish to consider. Based upon individual needs, estimate the proportion of your assets each beneficiary should receive. (Set up a worksheet.)

3. Estimate approximately the cash required to cover costs of last illness, funeral expenses, and settlement costs. Remember that costs of illness may be covered in part or in full by medical insurance. (See Chapter 9.) $_____

4. List the names, addresses, and telephone numbers of two or three lawyers in your area who specialize in estate planning. You will need a lawyer's assistance in selecting appropriate estate planning tools.

    a. _____

    b. _____

    c. _____

WILLS

A *will* is a legal document, almost always in writing and properly executed, which describes how a person (known as the *testator*) wants his or her property to be distributed after death, and which designates the person or institution that will carry out the terms of the will. In effect, your will is the center of your estate plan.

Basic Content of a Will

The basic content of a will includes the following:

1. Place of residence: full address and state in which the will is drawn.
2. Statement revoking all previous wills.
3. Instructions for the payment of taxes, outstanding debts, costs of administration, and funeral and burial expenses.
4. Specific bequests: a listing of particular items to be given to specified individuals.
5. General bequests: a listing of general sums to be given to specified individuals.
6. Bequests to charities.
7. Allocation of residual estate: a statement as to how the balance of the property is to be distributed.
8. Establishment of a trust or trusts, if any, and the naming of a trustee or trustees.

9. Naming of executor or executors and alternates.
10. Naming of a guardian or guardians and alternates to raise minor children, if any.
11. Statement on disposal of assets if a couple and children die in a common accident.
12. Names, addresses, and signatures of witnesses.

Why Make a Will?

A duly-executed will reflects your wishes as it applies to your property and your family situation. Having a will offers the following advantages:

1. It will guarantee that your property is distributed according to your wishes, which were based upon thoughtful planning.
2. It will minimize taxes and other expenses in the distribution of your assets.
3. It will accomplish the transfer of your estate to your heirs with a minimum of delay.
4. It will take care of special problems, such as provision for children or an incompetent dependent.
5. It will minimize the possibility of costly and family-disrupting lawsuits.
6. It can provide for continued income to the family during the period in which the estate is being settled.
7. It can direct that particular beneficiaries receive specified assets, known as *bequests*.
8. It is the appropriate means for setting up a trust after death.

Some assets cannot be bequeathed or disposed of through your will because the beneficiaries for these assets have already been named. These assets include life insurance, pension benefits, and jointly-owned property.

Types of Wills

A will can take many forms. Among them are the following:

Do-it-Yourself Will

How often the question is asked: "Why do I need an attorney to help me write a will? I know what I want." The answer is simple: You do not need an attorney to help you write your will. You can do it yourself. A printed-form will can be bought in a stationery store. Writing your own will would, of course, save time and money, but it could also create serious problems for your heirs. These could be costly, time-consuming, and evoke family squabbles.

The State of California became the first state to approve a legal, standard will. It costs $1, and became effective January 1, 1983. It is called a *fill-in-the-blanks will*, and is intended for low-and middle-income people with fairly simple legal needs. The document was drawn up by the State Bar of California and approved by the Legislature. The Bar still recommends that people see a lawyer before filling in the blanks. The terms of the document apply only to California residents.

A Handwritten Will

A handwritten will is known as a *holographic will*. It is fully handwritten and in the states where it is recognized, does not require witnesses. The risks and hazards of a holographic will are numerous. Only about half of the 50 states recognize them. Lacking legal knowledge, you may fail to use language which would guarantee that your estate is handled in the manner you intended. You might include an instruction in your will that would invalidate it, such as providing for an action that is not permitted by your State's law. A seemingly inconsequential error, such as failure to include the date, or part of the date, or use of a stamped date, may make such a will worthless under the law.

Other technicalities by which a handwritten will may be invalidated are listed below:

1. Part of the will is handwritten and part is typed. How can anyone know whether the typed part was put in by you?
2. A sentence is deleted by crossing it out, but no initials appear next to it showing that you approved the deletion. Anyone could have deleted the sentence, not necessarily the maker of the will.
3. After you have signed the will, an additional paragraph is added leaving some of your property to another person. Could this individual have added this paragraph after you had signed the will?

An Oral Will

An oral will is one made in military combat and within hearing of two witnesses. It is used primarily by soldiers or sailors in active service or by mariners at sea. Oral wills may be recognized only for a short time after discharge and usually provide for minimum estates. They always bear the risk that the witnesses may not recall accurately what was said.

A Will Drawn Up By Your Lawyer

Everyone needs a legally valid will; it is not a do-it-yourself activity. Executing a legally valid will is the job of a professional, and having a will can save your heirs numerous problems after your death and ensure that your property goes to the people you want to have it. A lawyer's fee for making a will may range from $75 to $250 and up, depending upon its complexity.

A will drawn up by a lawyer will meet the legal requirements for being valid, especially if the lawyer specializes in this area. He or she has a knowledge of the laws of the state in which you reside, and is trained to give you advice and guidance to meet your goals.

A Living Will

Many states have passed *right to die* or *natural death laws,* recognizing the right of an individual to make a *living will.* A living will specifies that an individual who has no chance of survival and is unable to speak for himself or herself will not be connected to a heart-lung machine or other devices to be kept alive by artificial means. The states that have enacted such laws include Alabama, Arkansas, California, Idaho, Illinois, Kansas, Nevada, New Mexico, North Carolina, Oregon, Texas, Vermont and Washington as well as the District of Columbia. A living will is binding and enforceable in these thirteen states and the District of Columbia. However, states that have no such law may permit the living will to be enforced even if it is challenged. You may wish to consider the sample living will on the following page.

A Living Will

TO MY FAMILY, MY PHYSICIAN, MY LAWYER, MY CLERGYMAN
TO ANY MEDICAL FACILITY IN WHOSE CARE I HAPPEN TO BE
TO ANY INDIVIDUAL WHO MAY BECOME RESPONSIBLE FOR MY
HEALTH, WELFARE OR AFFAIRS

Death is as much a reality as birth, growth, maturity, and old age—it is the one certainty of life. If the time comes when I, _____ , can no
(please print)
longer take part in decisions for my own future, let this statement stand as an expression of my wishes, while I am still of sound mind.

If the situation should arise in which there is no reasonable expectation of my recovery from physical or mental disability, I request that I be allowed to die and not be kept alive by artificial means or "heroic measures." I do not fear death itself as much as the indignities of deterioration, dependence and hopeless pain. I, therefore, ask that medication be mercifully administered to me to alleviate suffering even though this may hasten the moment of death.

This request is made after careful consideration. I hope you who care for me will feel morally bound to follow its mandate. I recognize that this appears to place a heavy responsibility upon you, but it is with the intention of relieving you of such responsibility and of placing it upon myself in accordance with my strong convictions, that this statement is made.

Date _____   Signed _____

Witness _____   Witness _____
(please print)   (signature)

Witness _____   Witness _____
(please print)   (signature)

Copies of this request have been given to _____

_____

Directions for the Living Will

1. Sign and date before two witnesses. (This is to insure that you signed of your own free will and not under any pressure.)
2. If you have a doctor, give him a copy for your medical file and discuss it with him to make sure he is in agreement. Also give copies to those most likely to be concerned "if the time comes when you can no longer take part in decisions for your own future." Enter their names on the bottom lines of the Living Will. Keep the original nearby, easily and readily available.
3. Above all discuss your intentions with those closest to you, *now*.
4. It is a good idea to look over your Living Will once a year, and redate it and initial the new date to make it clear that your wishes are unchanged.
5. Make a copy of the living will above for your spouse, if he or she desires. Attach the copy to this page for future reference.

The *Living Will* and Directions appeared in *Your Vital Papers Logbook,* 1981 edition, and are reprinted with the permission of Action for Independent Maturity, a division of the American Association of Retired Persons.

Types of Fiduciaries

The directives which you set forth in your will are not self-executing. Someone has to put them into effect. This individual or institution is referred to as a *fiduciary*. As lawyers use the term, a fiduciary is the individual or institution to whom you grant specific rights, duties, and powers to act for you or in your behalf to carry out the provisions stipulated in your will.

Fiduciaries serve in different capacities. Their titles include an *executor* (a woman would be called an *executrix*) or *executors*, to carry out the directives of a will; a *guardian* or *guardians*, to care for minor children; a *trustee* or *trustees*, whose function is to administer a *trust;* and an *administrator*. An administrator is a court-appointed executor who is designated to serve when someone dies without a will (intestate); when a will does not name an executor; when the named executor cannot or will not serve; when a will cannot be located; or when a will is declared invalid. The responsibilities of an administrator and an executor are the same.

The Executor

An *executor* or *executrix* is the person responsible for the management of the property specified in the will until disposition of the estate is completed. The executor serves in a *fiduciary relationship* to the beneficiaries of the estate, meaning that the executor must comply with high standards of integrity and responsibility in managing the estate's property and carrying out the provisions of the will. The executor must make periodic reports to the probate court and actually make a final accounting to the court before being released from the fiduciary relationship.

The responsibilities of the executor are listed below.

1. To prepare an inventory of all estate assets.
2. To pay all Federal, state, and local taxes owed by the estate.
3. To pay all of the estate's debts and expenses incurred during the administration.
4. To decide on the validity of claims against the estate.
5. To defend the estate against lawsuits.
6. To fund and establish any trusts created under the will.
7. To manage any other estate financial matters.
8. To keep complete records of all transactions made on behalf of the estate or in accordance with the will.
9. To distribute the remaining estate assets according to the terms of the will after all of the estate's settlement obligations are met and all specific bequests are satisfied.
10. To make a final accounting to the court and the decedent's beneficiaries.

Who should be the executor of a will? The first consideration is the size of the estate. If the estate is relatively small, a spouse, a son or a daughter could be the executor. If the estate is large, involving difficult tax and investment decisions, it would be best to select an estate lawyer or the trust department of a bank. A spouse may be called upon to serve as a coexecutor.

Special qualities of an executor which should be examined include the ability to get along with your heirs; the ability to command respect; availability, or having the time to get the job done; and finally, executive and administrative ability.

Before you select a professional fiduciary, discuss the fees, philosophy, and method of operation to be sure the individual meets your needs and those of your beneficiaries. You can change an executor during your lifetime, but once you die your will is irrevocable and it is then very difficult to make a replacement.

Fees or commissions for executors vary from state to state. The commission is computed on the gross value of the estate including income which passes through the executor's hands, and is deductible for tax purposes. The commission is fixed by state law and is payable only once during the administration of an estate. An example of an executor's commission charge is as follows:

5% on the first $100,000, or $5,000
4% on the next 200,000, or $8,000
3% on the next 700,000, or $21,000
2.5% on the next 4,000,000
2% on the excess over 5,000,000

The commission on a $300,000 estate would be $13,000.

Guardian

A *guardian* is a person who has the responsibility to care for a minor, or an incompetent adult, or to control his or her property, or both. A will usually nominates a guardian of minor children in the event of the death of both you and your mate. The court has the power and authority to disregard the nomination set forth in the will and to appoint another guardian who will serve the best interests of the individual requiring this care.

In naming a guardian, many gravitate toward relatives, particularly their own parents. But estate attorneys caution against this. Your parents may make wonderful grandparents, but they may not wish or be able to assume the responsibility of child rearing. Moreover, do not assume that a married sibling who is childless will want to act as guardian. Often, friends with children of about the same age are an ideal choice. Frequently, friends make reciprocal agreements, in which each couple agrees to act as the guardian of the other's children. In any case, be sure that you check with the persons you have selected before you name them in your will. It is a good idea to name *successor guardians* in case your initial choices die or become divorced. Some lawyers think it wise to name guardians who reside in the same state because legal complications may arise if you select nonresidents.

Guardianship lasts only until a child reaches the age of majority, typically 18. At that age, the child becomes fully entitled to whatever property is in the estate. In many cases, it is wise to establish a trust, stipulating that a child receive one-third of the assets at age 25, half the balance at 30, and the remainder at 35.

Where Should My Original Will Be Kept?

You have several choices for the safekeeping of your will. Among them are the following:

1. In a safe deposit box at a bank.
2. At your lawyer's office if your lawyer is named as executor.
3. At the trust department of a bank if the bank is named as your executor.
4. With the clerk of the probate court where this is permitted.

In some states, such as New York, your safe deposit box is sealed on your death, and the box may be opened only when a representative of the state's Tax Department is present to examine and inventory the contents. This could delay obtaining the will. To prevent such delay, your will should be kept in a box rented in your spouse's name and your spouse's will should be kept in a box rented in your name.

Risks of Dying Without a Will

When someone dies without a will, the individual is said to have died *intestate*. If you die leaving a valid will, you are said to have died *testate*. If you die intestate, the laws of the state in which you lived at the time of your death will provide for the distribution of your assets. These state laws determine who will inherit your property, which property, in what proportions, when, under what conditions, under whose auspices, and subject to what Federal, state, and local taxes. This may not be the way you want your assets distributed, and may result in many inequities.

Dying without a will may create serious problems for your survivors. For example:

1. If you have a wife and three grown children, you may want your assets to go to your wife to support her for the rest of her life. Without a will, she may get only one-half or one-third, with the rest divided among the children. If your wife cannot live on her share, it would be necessary for the children to support her, working a real hardship on everyone.
2. If you are married and have no children, money meant for your wife might go instead to your parents or even your brothers and sisters, who may feel no obligation to support her.
3. Without a will, adopted children or stepchildren may inherit nothing.
4. Where no will exists, the court appoints an administrator to manage and distribute your estate. The fees he collects may be greater than the cost of making a will and then having the survivors pay probate costs.

The distribution of assets *by intestacy*, applicable to many states but not all, gives you a general idea of what could happen to your property. The wishes or financial needs of the survivors are not taken into account by your state's law, and this may not be the way you want your property distributed. Even if you have not made a will, your state has one tucked away for you. Table 6.1 illustrates one state's distribution of assets by intestacy.

Supplemental Letter of Instructions

The process of administering an estate begins with locating the will and then determining what assets the deceased has left. You should leave a *supplemental letter of instructions* to assist the individual who must begin to administer the will. It should contain the following types of information.

1. Names, addresses, and telephone numbers of those persons to be notified at the time of death. Relatives, friends, associates, others.

2. Location of the will. Include the name, address, and telephone number of your lawyer and the executor of your will, as well as the location of the will.

Table 6.1
Example of Distribution of Assets by Intestacy

Status of the Deceased	Division of Assets
Married	Spouse, 100%
Married, one child	Spouse, 50% Child, 50%
Married, two or more children	Spouse, 33% Children, 67%
Married, no children, but parents surviving	Spouse, 75% Parents, 25%
Unmarried, parents surviving	Parents, 100%
Unmarried, no parents surviving, but brothers and sisters surviving	Brothers and sisters share equally

3. Location of vital documents. These include certificates of birth, marriage, veteran's discharge; Social Security number and location of card; past tax returns, paid bills, cancelled checks and bank statements for the last several years.

4. Location of assets. Safe deposit boxes, stock and bond certificates, insurance policies, pension documents, bank accounts, real property documents, such as mortgages, deeds, and title policies.

5. Names, addresses, and telephone numbers of your accountant, stockbroker, and insurance agent.

6. Employment or business information. Name, address, and telephone number of present or last employer; instructions relative to any business enterprises you may own or in which you have an interest.

7. Funeral and burial instructions. The testator should spell out instructions for disposition of the body; type of service desired; memorial donations to a selected charity.

The original supplemental letter of instructions should be kept with your original will. Make one copy for the executor of your will, and one for you and your spouse so that it may be reviewed periodically and kept up-to-date.

Basic Advice on Wills

It is important to be aware of some general suggestions relating to wills. These include the following:

Make a Will If You Have None

Whether you are married or single, it is exceedingly important for you to have a will. If you die *intestate*, that is, without leaving a valid will, the laws of the state in which you lived at the time of your death will provide for the distribution of your assets. This may not be the way you want your assets distributed, and may result in inequities. A will spells out exactly how you want your assets distributed to your heirs after your death. If you do not have a will, start the process immediately.

A Wife Should Have Her Own Will

Even when the husband has been the major provider, both husband and wife need a will. First, a wife may have property to bequeath even though it may be only a small amount. A wife usually has some personal property, such as jewelry or antiques. Moreover, the property which a wife will inherit from her husband must be redistributed at the wife's death. Second, if her husband dies, leaving everything to her, and she dies with him in an accident, or shortly thereafter without having the opportunity to draw a will, then her assets and those inherited would be distributed according to the laws of intestacy. The provisions of both the husband's and wife's will should conform. Both wills should name the same executor or alternate and the same guardian, just in case both die at the same time.

Hire a Lawyer to Draw up a Will

Executing a legally valid will is the job of a professional. Since the laws of the fifty states vary, a lawyer in the state where you reside is the only individual qualified to handle your particular needs in relation to the state's laws. The small cost of a legally valid will is well worth the investment. Fees range from $75 to $250 and up, depending on the complexity of the will. Select a lawyer who specializes in estate planning and taxes. Do not write your own will. It could be declared invalid, it may not meet your needs, and you may forfeit tax savings.

How to Safeguard Your Will

Your will is a valuable document and should be safeguarded. Depending on the rules and regulations in your state, a safe deposit box is probably the safest place to keep your will. Or, if you name your lawyer or the trust department of a bank as your executor, you may wish to leave your will with your lawyer or your bank. Where it is permitted, you may leave your will with the clerk of the probate court. If your executor is someone other than your lawyer or the trust department of a bank, make a copy for your executor and another to be kept at home easily accessible to you and your spouse.

Review Your Will Periodically and Keep It Up-To-Date

A will should be checked every two or three years to make sure that the provisions conform with changing Federal and state laws, and your own resources and wishes. Schedule the review of your will with the same lawyer who drew your will if you are satisfied with his or her ability as a specialist in estate planning. You should certainly revise your will if you move to another state of residence. This is especially true if you move to one of the popular states for retirement, such as Arizona, California, Idaho, Louisiana, Nevada, New Mexico, Texas, and Washington, which are community property states. This type of property ownership is discussed in Chapter 7.

Choosing an Executor

It is important to choose an executor who is competent and has your confidence. You should also choose an alternate. Make sure in advance that the executor and alternate are willing to serve in this capacity. You may wish to name your spouse or an adult offspring as executor. If the estate is large, name your spouse as coexecutor with perhaps a bank as executor. Selecting an adult offspring as executor may cause a problem with other family members.

Make Bequests as Percentages

Because of the continuing problem of inflation, it is suggested that bequests be made as percentages of your estate, rather than in dollar amounts. Specific items of sentimental value should be left to specific individuals to insure your intentions will be carried out.

SELF-STUDY: DATA FOR MY WILL

1. If you have no will, and wish to have a lawyer draw up a will for you, you should contact a qualified lawyer and arrange to have an estate planning conference. In preparation for this conference, you should assemble all the facts concerning your estate and your family. Following is a list of the types of data you should assemble:
   - family information
   - beneficiary information
   - executor, guardian, trustee information
   - property information.

   Worksheet 6.1 provides space for you to record these data.

2. If you have a will, check your answers to the following questions. You may have to make an amendment to your will, known as a *codicil*. A codicil must be signed with the same formality as a will. If the changes are major, it may be wiser to draw up a new will.
   a. Are the beneficiaries named still alive and still worthy of your bequest?
   b. Have you moved to another state since making this will?
   c. Are you now living in a community property state?
   d. Do you still want to keep the same executor and alternate executor?
   e. Do you still own the same properties mentioned in your will?
   f. Do you wish to take advantage and are you taking advantage of the maximum marital deduction allowable under the Economic Recovery Tax Act of 1981? (See section on estate taxes.)
   g. Should this will be reviewed with your lawyer?

Worksheet 6.1

Basic Information for Estate Planning Conference

Family Information

Date _____

Full legal name _____

Address and phone number _____

Birth date _____ Social Security number _____

Employers (last 10 years)

_____

_____

_____

Veteran? _____ Service number _____

Disability: Service connected or non-service connected _____

Marital status: Single, Married, Widowed, Separated, or Divorced _____

Do you have a will _____

Legal name of spouse _____

Address and phone number _____

Birth date _____ Social Security number _____

Does spouse have a will? _____

Children, including those legally adopted:

Full name	Full address	Birth date	Extent of dependence
_____	_____	_____	_____
_____	_____	_____	_____
_____	_____	_____	_____

Other dependents:

_____ _____   _____ _____

_____ _____   _____ _____

Annual income: Salary _____ Investment income _____

Beneficiary Information

Names of individuals or charities	Bequest: Dollars or percent of estate
_____	_____
_____	_____
_____	_____

Executor, Guardian, Trustee Information

(1) The following person and/or bank trust department should be the executor of my estate:

Name and address of person and/or bank _____

Name and address of alternate executor _____

(2) The following person(s) should be the guardian(s) of my children:

Name and address _____

Name and address of alternate _____

(3) The following person and/or bank trust department should be the trustee for any trust that may be established.

Name and address _____

Name and address of alternate _____

Property Information

Real estate:

Description and location	Market value	In name(s) of	Amount of mortgage
_____	_____	_____	_____
_____	_____	_____	_____

Leases: _____

Bank accounts: _____

Stock and bonds: _____

Other assets: _____

Pension benefits: _____

3. Prepare a Supplemental Letter of Instructions (see Worksheet 6.2) by filling in the required information. Data for the Supplemental Letter of Instructions can be taken from Appendix A, Inventory of Personal and Financial Data. After it is completed, make two copies and file the original with your will. Give one copy to your executor and retain one accessible to you and your spouse so that it may be kept up-to-date. If you are single, give one copy to your executor and/or to a close friend or relative. Retain one for yourself so that you may keep it up-to-date.
4. Have you considered drawing up a Living Will?   ☐ Yes   ☐ No

Worksheet 6.2

The Supplemental Letter of Instructions

_____   _____
(Name of husband or individual)   (Name of wife or individual)

Legal name   _____   _____

Permanent address   _____   _____

                            _____   _____

(Name of husband or individual)   _(Name of wife or individual)_

1. Persons to be notified of death

(Name, address, and telephone
number of each entry)

_____   _____

_____   _____

_____   _____

_____   _____

2. Location of the original will

(Name, address, and telephone)

_____   _____

_____   _____

_____   _____

☐ Safe deposit box   _____   _____

☐ Lawyer   _____   _____

☐ Bank trust department   _____   _____

☐ Executor: _____   _____

3. Vital document information

Birth certificate location   _____   _____

Birthdate   _____   _____

Birthplace   _____   _____

Father's name   _____   _____

Mother's name   _____   _____

Marriage certificate location   _____   _____

Date married   _____   _____

Place married   _____   _____

	(Name of husband or individual)	(Name of wife or individual)
Prior marriages Names; dates		
How terminated		
Veteran's discharge certificate Location		
Service serial number		
Date discharged		
Place discharged		
Social Security: card location		
Social Security number		
Financial documents: Location of paid bills		
Location of past tax returns		
Cancelled checks		

4. Location of assets

Safe deposit boxes		
Stock and bond certificates		
Insurance policies		
Pension documents		
Bank accounts and books		
Real property documents		

_____   _____
(Name of husband or individual)   (Name of wife or individual)

5. My professional advisors
(Name, address, phone number)

Lawyer

Accountant

Insurance agent

Broker

Banker or trust officer

Minister or rabbi

6. Employment or business data

Present or last employer
(Indicate which)

Name, address, phone number

Instructions re: business enterprise

7. Funeral and burial instructions

Include disposition of the body
(burial, cremation, donation of body or
parts); type of burial service desired
(religious or nonreligious); recipient of
memorial donations; flag for casket
from Veterans Administration.

_____   _____
(Signature)   (Signature)

_____   _____
(Date)   (Date)

TRUSTS

The *trust* is an important tool of estate planning, and is usually set up in the will. Holding property in a trust is a form of ownership that may result in tax savings. It is similar to a life insurance policy in that the trust property is ultimately distributed to beneficiaries under the terms of the trust agreement. Trust property passes to beneficiaries outside an individual's will and avoids probate.

What is a Trust?

A *trust* consists of assets which are set up as a legal entity. This entity is administered by an individual or an institution, known as the *trustee,* for the benefit of yourself and/or others. Any asset you may own can be put into a trust, including cash; proceeds of life insurance, annuities, and pension funds; securities; and real estate. No rules limit the size of a trust.

Trusts are set up to protect assets against loss or dissipation due to poor management at the same time that they can provide income to certain individuals of your choice. An attorney, a bank, or anyone else can serve as a trustee.

If you choose a bank as trustee, you should be aware of bank requirements. Small banks may accept individual trusts of $50,000 as a minimum. Larger banks usually require that individual trusts start at $100,000 to $200,000. The trust department of a bank handles this function. For investment purposes banks aggregate smaller trusts into *pooled funds* which operate much like mutual funds, investing the money for fixed income, income and growth, or tax-exempt income. You can choose the goal which you prefer.

Banks and attorneys charge a management fee for administering a trust. A husband may serve as trustee for a wife's trust and vice versa. While this may achieve savings of the management fee, the lack of professional administration may be costly in the long run.

Uses of Trusts

Among possible uses of trusts are the following:

1. ***To provide management of funds left to a spouse.*** A spouse may lack the ability or the knowledge to manage a large sum of money effectively. In such a case, assets can be set up in a trust to be managed by a trustee who does have this specialized knowledge and experience. The spouse is thus guaranteed income for life, and at the spouse's death, the assets in the trust can be distributed to your children and/or grandchildren, or any other beneficiary you name.

2. ***To hold money until a child reaches maturity.*** Funds can be set aside in a trust until a child reaches maturity, usually 18 years of age. If you believe that this is too tender an age to assume the responsibility of money management, you can provide that the funds be paid out in installments, such as one-third at age 25, one-third at age 30, and the last third at age 35. Or, you can provide that the funds be paid out in one lump sum, at a specified age, or paid out at the discretion of the trustee.

3. ***To provide for a retarded or physically-handicapped child.*** In the case of a retarded child, you may wish to set up a trust which would provide income for the

life of the retarded person to insure that the individual will have spending money, clothes, and incidentals. Federal and state programs pay for basic residential and medical costs for retarded children and adults.

4. ***To save on estate taxes.*** The Economic Recovery Tax Act of 1981 provides for an unlimited marital deduction which means that assets left to a spouse go completely untaxed. However, when the spouse dies, if the amount in the estate exceeds the limits set up by law, then taxes are imposed. This is discussed in the section on estate taxes. However, the spouse's will can set up a trust for the children and/or grandchildren for the amount which exceeds the tax-free portion. For 1987 and thereafter, the amount of an estate which can pass to heirs tax-free is $600,000.

5. ***To protect the children of a first marriage when a second marriage takes place.*** Before marrying a second time, it is essential that you protect the children of your first marriage. This can be done by setting up a trust which will provide them with income, particularly during their college years, and ultimately with the principal at some specified time.

6. ***To pay for a child's college education or other needs.*** Property may be placed in a trust to benefit a minor child for the purpose of financing education or for other needs, such as medical emergencies. The trust can be set up so that income from trust property may be distributed to the child while he or she is a minor, and at age 21 the beneficiary may receive all the trust assets and accumulated trust earnings.

7. ***To avoid probate.*** Probate, the court procedure for validating a will, is often a very costly and time-consuming process. Many people, seeking to bypass probate, place assets in a living trust in order to transfer ownership to others and at the same time avoid probate.

Any of these goals can be achieved through setting up a trust. It is not a do-it-yourself project. You should call upon an experienced lawyer who specializes in estate planning and trusts to guide you.

Types of Trusts

The two major types of *trusts* are (1) a *living trust*, also known as an *inter vivos trust*, which is created while you are still living. The Latin words *inter vivos* mean *among the living*. (2) a *testamentary trust* which is arranged for in your will, and comes into being after your death.

Living Trusts

Living trusts are of two types. A *revocable living trust* is one that can be changed or cancelled during your lifetime. This is a distinct advantage. Another advantage is that if you, the *trustor* (or maker of the trust), die, the properties held in a living trust are not subject to the formalities of *probate*, the legal procedure for determining the validity of a will and disposing of an estate at death. An *irrevocable living trust* is one that cannot be amended or revoked during your lifetime. Among the advantages of an irrevocable living trust are the following:

- Savings in income taxes. Income taxes can be saved by shifting income from the maker of the trust, who is in a high tax bracket, to the beneficiary who pays taxes at a lower rate.
- Savings in estate taxes. The appreciation of the principal over the years is not subject to the estate tax and the transfer of property to the trust reduces the size of your estate.
- Avoids probate. The property in the trust is no longer yours and therefore, on your death, would be transferred to your beneficiaries outside of probate.

The disadvantages of an irrevocable living trust are as follows:

- May not be revoked. You will lose control of the asset forever.
- Subject to income taxes. If property is sold after your death, the profit is subject to income taxes.
- Costs are involved. The costs include a legal fee for preparing the *trust agreement*, and an annual commission charged by the trustee.

Testamentary Trusts

A *testamentary trust* is created by the terms of a will. It therefore takes effect some time after death and consequently is irrevocable. Estate planning is usually directed toward the creation of testamentary trusts rather than living trusts.

Examples of some testamentary trusts include the following:

Sprinkling Trust. A *sprinkling trust* allows the trustee to distribute income to the children or to other beneficiaries according to their needs rather than according to some specific formula. If one beneficiary has a greater need than another, the trustee has the power to *sprinkle* more of the money to the needier beneficiary.

Standard Marital Trust. A *standard marital trust* provides the surviving spouse with the full benefits of receiving income from the trust for the remainder of his or her lifetime. After the death of the surviving spouse, the surviving children and/or grandchildren become the beneficiaries.

Qualified Terminable Interest Property Trust (or Q-Tip). Trust lawyers refer to the *qualified terminable interest property trust* as Q-Tip. The Q-Tip enables you to provide income for your surviving spouse for his or her lifetime, but upon his or her death the maker of the trust has the right to designate to whom the property shall be distributed. In the conventional trust the surviving spouse had the right to designate the beneficiaries. The Q-Tip enables you to protect your assets from going to someone your spouse later marries. The Q-Tip can also be used in a second marriage to provide for your second spouse, but it is stipulated that, after the death of the second spouse, the assets go to the children of your first marriage.

Life Insurance Trust. The *life insurance trust* is designed to accept the proceeds of a life insurance policy of the decedent. The trustee has a great degree of flexibility in increasing allowances to assist a child in paying college expenses or to provide increased benefits as a special need arises.

Other Types of Trusts

Some trusts have characteristics of both the irrevocable and revocable trusts and others are simply custodial accounts for minors. Examples of some of these are the following:

Clifford Trust. The *Clifford Trust*, named after the taxpayer who developed it (Helvering v. Clifford), is an irrevocable living trust for at least ten years and one day, and then the assets revert back to the maker of the trust. It is designed for parents who wish to establish an education fund for a child or children. The income generated by the trust goes to the child or children until the trust ends, at which point the assets revert back to the parents. The assets are not part of the donor's estate during the irrevocable period. The parents may serve as trustees, although a lawyer or bank may be designated as trustee.

The Tax Reform Act of 1986 repeals the use of a Clifford trust as an income shifting device. The income generated by such trusts set up after March 1, 1986 is taxed at 15 percent and 28 percent, the two-bracket structure of the 1986 law, but the tax is levied on the first $5,000 of annual trust income and rises on higher trust income, resulting in very high taxes. While the new law does not prevent the creation of the Clifford trust, it simply eliminates the income tax benefits of doing so.

The 1986 law also changes the rules for Clifford trusts created prior to March 1, 1986. Income is taxed at the maker's rate until the beneficiary, usually a child, reaches age 14. After that, the child's rate applies. But with the higher rates on trust income, the Clifford trust is no longer useful as a tax shelter.

Charitable Remainder Trust. The *charitable remainder trust* can be set up as a living trust or as a testamentary trust. As a living trust you get an immediate tax deduction for your charitable contribution and also provide income for yourself and/or your family while the property is in trust. In the trust agreement, you can arrange for the charity or institution to get the trust's assets at some future date, say at your death, or ten, twenty, or twenty-five years hence. If you set it up as a testamentary trust, you can specify that the trust provide income to your beneficiary for life, with the remainder of the trust's assets to go to a specified charity or institution at the beneficiary's death.

Totten Trust. A *Totten trust* is a bank account that is "in trust for" a named beneficiary, such as "Jack Smith in trust for Jane Smith." If Jack Smith dies, the bank account belongs to Jane Smith. As long as Jack Smith lives, he maintains control over the account with the right to withdraw funds. Jane Smith has no right to the funds in the account until Jack Smith dies, at which time the funds in the account go directly to Jane Smith, avoiding probate. Certificates of deposit and other investments can be registered in this manner. The Totten trust is an alternative to putting savings in joint tenancy, discussed in Chapter 7.

Uniform Gifts to Minors Act. Under a state's *Uniform Gifts to Minors Act*, parents can plan ahead to help their children through the financial burden of the college years.

A donor can contribute up to the gift maximum of $10,000 a year and a couple can contribute up to $20,000 a year to each minor and avoid income, gift, and estate taxes. A beneficiary need not pay an income tax on the gift unless his or her income is in excess of the IRS allowance of $3,430 in 1985. When a minor is entitled to a distribution from an estate, under this law the executor of the estate can give cash, stocks, bonds, and, in some states, insurance policies to an adult who will serve as custodian for the minor. If you die while serving as a custodian, the property is included in your gross estate, even though the legal owner of the gifted property is the minor. This can be avoided by having your spouse or other relative serve as custodian. When the child reaches 18 or 21, depending on state law, the property belongs to the minor. This type of gift can be arranged through your bank, stockbroker, or insurance agent.

The Tax Reform Act of 1986 makes no change in gift giving within the $10,000 (or $20,000) limit per year. However, if the child is under 14, only the first $1,000 of income from new and existing accounts is taxed at the child's rate. Income amounts above $1,000 are taxed at the rates of the parent/custodian until the child reaches age 14. When the child becomes 14, income from the account is taxed at the child's personal income tax rate. This provision of the 1986 Tax Reform Act is known as the Kiddie Tax.

The Role of a Trustee

Since the job of a trustee is generally long-term, every trust requires maintenance of records, keeping custody of securities, and filing whatever tax returns are necessary. When very long service is required, the testator, or maker of the will, may designate an individual as the *first trustee* and another individual or a bank as a *contingent* or *successor trustee.*

An individual can act as trustee of his own trust in the case of a living trust which is created during his or her lifetime. In this case, the individual does not want to give up management of his or her own affairs, but wants to be sure that if he or she becomes ill, incapacitated, or dies suddenly, the terms of the trust will be carried out. Thus, a *successor trustee* or *alternate trustee* is available to step in and carry on.

The most important job of a trustee is to manage the assets of the trust carefully and prudently for the benefit of the beneficiary or beneficiaries. Often, a trustee is given discretionary authority in deciding to whom to pay out income from a trust or even in some cases to dip into the principal if income is insufficient to meet a beneficiary's needs. If, for example, an elderly person is in a nursing home and for a time has extremely large medical bills, then the trustee may use not only the income from the trust, in the case of a Sprinkling trust, but also some of the principal to pay the medical bills.

Choosing a Trustee

Many individuals choose a relative or close friend as a trustee. If you are considering doing this, weigh the decision carefully. An individual may not have the time or inclination to properly manage a trust fund and, even more important, might not have the background and knowledge to do so.

If you do name an individual, remember to name a successor or alternate in case the first individual cannot fulfill the obligation. It is wise also to include a provision that, after your death, your spouse or other heir can name a successor or alternate to the original trustee.

While an individual family member or trusted friend probably would charge little or nothing to manage a trust, institutional managers do charge for this service. Any fees paid are tax deductible, however, and you would have several important advantages:

1. The institution will undoubtedly continue doing business in the same city and state for many years to come, while an individual may move.

2. Trust officers devote their time to managing money and are among the most knowledgeable people in handling trust funds.

3. Your money is protected because banks and other financial institutions are subject to periodic state and Federal audits, whereas individual trustees are not under any such scrutiny.

4. An institution provides continuity in the management of your funds. Even if your trust officer is unable to continue handling your account, another trained and knowledgeable individual would be available.

SELF-STUDY:
SHOULD YOU SET UP A TRUST?

1. Based upon your reading of this introduction to the subject of trusts, do you believe that you have need for a trust in your estate plan?   ☐ Yes   ☐ No
    If yes, what type of trust are you considering? _____

    _____

2. Do you have a relative, or close friend qualified to serve as a trustee?   ☐ Yes   ☐ No

    If yes, who? _____
    If no, you have the choice of any bank trust department.

    List your first choice _____

    List your second choice _____

    Present the above choices to your lawyer when you discuss your estate plan and will.

3. Ideas for charitable bequests.
    a. Help the causes you have always supported, the ones that will miss your help when you are gone.
    b. Consider a charitable gift as a living memorial for a loved one.
       What charitable causes have you always supported?

PROBATE

Probate is a state's court procedure for establishing the validity of a will and supervising the distribution of an estate's assets. The laws of probate have evolved over centuries and operate in all fifty states. Basically, the probate process serves an important function, namely, to make certain that your assets are distributed as specified in your will, thus protecting the interests of your beneficiaries. The probate process also serves to insure that the property of an individual who dies without a will is distributed in accordance with the laws of the state.

Criticisms of the probate process over the years include high costs, a slow and cumbersome system that is too time-consuming, and corruption among probate lawyers and probate judges. As a result much has been written on how to avoid probate. The thrust of much of the writing is that the average layman can probably handle whatever probate proceedings are required without the assistance of a lawyer; and that assets can be legally transferred without going through probate.

With a little time and effort and a willingness to study a state's probate laws and procedures, a survivor can probably deal with the details of settling an estate as a do-it-yourself project. Relevant material on handling the simple, routine tasks can be found at your local library. Moreover, personnel at local probate courts are usually cooperative and would assist you in filling out and filing required forms. Even if you ultimately seek the assistance of a lawyer, you can probably complete most of the routine, preliminary paper work, thus reducing your lawyer's workload. This would significantly reduce the lawyer's fee, yielding large savings to you.

Methods of Transferring Property Outside Probate

To bypass the probate process you can arrange to transfer property to a beneficiary outside your will. Among the methods available are the following:

1. *Joint Ownership.* When you die, all property held in joint tenancy with the right of survivorship automatically goes to the survivor, usually your spouse, outside the probate process. Usually, joint ownership is used for your home, but the technique of joint ownership can be applied also to other types of property such as stocks and bonds, bank accounts, and mutual funds.

2. *Living Trusts.* The two types of living trusts, revocable and irrevocable, can also be used for transferring property outside the will and the probate process. The trust instrument specifies who shall receive the property when death occurs.

3. *Life Insurance.* Life insurance is not part of a probate estate because when you die the proceeds of the policy are paid directly to a named beneficiary. The money is transferred by contract and is therefore nonprobated property.

4. *Gifts.* By giving gifts to your heirs before your death you will reduce the size of your estate. Your gifts may be subject to the Federal gift tax, but the gifts themselves are not part of the probate estate.

5. *Other.* Other transfers by contract as nonprobate property include money in a corporate profit-sharing or pension plan, savings bonds, and some business assets of partnerships.

Role of a Probate Court

A probate court not only validates the will but also serves as a referee, resolving questions of interpretation of the wishes expressed in the will. A will may be poorly worded, and the heirs may question the interpretation. Other aspects of a will which must be considered are whether undue influence was used to obtain particular benefits, whether the maker of the will was of sound mind, or whether the executor is handling the estate properly.

It has been estimated that almost three-quarters of the people who die each year leave no will, mainly wives and single people. In these cases, the probate court has the responsibility of appointing an administrator who must inventory the decedent's assets and then have them appraised to get an accurate value. The property is then distributed according to prescribed state law. No one knows what the wishes of the decedent were, nor is it possible to make allocations according to need. The law spells out what the spouse receives and what each child receives. The eight-year-old gets the same amount as an adult child, or the affluent adult child gets the same amount as the retarded child, for whom the decedent should have been more generous.

The role of a probate court is to study the will of a decedent. It must be proven to the satisfaction of the court that the instrument before it is the decedent's valid will. If the court accepts the will as valid, then the property owned by the decedent in his or her own name as the sole owner at the moment of death is distributed. If the court rejects the will as invalid, the property of the decedent is distributed in accordance with the state's law of *intestacy*.

What Makes a Will Invalid?

The will may have been handwritten in a state that does not accept handwritten wills. Or, the will may not have been properly witnessed: maybe too few witnesses, or one of the witnesses may also be a beneficiary. Possibly all the heirs named in the will are deceased, or the property that was bequeathed in the will has been sold.

The probate court will generally try to weed out any parts of a will which are invalid and then try to honor your instructions as closely as possible in the rest of the will. If this is not possible, the court may declare the entire will invalid and proceed as if you had died without a will, distributing your assets according to the law of *intestacy*.

If you wish to avoid this possibility, make certain that your will is valid and that it stays valid by having it drawn up by a qualified lawyer. Then, keep it up-to-date by reviewing it every two or three years.

Advantages and Disadvantages of Probate

The advantages of using the probate process are as follows:

1. Determines the validity of a will.
2. Serves as a forum for settling disputes on the interpretation of a decedent's wishes.

3. Protects your beneficiaries by honoring the directives in your will.
4. Distributes property of an individual who dies without a will according to state law.

The disadvantages of using the probate process are as follows:

1. The probate process is expensive, involving legal fees, executor fees, court costs, and other fees and expenses.
2. The probate process takes a long time, possibly years, if the estate is diverse, if tax problems exist, or if disputes occur.
3. Records of the probate court are open to the press and public, leading to unwelcome publicity.
4. Charges are frequently heard that a particular probate system is corrupt.

MINIMIZING ESTATE, INHERITANCE, AND GIFT TAXES

The *Federal estate tax* is paid to the Federal government by the executor of the decedent's estate. Some states also tax estates, but most states levy an inheritance tax, which is paid by the inheritor rather than the estate. Some wills specify that the inheritance taxes be paid out of the estate's funds in order to minimize the shrinkage of an individual's inheritance. The Federal estate tax and state inheritance and estate taxes are referred to as *death taxes*.

In addition to taxing estates, the Federal government levies a gift tax which applies to transfers, that is, gifts between living individuals. Gift taxes are imposed in order to make the taxation of estates and gifts equitable. If there were no gift tax, wealthy individuals could make large gifts immediately prior to death, thus reducing their estates and paying a lower estate tax, while the average citizen, who has to maintain maximum assets until death, would have to pay an estate tax on all accumulated propertry at death. In 1976 the Federal government combined the gift and estate tax schedule and created a single, unified tax credit which minimizes the tax liability either on taxable gifts or on an estate.

The Federal estate tax dates from 1916 and the Federal gift tax from 1932. Estate and gift taxes produce between one and two percent of revenue for the Federal government. Although the volume of wealth transferred each year is large, most of these transfers escape taxation because substantial exemptions and deductions are allowed. Most of the revenue actually collected comes from the few very large estates transferred each year.

The Federal Estate Tax

Prior to the Economic Recovery Tax Act of 1981, known as ERTA, you were allowed to leave your spouse tax-free either half of your estate or $250,000, whichever was larger. The remainder was subject to estate taxes. The progressive rate taxed larger estates more heavily than smaller ones. The 1981 law made several sweeping changes that not only affected estates and estate taxes but also gift taxes.

Unlimited Marital Deduction

The single most significant change in the tax structure is the unlimited marital deduction. As of January 1, 1982 all transfers between husband and wife are free of estate taxes.

This allows estates of *any* size to be passed tax-free. This change simplifies estate planning for the initial transfer from one spouse to another, but requires very careful planning for the transfer when the second spouse dies.

Tax-Free Estate Transfers to any Beneficiary Aside from Spouse

The 1981 law increases the amount of an estate which can pass tax-free to any beneficiary, other than the spouse, from $225,000 in 1982 to $600,000 in 1987 and after. An estate tax return must be filed only if the decedent's estate exceeds the amounts shown below:

Year of Death	Amount of Estate that Can Pass Tax-Free
1981	$175,625
1982	225,000
1983	275,000
1984	325,000
1985	400,000
1986	500,000
1987 and after	600,000

Increase in Annual Gift Tax Exclusion

Under the old law, gifts of $3,000 or less per year per donee were excluded from the gift tax. Starting January 1, 1982 the new law increases the gift tax annual exclusion to $10,000 per donee. This means that, if a married couple agrees to make a split gift, they can give up to $20,000 per donee, each and every year without incurring any gift tax.

Maximum Estate and Gift Tax Rates are Reduced

The maximum tax rate on estates and gifts is reduced from 70 percent to 50 percent over a four-year period as follows: 1981–70 percent; 1982–65 percent; 1983–60 percent; 1984–55 percent; 1985 and after–50 percent. This change has a significant impact on estates of $2,500,000 and over. Nevertheless, the liberalization of the law benefits estates of all sizes, and married couples, with proper planning, are able to protect the entire estate of the first spouse who dies.

Taxable Gifts

Under current law a taxable gift is any gift of more than $10,000 (or $20,000 if each spouse makes a gift) made in any year after 1981. If you make one or more such gifts above the exempt amount, you must file a Federal gift tax return so that the IRS can charge them against your exemption, the amount of your estate that can pass tax-free, shown previously. Gifts to a spouse are exempt from these limits, and gifts to others are also exempt as long as they do not exceed the limits noted above.

If you exceed your annual exemption of $10,000/$20,000 per recipient, and file a Federal gift tax return, no tax is payable until you exceed your lifetime exemption, either during your lifetime or after your death, when the value of your estate must be determined. Therefore, grandparents giving a joint gift can transfer to each of their children and grandchildren up to $20,000 a year.

Inheritance Tax

The inheritance tax differs from the estate tax in that the individual who inherits property pays the tax. States impose inheritance taxes which vary greatly among the states. The state inheritance tax applies when the decedent lived in the state at the time of death, or if the property of the decedent is located in the state which levies the tax. The only state that does not levy a tax on inheritances is Nevada. The Federal estate tax computation allows a credit for any inheritance taxes actually paid to any state or to the District of Columbia.

SELF-STUDY:
UNDERSTANDING MY ESTATE TAXES

1. Assume that your estate is worth $350,000. Will the Federal government levy an estate tax?
    ☐ Yes   ☐ No

    Explain. _____

    _____

    _____

2. Would your answer change if the estate were worth $1,500,000? Explain. _____

    _____

    _____

GLOSSARY

Administrator. The person appointed by a court to administer and settle the estate of a person dying without a will or the estate of a person whose will appoints an *executor* who cannot serve. (See Executor.)

Assets. All money, investments, and other property owned by an individual, a family, or a business. (See Liabilities, Net Worth.)

Beneficiary. A person or organization you designate to receive the income from a policy or a *trust*.

Bequest. A gift of property by *will.* Same as Legacy.

Buy-Sell Agreement A tool for transferring the portion of an individual's ownership of a business to designated heirs with the surviving owners retaining control of the business. An important area of concern in *estate planning.*

Charitable Remainder Trust. An arrangement with a charity under which it pays income to one or more persons for the lifetime of the persons named and at some future date, say at your death, or 10, 20, or 25 years hence, the charity receives the trust's assets.

Clifford Trust. The placement of money or property under a *trustee,* who is required to pay the income to another person for at least 10 years and one day, and at the end of the time period, the money or property reverts back to the person or persons making the *trust.*

Codicil. An amendment to a will that must be signed and witnessed with the same formality as a will.

Coexecutor. An additional executor, perhaps your spouse, to work with the *executor.*

Curtesy. The common-law right of a husband in his wife's property which arises from the marriage. (See Dower.)

Death Taxes. Those taxes imposed on the property that is transferred to another upon the death of an individual. Death taxes include the Federal estate tax and state inheritance and estate taxes.

Donee. A person to whom a gift is made.

Donor. A person who makes a gift.

Dower. The common-law right of a wife in her husband's property which arises from the marriage. (See Curtesy.)

Estate. The assets you leave to your heirs.

Estate Planning. The process of analyzing your assets and liabilities, managing them effectively during your lifetime, and disposing of them at your death through a will so as to best serve the needs of your beneficiaries. (See Will.)

Estate Tax. A tax levied upon the gross estate of a deceased person prior to its division. (See Inheritance Tax.)

Executor (Executrix, if a woman). A person nominated by the individual who writes a *will* to carry out the directions and requests in the will. (See Administrator.)

Fiduciary. The individual or institution to whom you grant specific rights, duties, and powers to act for you or in your behalf to carry out the provisions stipulated in your *will*. (See Administrator, Executor, Guardian, Trustee.)

Gift. A voluntary transfer of property from one person to another. Gifts can be given while you are still living to your children, grandchildren, relatives, other people, or charities, or they can be given after your death through a charitable foundation or trust. A charitable foundation can be created during your lifetime or through your *will.*

Gift Tax. A tax levied upon the value of a gift after certain specified exemptions. Under Federal law an individual may give away to one or more persons a total of $10,000 each per year. A couple, giving a joint gift, can give a total of $20,000 to each individual per year, which is tax-free to both donor and recipient. Amounts above these are subject to a gift tax.

Guardian. A person who has the responsibility to care for a minor or an incompetent adult or to control the property of such an individual, or both. (See Successor Guardian.)

Heirs. Those who inherit your property.

Holographic Will. A handwritten will that is signed and dated by the person writing the will. Recognized in about half the states, *holographic wills* require no witnesses.

Inheritance Tax. A tax levied upon the property which individual beneficiaries receive from the estate of a deceased person. (See Estate Tax.)

Inter Vivos Trust. Created while you are still living. The Latin words *Inter Vivos* mean *among the living.* (See Living Trust.)

Intestate. One who dies without leaving a valid *will.* (See Testate.)

Irrevocable Living Trust. A trust that cannot be changed or cancelled during your lifetime. (See Living Trust, Revocable Living Trust.)

Joint Tenancy with Right of Survivorship. Two or more individuals holding property jointly with equal rights to share use of the property during their lifetimes. When one dies, the survivor receives the entire property. Property held this way avoids *probate.*

Legacy. A gift of property by *will.* Same as Bequest.

Liabilities. All forms of indebtedness for which an individual, a family, or a business is legally liable. (See Assets, Net Worth.)

Life Insurance. Insurance to pay a named beneficiary or beneficiaries a specified dollar amount at the death of the insured. A life insurance policy can be used to provide income for the family at your death, or can be used to fund a trust or a business agreement.

Living Trust. Created by an individual who is living to be effective during the maker's lifetime. The property is placed in the hands of a *trustee* to be managed by the trustee for the benefit of one or more individuals. (See Revocable Living Trust, Irrevocable Living Trust.)

Living Will. A written request that the life of the individual not be prolonged by artificial means when death is inevitable.

Marital Deduction. The amount of property that can be left to a spouse tax-free. The Economic Recovery Tax Act of 1981 permits an *unlimited marital deduction.*

Net Worth. Monetary value of an individual, a family, or a business. It is equal to total assets minus total liabilities. (See Assets, Liabilities.)

Oral Will. Made in military combat and within hearing of two witnesses, it is used primarily by soldiers, sailors in active service, or mariners at sea.

Power of Appointment. A power granted by one person to another person to name a beneficiary.

Probate. The judicial process of establishing the validity of a will and supervising the distribution of an estate's assets.

Probate Court. Acts as a referee and decision maker by answering pertinent questions and resolving conflicts of interpretation of a will.

Property. Includes cash, securities, real estate, and any other possessions.

Qualified Terminable Interest Property Trust (Q-TIP). An arrangement by which the surviving spouse has a right to the income from the principal for life, but has no access to the principal. On the death of the surviving spouse, the property goes to such person(s) or organization(s) as determined by the spouse whose property it was and who was the first to die. The concept was developed by the Economic Recovery Tax Act of 1981 (ERTA).

Residuary. Property left in your estate after payment of your debts and distribution of specific bequests.

Revocable Living Trust. One that can be changed or cancelled during your lifetime. (See Living Trust, Irrevocable Living Trust.)

Sprinkling Trust. The trustee has the power to make distributions according to a standard such as need rather than according to a preset percentage. This gives a trustee the power to distribute income, and possibly principal, according to the needs of each beneficiary.

Successor Guardian. An additional guardian listed in a will, who can assume the responsibilities of guradian in case your initial guardian dies or is otherwise unable to perform the functions.

Successor Trustee. An additional trustee listed in a will, who can assume the responsibilities of trustee in case your initial trustee dies or is otherwise unable to perform the functions.

Supplemental Letter of Instructions. A memorandum of personal details that should be attached to your will with a copy to your executor and one for you and your spouse so that it may be kept up-to-date. The Supplemental Letter of Instructions should include such information as location of the will, location of vital documents, location of assets, employment or business information, and funeral and burial instructions.

Testate. One who dies leaving a valid will. (See Intestate.)

Testator (Testatrix, if a woman). The person who makes a will.

Totten Trust. A *payable on death* bank account. The bank account will usually read *John Smith in trust for Jane Smith,* or vice versa.

Trust. A legal entity (the *trust*) created by the owner of property for the purpose of administering and distributing such property for the benefit of the owner and/or other persons.

Trustee. The person who holds legal title to property for the use and benefit of another person who is the beneficiary.

Unified Tax Credit. The amount that can be deducted from the gross estate tax. This deduction is applied against both estate and gift taxes due the government, thus shielding both transfers from taxation. This tax credit is a direct reduction of the total taxes due, saving the taxpayer thousands of dollars. Approved by Congress in 1981, the *unified tax credit* increases from $62,800 in 1982 to $192,800 in 1987 and later years.

Unlimited Marital Deduction. Under present law no limit exists on the size of the estate that one spouse can leave for the other, and the transfer is free of estate taxes. This change became effective January 1, 1982.

Ward. A person incapable of managing personal affairs and for whom a court has appointed a guardian.

Will. A legal document, almost always in writing and properly executed, which describes how a person wants his or her property distributed after death, designating an executor, the person or institution that will carry out the terms of the will.

Chapter 7
Handling Legal Affairs

Although you may consider yourself a free and independent spirit, you are nevertheless a member of a society which is directed by law, and it is this law that directs an extraordinary part of your activity. Whether it is a birth certificate, marriage certificate, or death certificate; whether it is enrolling in school at a set age for a specified number of years; paying taxes or signing documents; filling out required forms for owning an automobile or paying a fine for a driving violation; taking out a passport to travel in a foreign country or fulfilling mandated health requirements—you are affected every day by laws already in existence or new laws that are under consideration. Your life would not be the same without such laws. Indeed, civilized society could not exist without them.

THE ROLE OF LAW IN RETIREMENT PLANNING

In this chapter the role of law will be reviewed in relation to retirement planning. Legal questions that may affect you as a retiree involve property ownership; premarital planning; age discrimination; arrangements with a paid companion; setting up a new business; personal bankruptcy; or involvement in a contract. A lawyer can play an essential role in many of these and in other areas. For example, laws regarding Social Security and pensions are complex, frequently requiring legal interpretation. Likewise, protection of your savings and investments may on occasion call for legal intervention. In estate planning, wills, and trusts, a lawyer is important in drawing up a will to assure that your bequests will be executed according to your wishes. Clearly, law plays just as important a role in retirement planning as it does in every other aspect of your life.

FORMS OF PROPERTY OWNERSHIP

The word *property* is a general term for things that people acquire for the purpose of ownership. The two basic types of property are *real property,* or real estate, which includes land and the buildings on it, and *personal property, tangible* and *intangible. Tangible personal property* includes things that you can touch, such as a car, a boat, clothing, or a stamp collection. *Intangible personal property* includes ownership of a right or an interest which is protected by law, such as an invention, a musical composition, a stock certificate, or a savings account.

Real or personal property may be owned or possessed in order to control or enjoy its private use. A person can possess property without owning it. A tenant in an apartment house or the driver of a rented car possesses the apartment and the car without owning them. Conversely, a person may own property without possessing it. For example, the landlord of the apartment building is the owner of the building even though he is not in possession of the apartment he has rented; and the car rental agency is the owner of the car which has been rented to the driver but is not in possession of the car until it is returned.

Property can be owned by an individual, a group, a corporation, or the state. When property is owned by an individual, it is known as *sole ownership*. If more than one person owns the same property at the same time, it is known as *concurrent ownership* or *plural ownership*. The types of concurrent ownership are *joint tenancy with right of survivorship, tenancy in common, tenancy by the entirety*, and *community property*. Each is treated differently at the owner's death.

Sole Ownership

The basic form of property ownership is *sole ownership*. In sole ownership one person owns and controls the property and has the right to leave it to chosen heirs at death. The owner has *title* to the property. Title is evidence of the right a person has to possess or enjoy property to the exclusion of all others and the right to dispose of property. Title to any type of property, real or personal, exists once it is owned by someone. Disposing the property is accomplished by *transferring the title*. The shell on the seashore, for example, belongs to no one, but once you pick it up for your collection, you have greater rights to it than anyone else.

A husband may be the sole owner of a couple's securities and automobile, and the wife may be sole owner of the couple's real estate. In many situations, even between married couples, sole ownership may be the wisest choice. The assignment of ownership of property to a husband and wife is a complicated matter and is treated differently in the various states.

Separate-Property System vs. Community-Property System

In 42 of the 50 states, the *separate-property system* is followed. Under this system, each spouse has *sole ownership* to property in his or her name, but real estate is generally owned jointly. The remaining eight states follow the *community-property system*, under which property acquired after marriage is owned equally, 50 percent each. The details are discussed in the following section, *ownership with others*.

Ownership with Others

Ownership with others exists when two or more persons have ownership rights in property. Types of ownership with others include *joint tenancy with right of survivorship, tenancy in common, tenancy by the entirety*, and *community property*.

Joint Tenancy with Right of Survivorship (WROS)

Joint tenancy WROS is a traditional way for husbands and wives to hold property; each owns 50 percent of the property. *With right of survivorship (WROS)* means that when one of the owners dies, the property goes to the surviving spouse free from the claims of heirs or creditors of the deceased co-owner.

If there are three joint tenants, each owns a third of the property. When one owner dies, the surviving co-owners own a half of the property each. When the second of the three co-owners dies, the last survivor becomes the recipient and owner of all the property.

Since property held as joint tenancy with right of survivorship passes to the surviving owners, it bypasses the directives of a person's will, thus eliminating probate proceedings. This is one of the principal reasons why so many people opt for this type of ownership. Nevertheless, it is wise to indicate in the will to whom the property should pass just in case both owners die simultaneously in an automobile accident or die within a short time of each other. Designating an ultimate beneficiary in the will is a prudent clarification of the owners' wishes.

Bank accounts are usually opened as *joint tenancy with the right of survivorship*. If you are considering this type of ownership, it is important that both parties understand that either owner of the account can withdraw all the funds at any time.

Advantages of joint tenancy with right of survivorship (WROS)

1. *A sense of togetherness.* A joint tenancy WROS indicates that marriage is a joint relationship in which two individuals share everything. It provides a feeling of unity, harmony, and security.

2. *Protection for a wife.* If a wife has no wealth of her own, joint tenancy offers her protection, because neither owner can sell the property or borrow against it without permission from the other.

3. *Automatic transfer to the survivor.* The property passes to the survivor automatically without probate when one owner dies.

4. *Protection from claims after death.* In many states, certain jointly-owned property is not subject to claims made by creditors nor by damage-injury claims against the deceased spouse.

5. *Avoidance of publicity.* Prompt transfer of ownership can be completed without the publicity that may accompany the probate of a will.

6. *Reduction of estate administration costs.* Since ownership of joint tenancy property passes automatically to the survivor, administration expenses of probate are not applicable to that part of the estate.

7. *Tax consideration.* Under the Economic Recovery Tax Act of 1981, effective Janaury 1, 1982, at the death of one joint tenant where the joint tenants are spouses, one-half of the value of the property for Federal estate tax purposes is included in the estate of the deceased joint tenant. In 1981 and prior years, the Internal Revenue Service generally presumed that property owned jointly belonged entirely to whichever owner died first. Any property still owned by the survivor at his or her death could be taxed again.

Disadvantages of joint tenancy with right of survivorship

1. ***Loss of right to dispose of property at death.*** A person who places property in joint ownership usually gives up the right to dispose of it in the will. This applies even though you state in your will that all property is to go to someone other than the co-owner.

2. ***Need for complete agreement.*** Decisions on how jointly held property is to be used, managed, and invested must be made harmoniously. Such unanimity may be difficult to achieve in case of a separation, a divorce, or an intrafamily dispute.

3. ***Heirs of a second marriage.*** If you have children from a first marriage, marry a second time, and place property into *joint tenancy with right of survivorship,* and then you die first, your second spouse will inherit all the property. This individual may not be concerned with the welfare of your children from the first marriage.

4. ***Loss of control.*** In most cases, joint tenancy reduces a person's legal control over property. If you have a joint bank account and become ill, the other joint tenant can withdraw sums of money from the account without your knowledge or consent. In the case of a marital dispute, you may find that your spouse has withdrawn all your money and left town.

5. ***Freezing a joint bank account.*** A joint bank account may be frozen in some states when one spouse dies in order to be sure all required taxes and claims have been settled. It may take some time for funds to be released. Each spouse should have some money in an individual account.

Tenancy by the Entirety

Tenancy by the entirety is a form of joint ownership in which a husband and a wife own property (usually real estate) jointly because each spouse owns the *entire* property in his or her own right. Under this arrangement the property passes to the surviving spouse in the same way as a joint tenancy with right of survivorship. Tenancy by the entirety is usually applicable only to real property, and the owners must be husband and wife. Some states do not recognize this type of holding.

Tenancy in Common

Tenancy in common is a form of joint ownership except that there is no right of survivorship or automatic transfer at death. If two people are co-owners of a property, each may own 50 percent or any other percentage of the total. If four people invest in some property as tenants in common, the first may own a 35 percent share, the second a 25 percent share, and the third and fourth co-owners a 20 percent share each. The portion owned by each person may be sold, given away, used as collateral, or passed through the particular owner's will.

In most cases, the share of the property belonging to a deceased tenant in common passes by means of a will. If the co-owner dies without a will, the property is disposed of according to applicable state laws. Ownership under tenancy in common is convenient for two or more friends or relatives where the owners wish to preserve their freedom to dispose of their individual shares as they like.

To inherit property under tenancy in common, a survivor must depend upon a will.

Community Property

In certain states the laws provide that property acquired after marriage is considered *community property,* which means that it is owned equally, 50 percent each, by both spouses no matter who contributes the money to pay for the property. Eight states follow community property laws: Arizona, California, Idaho, Louisiana, Nevada, New Mexico, Texas, and Washington. All other states determine property rights according to *common law.* In common law states two rules apply to property acquired after marriage. In some, property acquired after marriage is owned solely by the husband even if the wife has provided money to purchase the property. In others, each spouse owns the property derived from his or her earnings.

In both common law and community property states, property owned by either spouse before a marriage is considered the sole property of the original owner. In addition, the income or capital gain produced by the premarital property is *separate property.* Excluded from community property rules in community property states is property acquired after marriage by gift or inheritance, which is also known as *separate property.*

Community property does not carry the right of survivorship. When one spouse dies, the other does not automatically assume full ownership. The deceased partner's half is disposed by will or the state's intestate laws if there is no will, and only that part is included in the estate for tax purposes. If, however, the property is willed to the spouse, then it qualifies for the unlimited marital deduction. Community property laws usually permit couples to set up other types of ownership, either separate or joint, but the laws in each of the eight states differ. If you move from a common law state to a community property state, or vice versa, be sure to have your will checked.

Which Type of Ownership is Best?

An estate attorney is the best guide to advise you on how various types of property should be held. The following are a few basic suggestions.

Individual Ownership

Some forms of property should be held in your own name because you have maximum flexibility in dealing with the property. You can sell it, use it as collateral, give it away, and ultimately pass it on to your heirs through your will. The following are examples of property for which individual ownership is suggested.

1. **Life insurance.** A life insurance policy can be written in the name of the insured or in the name of the insured's spouse, with the same beneficiary or beneficiaries. Putting the policy in the name of the insured's spouse is done in order to keep the proceeds of the policy out of the estate of the deceased. This is no longer necessary because of the unlimited marital deduction. However, the proceeds of a life insurance policy pass to the beneficiary or beneficiaries outside the will.

Holders of large amounts of life insurance may wish to consider creating a life insurance trust to insure a source of steady income to a surviving spouse with the proceeds passing to children at the death of the surviving spouse.

2. **Stocks and bonds.** Individual ownership makes sense for stocks and bonds. It increases the degree of flexibility in the process of buying and selling. Joint ownership restricts flexibility in buying and selling because both signatures are needed. The couple can agree to split ownership of these assets, each owning about 50 percent.

3. **A car.** Individual ownership is suggested for a car. In case of suit for damages, only the assets of the owner are subject to damages. The drawback of joint ownership is that the assets of both owners could be vulnerable to a suit for damages.

Joint Ownership

Some forms of property should be held in joint ownership. The following are a few basic suggestions.

1. **A house.** Joint ownership with the right of survivorship is the usual method of ownership in the case of a home. Home ownership is considered a joint effort and when one spouse passes away, the surviving spouse and children, if any, are guaranteed that they will have a roof over their heads. A jointly owned house passes to the survivors outside the will.

2. **Savings and checking accounts.** Joint accounts are convenient so that either spouse has access to the account. In some states, however, savings and/or checking accounts may be frozen at the death of either owner if the bank learns of the death. Sometimes, an alert survivor who is aware of this possibility withdraws the money immediately. It is generally advisable for each spouse to maintain a small, individual account of a few thousand dollars so that cash is readily available if a bank freezes a joint account.

3. **Safe deposit box.** Most couples keep a safe deposit box in joint ownership so as to provide equal access. In case of death, the surviving spouse may empty the box immediately, because in some states the bank will seal a jointly owned box until the tax authorities take inventory of the box's contents and collect whatever taxes are due. To avoid the problem of a sealed box, a married couple should store the husband's will and valuables in a box rented in the wife's name, and her will and valuables in a box rented in his name. It is also usually possible to name a deputy (an adult child, relative, or friend) who has access to the safe deposit box.

ASPECTS OF RETIREMENT WITH LEGAL IMPLICATIONS

Situations may arise in the course of the retirement years that require legal assistance. In the case of a second marriage or a first time marriage in the retirement years, a legal agreement should be made prior to the marriage to protect the property rights of one or both partners or their children. Another situation with legal implications can occur if you ask someone to care for you and/or to handle your financial affairs during an illness, or similarly if you are called upon to be responsible for someone else. Problems associated with age discrimination, bankruptcy, setting up a new business, or entering into a contract are other areas that require knowledge of the law. An analysis of these situations and their legal implications follows.

A Late or Second Marriage

If you marry late in life for the first time or for a second time, you should be aware of potential legal problems, especially relating to property. Take the case of a second marriage in which each spouse has children from a previous marriage. On the death of the first spouse, the second spouse inherits all the property. The surviving spouse then draws up a will leaving all the property to his or her children with nothing going to the children of the deceased.

The couple should have obtained the assistance of a lawyer to draw up an *antenuptial agreement* or *premarital agreement.* Such an agreement is entered into before marriage. It is a contract between a man and a woman in which the property rights and interests of either the prospective husband or wife, or both, are determined, or in which property is guaranteed to one or both, or to their children.

Such an agreement may be supplemented by a *trust agreement.* By leaving the assets in a trust, the first spouse to die can guarantee that the surviving spouse will enjoy the income from the trust for his or her lifetime, but that on his or her death part of the remainder will go to the first spouse's children and part to the second spouse's children; or all to the first spouse's children; or any other arrangement desired. This type of agreement provides control in the ultimate distribution of an individual's assets.

A lawyer can advise you and your future spouse of potential financial and/or legal problems which may arise unless valid legal agreements are made before marriage.

Someone to Care for You

Usually at retirement you are in good health and fully capable of handling all sorts of activities, such as managing an investment portfolio, depositing monthly Social Security and pension checks, paying the bills, taking care of house chores, and walking the dog. Then suddenly you suffer a mild stroke, spending time in the hospital and then several months recuperating. Who is going to handle the myriad daily activities requiring attention? You can plan ahead so that everything can be taken care of the way you want it to be until you are once again able to take over.

Informally, you can arrange with your spouse, or with another relative or a friend who knows your economic affairs, to step in when such a crisis arises. Or, you may wish to handle this possibility more formally by granting the *power of attorney* to a person of integrity to take care of these matters for you while you are incapacitated.

A *power of attorney* is a legal document by which the principal (you, the signer) designates another person (such as your lawyer, a relative, or a friend) to act for you in all or some transactions. A *general power of attorney* gives an individual the right to handle all your financial affairs, including depositing and withdrawing money from your bank accounts, buying and selling property or securities in your behalf, and negotiating contracts for you. A *limited* or *special power of attorney* restricts your agent to certain specific actions in your behalf, such as receipt of money due you and payment of current bills.

Your lawyer should prepare the power of attorney. Do not buy a printed form and fill it in yourself. A properly executed power of attorney not only protects you but also your agent and those with whom this person deals.

Caring for Someone Else

Preretirees or retirees may have an elderly parent, relative, or friend who is unable to handle his or her affairs because of illness or senility. In such a case, it may become necessary for you to petition a court to appoint you or some other member of the family as that person's *guardian* or *conservator*. In terms of function, both are the same, but to be appointed a guardian, the *ward* must be proved *incompetent*.

The functions of guardian/conservator include the responsibility for handling all monies as well as real and personal property of the ward, and the maintenance of an accurate record of income and expenditures. Basic decisions include where the ward will live, medical and/or nursing home requirements, and proper provision of food and clothing. To have an individual declared incompetent requires the services of an attorney since so many legal responsibilities are involved.

Age Discrimination

Almost all Americans are covered by the Federal *Age Discrimination in Employment Act* (ADEA) of 1968, as amended in 1978. ADEA makes it illegal for employers or potential employers to refuse to hire an individual based on his or her age if that person is between 40 and 70. It applies to private employers who employ 20 or more people in an industry affecting commerce. Most Federal, state, and local government employees are covered, as are employment agencies serving one or more covered employers, and labor unions representing 25 or more members or functioning as hiring halls.

ADEA also makes it clear that employers cannot require employees to retire before they are 70. Mandatory retirement at any age is forbidden for many government employees. In general, the Act also prohibits discrimination in hiring, job retention, promotions, compensation, or other terms or conditions of employment. People who believe that their rights have been violated under the Act can file a charge with the Equal Employment Opportunity Commission.

On October 31, 1986 President Reagan signed the Age Discrimination in Employment Act Amendments of 1986. Effective January 1, 1987, the Amendments eliminate mandatory retirement at any age by removing the age 70 cap for employees protected by the law. One of the exceptions continues to allow compulsory retirement of any tenured college professor who attains age 70. This special rule, however, will expire on December 31, 1993.

The Federal ADEA and its 1986 amendments, if less liberal than state law, do not preempt state age discrimination laws. Therefore, employers located in states having age discrimination laws are subject to both the Federal and state laws, and must generally comply with the most liberal provisions of each. For example, if a state law does not permit the tenured employee exemption then the state law applies.

The *Age Discrimination Act* of 1975 is different from the *Age Discrimination in Employment Act.* The ADA's prohibition against age discrimination, effective July 1979, affects Americans of *every age* and forbids most age discrimination in programs and activities receiving Federal financial assistance. The effects of the ADA are potentially widespread, as many institutions receive Federal money in some form.

Complaints under the ADA can be filed with any or all agencies that provide money for the program. All complaints within the jurisdiction of the Act will be referred to the Federal Mediation and Conciliation Service, which will try to reach a solution satisfactory to both parties.

Bankruptcy

Occasionally an individual planning retirement or already retired becomes mired in debt. Whatever the reasons responsible for this unfortunate situation, the individual may have no alternative but to declare in a bankruptcy court that accumulated debts cannot be paid. Legally, bankruptcy is a constitutionally guaranteed right of Americans.

Federal bankruptcy law was significantly revised by the *U.S. Bankruptcy Reform Act of 1978,* which became effective October 1, 1979. The law expands the rights of individual debtors, streamlines bankruptcy procedures, and gives bankruptcy judges more status, staff, and power. Under this law bankruptcy can take one of two forms for an individual: the first is *straight bankruptcy* (Chapter 7 of the Bankruptcy Act), and the second is the *wage earner's plan* (Chapter 13 of the Bankruptcy Act). Under straight bankruptcy, the court appoints a trustee to list all the debts; to determine whether repayment can be made; and, if the debts cannot be repaid, to sell an individual's assets to repay as much of the debts as possible. This wipes out the debts and the bankrupt individual is then judged free and clear, but cannot declare bankruptcy again for six years. If you file under Chapter 7, an individual or individual and spouse may retain a specified equity in a home as well as other specified amounts of property exemptions in a car, furniture, appliances, clothing, jewelry, and tools used for a livelihood.

Under the wage earner's plan, you are permitted to keep your property, but you must set up a monthly budget plan, approved by the court, to pay off your creditors within a three-year period. Your budget indicates how much you can afford to pay your creditors after paying your living expenses. Your payback may be 10 cents on the dollar or more, depending on your income and essential living expenses. While repaying part or all of your debts, your creditors may not contact you about your financial obligations, and, after the plan is completed, whatever debts you had are considered as having been eliminated. Some debts cannot be erased, including taxes, fines, alimony, and child support.

In some states if you file for bankruptcy, your private pension accounts, including IRAs and Keoghs, may be subject to creditors' claims if you have access to the money, even with a penalty. Under the rules of bankruptcy, payments from stock bonus, pension, profit-sharing, annuity or similar plans are exempt only to the extent that they are necessary to support the account owner and his or her dependents.

If you have no alternative and are considering bankruptcy, contact a lawyer for advice and guidance even though you are permitted to file for bankruptcy on your own. The law is complex, and a lawyer can help you to protect your property and to advise you whether to file under Chapter 7 or Chapter 13.

Setting up a New Business

Some retirees set up a small business to keep themselves occupied, to enjoy personal satisfaction, and/or to earn extra money. Free advice and guidance on small business is available from the Federal government's Small Business Administration, 1441 L Street, N.W., Washington, D.C. 20416, or from any one of its field offices.

If you decide to set up a business, you can structure your business as an individual enterprise, a partnership, or a corporation. In both the individual enterprise and partnership, your liability is unlimited, which means you are responsible to the full extent of your assets, both personal and business, for any debts incurred by the business. Under *limited liability*, the principal advantage of a corporation, in case of a business failure, you are liable only for the money you invest and not any of your personal assets which cannot be touched. To set up a corporation your lawyer must draw up incorporation papers and other documents. In a partnership, it is necessary to draw up a detailed partnership agreement to cover all aspects of the business relationship, including a suitable escape clause in case the partnership is dissolved.

Some points to check before starting a small business include the following:

- **Taxes.** You will need a tax number for filing reports; a sales tax number for purchasing materials; and special records for state income and sales taxes as well as for local taxes. Also, you must pay Social Security taxes for yourself and your employees.
- **Insurance.** You will have to purchase fire and liability insurance as well as workmen's compensation if you hire anyone.
- **Licenses and Permits.** You may need a special license or permit to operate your business.

In any case, it is essential that you obtain the services of a lawyer who is knowledgeable in the field of business law and regulations in your city and state.

An Expenditure Involving a Contract

You may wish to spend part of your retirement income to join a social club, to register in an exercise program, or to buy hobby equipment. These purchases may involve you in a contract requiring the payment of a large sum of money either in advance or on the installment plan. You must remember that a contract is a binding legal agreement. Before you sign it, be sure you understand what it means. You have the right to read the contract carefully and to check it with your lawyer.

A widely used type of contract is the *conditional sales agreement*. If you sign such an agreement, you are committing yourself to pay an agreed amount per month for a given number of months. The buyer takes possession of the item—whether it is an automobile, home appliance, or furniture—but ownership or *title* remains with the seller until the final installment has been paid. Failure to meet the payments gives the legal owner, or seller, the right to repossess the goods, resell them, and sue you for any deficiency, plus whatever costs were incurred in the course of the court procedure.

In some cases a *chattel mortgage* is used. The buyer acquires title to the property but pledges it as security for the balance due. Again, failure to meet the payments gives the lender, usually a bank or finance company, the right to foreclose the loan, repossess the goods, and sue for the remaining balance, plus court costs.

Some Tips on Contracts

Because contract law is an area that most closely touches your everyday life, it is important for you to be aware of major pitfalls and how to avoid them. The following are a few basic tips that can save you time and money in the long run.

- **Watch for blank spaces.** Do not sign a contract with blank spaces in it. Be sure every space is filled in to your satisfaction.

- **Right to change a printed form.** You have the right to change a printed form to make the agreement conform to the terms you are willing to accept.

- **Reject oral promises.** Every provision agreed upon must be written into the contract in order to be enforceable. Do not accept oral promises.

- **Check with your lawyer.** Most important, before you sign a contract, check it out with your lawyer. Failure to do so can be costly and time-consuming.

CHOOSING AND USING A LAWYER

A lawyer is a highly trained professional who is qualified to assist you in handling your financial resources, property, housing arrangements, estate planning, and a variety of family affairs. Some lawyers specialize in one or more of these areas, and with their academic and legal training are able to guide you when you begin planning for retirement. Making a wrong decision can be very costly, and when you pass age fifty, the opportunities for correcting costly errors are fewer. Therefore, it is wise to obtain as much expert legal advice as possible to assure yourself a problem-free retirement. Correct planning decisions will insure your independence, security, and peace of mind.

Laws today are much too complex to be correctly interpreted and applied by the layman. Individuals attempting to practice do-it-yourself law have found that they have multiplied both their problems and the legal fees they must ultimately pay to get the problems resolved. If you do not already have a lawyer, choose one to give you a legal checkup in the various areas of retirement planning: financial, estate planning, buying or selling a home, civil or criminal court actions, starting a business, and tax consequences of charitable contributions, bequests, medical expenses, and trusts.

More and more people, as they plan for their retirement and after retirement, are turning to lawyers for help. Many older citizens' problems center on the uncertainties and inequities in the government assistance programs, such as Medicare, Medicaid, and, on occasion, Social Security. Constantly changing rules and regulations make professional assistance mandatory.

Choosing a Lawyer

One way to select a lawyer is to find a satisifed client. You may be able to get a lead by talking to your family and friends. Be sure that the lawyer you choose handles your particular problem since lawyers in larger cities generally specialize in a certain branch of the law.

If you live in a rural area or small town, contact your local bank for the names of a few reliable attorneys. In larger towns or cities, call your local bar association. Most bar associations sponsor a lawyer referral service. For a small fee you can arrange an interview to discuss your problem, and at the same time you can get to know the individual. If for any reason you are dissatisfied, you can try someone else.

Your local library has a copy of the *Martindale-Hubbel Directory,* which lists lawyers, their specialties, and their ratings. Other directories include *Sullivan's Probate Directory, Markham's Negligence Counsel,* and *Best's Recommended Insurance Attorneys.* If you cannot afford a lawyer, contact your local legal aid society, which offers free legal services.

Legal Fees

Fees vary according to the area in which you live and the complexity of the case. Ordinarily, a lawyer charges on the basis of the amount of time he spends in serving you. This includes the time he spends in talking to you in his office and on the telephone, looking up the law, preparing legal documents, writing letters, and negotiating with others in your behalf.

Sometimes a lawyer sets a flat fee for certain types of work, such as a real estate transaction, drawing a will, or probating an estate. Many county and state bar associations establish minimum fee schedules for most common types of legal work. However, at your first contact with a lawyer, you should ask him or her how much the charge will be in your particular case and what the method of payment will be. Payment possibilities include payment in advance, or a deposit with the balance to come at the conclusion of the work, or periodic payments. A financial arrangement in advance will avoid the possibility of disagreement and confusion later on. If you believe that a particular lawyer's fee is too high and you cannot afford it, you are free to solicit another lawyer whose charge may be more modest.

For certain kinds of legal work, a lawyer's fee is subject to approval by a court or by a state or Federal agency. For example, the lawyer's fee is controlled in cases involving guardianships and estates of deceased persons, and in proceedings concerning certain types of retirement benefits, such as Social Security.

Know Your Rights

Many new rights and protections have been extended to older Americans by recent Federal laws, as well as by state and local laws. If you believe that any of your rights have been violated, the laws spell out the ways in which you can obtain redress. Many of the laws permit you to file a suit against the party that you believe has injured you. However, filing a suit can be expensive and time-consuming and does not guarantee that you will win your case. Initiation of a lawsuit should be made with great care and in consultation with your lawyer.

Factors to be considered before filing a lawsuit include:

1. *Violation of a Law.* You must consider with your lawyer whether a law has been violated. Even though you may not like something or think that it is unfair, it does not mean that a law has been violated. Your lawyer must carefully check the law's provisions.

2. *Payment of Your Legal Expenses.* If you win your case, the court may require the losing side to pay for your legal expenses. This is not guaranteed in advance, and

there is also the possibility that you may lose your case. You must decide whether initiation of the lawsuit is worth the high cost.

3. ***Proving Your Case.*** In a lawsuit you are required to prove to the satisfaction of the court that you have been harmed. You may be certain that you have been injured, but you must be able to prove it.

4. ***Time and Aggravation.*** You must carefully weigh whether the time, cost, and aggravation of a lawsuit are worth the redress you *may* win. As you deliberate, you must also bear in mind that you *may* lose.

SELF-STUDY: EVALUATING A LAWYER

1. Which of the following qualifications do you consider essential in a lawyer?

	Check	
Qualifications	**Yes**	**No**
Competent	☐	☐
Forceful	☐	☐
Honest	☐	☐
Knowledgeable in field	☐	☐
Up-to-date	☐	☐
Discreet	☐	☐
Independent	☐	☐
Compassionate	☐	☐
Respected	☐	☐
Communicative	☐	☐
Reasonably priced	☐	☐

2. To what extent does your current lawyer meet these standards?

GLOSSARY

Age Discrimination. When someone makes a decision against hiring an individual because of age alone, overlooking individual merit or competence. (See Age Discrimination in Employment Act.)

Age Discrimination in Employment Act (ADEA). A Federal law, passed in 1968 and amended in 1978, that makes it illegal for employers to refuse to hire any individual because of the person's age, up to age 70.

Antenuptial Agreement. Usually prepared prior to entering into a second marriage, it sets forth the details of property distribution in case of the death of one of the partners. Also known as a *premarital agreement.*

Bankruptcy. A court proceeding in which an individual declares that he or she is unable to pay his or her debts, and seeks the court's guidance in an effort to remove or reduce those debts. (See Straight Bankruptcy, Wage Earner's Plan Bankruptcy.)

Chattel Mortgage. The buyer acquires *title* or ownership to the purchased property but pledges it as security for the balance due. Failure to meet the payments gives the lender, usually a bank or finance company, the right to foreclose the loan, repossess the item, and sue for the remaining balance plus court costs. (See Conditional Sales Agreement.)

Community Property. In eight states (Arizona, California, Idaho, Louisiana, Nevada, New Mexico, Texas, and Washington) the laws provide that property acquired after marriage is considered to be equally owned, 50 percent each, no matter who contributes the money to pay for the property. (See Joint Tenancy with Right of Survivorship, Tenancy in Common, and Tenancy by the Entirety.)

Concurrent Ownership. (See Plural Ownership.)

Conditional Sales Agreement. A type of contract in which the buyer of an item agrees to pay a specified amount of money per month for a given number of months. Ownership or *title* remains with the seller until the *final installment* has been paid by the buyer. Failure to meet the payments gives the seller the right to repossess the item. (See Chattel Mortgage.)

Conservator. (See Guardian.)

Consideration. Something of value that makes a contract legally binding, usually some value agreed upon by the individuals entering the agreement.

Contract. A legally binding agreement between two or more parties in which, for a *consideration,* one or more of the parties agrees to do or not to do a certain thing.

Corporation. A legal entity which, within the scope of its charter issued by a state, is treated as a natural person. It may make contracts; own, buy, and sell property; incur debts; sue and be sued in a court of law. The corporation enjoys perpetual life, and the stockholders enjoy *limited liability.* (See Limited Liability.)

Form of Business Organization. The various ways in which business enterprises may be organized. (See Individual Proprietorship, Partnership, Corporation.)

Guardian. A person who has the responsibility to care for a minor or an incompetent adult, or to control the property of such an individual, or both. Also known as *conservator.* (See Ward.)

Individual Proprietorship. A form of business organization in which one individual owns and manages, assumes all the risks of, and derives all the profits from, an enterprise. (See Partnership, Corporation.)

Joint Tenancy with Right of Survivorship. A form of joint ownership in which each spouse owns 50 percent of the property. When one owner dies, the property automatically passes to the survivor(s) outside a will. (See Community Property, Tenancy by the Entirety, Tenancy in Common.)

Limited Liability. The legal condition which exists when a stockholder cannot be held personally liable for the debts of a corporation beyond the amount that he or she has already invested in the enterprise. (See Unlimited Liability.)

Partnership. A form of business organization created through a contractual arrangement between two or more individuals, each of whom assumes full personal liability for the debts of the joint enterprise. (See Individual Proprietorship, Corporation.)

Personal Property. The two types are *tangible personal property,* which is something you can touch, such as clothing, a car, a boat; and *intangible personal property,* which is the ownership of a right or an interest that is protected by law, such as an invention, a stock certificate, or a savings account. (See Real Property.)

Plural Ownership. Ownership and control of property by more than one person. The different types of ownership are treated differently at death. Also known as *concurrent ownership.* (See Community Property, Joint Tenancy with Right of Survivorship, Sole Ownership, Tenancy by the Entirety, Tenancy in Common.)

Power of Attorney. A written instrument by which one person as principal appoints another as agent with authority to perform certain specified acts on behalf of the principal.

Premarital Agreement. (See Antenuptial Agreement.)

Property. Things or rights that people acquire for the purpose of ownership. (See Real Property, Personal Property.)

Real Property. Includes land and the buildings on it. It is referred to as real estate. (See Personal Property.)

Sole Ownership. Ownership and control of property by one person who, upon death, leaves it to chosen heirs. (See Plural Ownership.)

Straight Bankruptcy. If the debts of an individual are greater than the ability to repay, a bankruptcy court orders the liquidation of a specified amount of an individual's assets to repay as much of the debts as possible. (See Bankruptcy, Wage Earner's Plan Bankruptcy.)

Tenancy by the Entirety. A form of joint ownership of real property in which each spouse owns the entire property in his or her own right. Property passes to the surviving spouse in the same manner as a joint tenancy. If either party wants to eliminate the other's right to survivorship, it can only be accomplished with the consent of both parties. (See Community Property, Joint Tenancy with Right of Survivorship, Tenancy in Common.)

Tenancy in Common. Each individual of the tenancy owns a specified percentage of the property but not a specific piece. In this form of joint ownership there is no right of survivorship or automatic transfer at death. The portion owned by each person may be sold, given away, used as collateral, or passed through the particular owner's will. (See Community Property, Joint Tenancy with Right of Survivorship, Tenancy by the Entirety.)

Title. Legal right to the possession of property, especially real property, or the instrument constituting evidence of such right.

Unlimited Liability The owners of an *individual proprietorship* or a *partnership* are personally responsible for the debts of the business to the full extent of their assets and personal wealth. (See Corporation, Limited Liability.)

Wage Earner's Plan Bankruptcy. If the debts of an individual are greater than ability to repay, a bankruptcy court allows an individual to retain his or her property, but requires the individual to set up a court-approved monthly budget plan in order to repay as much of the debts as possible within a three-year period. (See Bankruptcy, Straight Bankruptcy.)

Ward. A person incapable of managing personal affairs and for whom a court appoints a *guardian.*

Chapter 8
Making the Retirement Housing Decision

Housing expenses are the chief concern of retirees living on fixed incomes. The problem is especially serious among widowed and unmarried older women. More than ever, community and government agencies are striving for solutions to the housing problem for those retirees who do not own a paid-up home. Housing cost problems become most acute during inflationary periods when the expenses of housing and maintenance increase at a higher rate than anticipated.

The basic ingredients of any budget are food, clothing, and shelter. The retirement budget, detailed in Chapter 5, distributes expenses for these three elements as 30 percent, 5 percent, and 35 percent, respectively, a total of 70 percent. Shelter is the largest budgetary component.

As you begin to plan for retirement and to study your assets, you will probably find that the family home is the largest single asset you own. Purchasing your present home undoubtedly was the greatest single investment decision you made. Mortgage interest rates, however, were low, and fixed monthly payments over the years became less and less burdensome as varying degrees of inflation helped you to pay off the debt with cheaper dollars.

Census statistics indicate that about three out of four householders at 65 years of age or older are homeowners, and about 85 percent have paid off their mortgages. If you sell your home or refinance it, the cash you derive can be used to buy a retirement home, which may better suit your retirement needs, and possibly provide a significant portion of retirement income.

DECIDING WHERE TO LIVE AFTER RETIREMENT

The most difficult decision to make, after you have decided to retire, is where to live after retirement. Over 90 percent of retirees choose to remain in the area in which they have been living, either in their own home or in a rented apartment. The rest move to a new location, a few to hundreds of miles away.

Should you stay where you are or move elsewhere? What type of residence should you choose? On what should you base your choice? Among the considerations in choosing a new residence are the following: type of ownership, size of residence, degree of privacy, and types of conveniences desired.

These issues must be resolved because the housing decision is at the heart of any financial retirement plan. The ensuing discussion may help you to decide where you want to live after retirement.

Your Housing Requirements

Before deciding on the type of retirement housing you desire and need, you should first review the specific characteristics you are seeking.

Size. How many bedrooms do you need? If you have children or other family members who visit you periodically and stay overnight for one or more days, you may require a second or third bedroom. Extra bedrooms generally require extra bathrooms. Also, do you need a dining room? Do you periodically entertain family or friends in a formal setting?

Layout. Should you seek a housing unit which is all on one floor, thus avoiding the need for walking up and down stairs? Do you or your spouse have any leg or back ailments which would require living on one level? Generally, a single-level home is more desirable for retirees who are 65 or older.

Extras. Do you favor a large kitchen with a great deal of counter space or would you settle for a smaller kitchen? Is a garage or fireplace essential to your lifestyle?

Climate. Northern states generally have very cold winters and heavy snows. People approaching retirement dream of the sun belt such as Florida, southern California, or southwestern states. Southern Florida and states bordering on the Gulf coast have very hot summers with extremely high humidity. Try living in the state of your dreams before making your housing decision.

Your Non-Housing Requirements

The dwelling in which you are now living has given you roots in a community that developed over many years. Your home or apartment may be close to your children and grandchildren as well as to your relatives, friends, and neighbors. Sickness or bereavement would highlight the importance of these associations. Moving more than 25 miles away from your present home would result in some loss of these close associations. Moving further away could completely sever these relationships. These *personal associations* represent a significant component of your non-housing requirements, and would have to be redeveloped in a long-distance move. Some other non-housing requirements which should be considered include those discussed below.

Professional Services. Over the years you have probably developed an association with a family physician, a family dentist, an attorney, an accountant, a stock broker and/or a banker. A physical ailment may require a particular type of medical treatment. If you move, new relationships will have to be made with one or more of these professionals.

Recreational Facilities. A neighborhood religious institution may offer recreational activities in addition to religious services. Such a center of activities may offer lectures, concerts, sports activities. Local libraries offer many intellectual activities. These facilities will have to be checked in a new community. Do you participate in civic, social, or political groups in your present community?

Should You Move or Stay in Your Present Housing Situation?

At the point of retirement, chances are that your children are on their own and the house or apartment that provided for everyone's needs is now too big. You and your spouse are probably overburdened with maintenance chores. On the other hand, you may like the community, have many friends and neighbors, and are accustomed to the comforts that your dwelling provides. If you list the reasons for remaining in your present housing, you should also list the reasons for moving. Take a close look at the reasons offered.

Reasons for Staying in Your Present Housing

If you are a homeowner or renter:

- You enjoy the space and have room for visits from children, grandchildren, and friends who can stay overnight.
- You get along well with your neighbors, and are participating in community activities.
- The neighborhood is still very nice since many of your friends and neighbors remain.
- Shopping and medical facilities are conveniently located.
- Your home or apartment is exactly the way you want it. The furniture fits in just right, and you can avoid the trauma of a move.
- The happy events you enjoyed make pleasant memories.

A homeowner has additional considerations:

- You have probably paid off the mortgage, and can afford to maintain it on your anticipated fixed income.
- If you ever need money, you can borrow against the equity in your home.

Reasons for Moving

If you are a homeowner or renter:

- Your house or apartment is too big, and is hard to keep clean.
- The neighborhood is changing—many of your friends and neighbors have moved.
- Your children have moved to distant states and visit infrequently.
- You live far from shopping and medical facilities.

A homeowner has additional considerations:

- Maintenance is a problem. Cutting the grass in the summer and snow removal in the winter are becoming harder, and hired help is expensive.
- Taxes, cost of utilities, and repairs keep rising every year as a result of inflation. These and other costs may become more than you can afford.
- Stairs are becoming a problem.
- If you sell, you can enjoy the $125,000 exclusion from income taxes.

Should You Continue to Own?

If you stay in your present housing or move elsewhere, the next basic question to consider is owning vs. renting. A mortgage-free home is cheaper than paying rent in most parts of the country. Against this you have to consider the loss of the interest or dividends that you would earn if you sold your home and invested the proceeds. Perhaps if this calculation were made, renting might actually be cheaper.

The Advantages of Owning. The advantages of owning your own home are the following:

- You are not subject to the terms of a lease and are free to do as you wish.
- Home ownership is a sound investment.
- You enjoy pride of ownership.
- Your living situation is more permanent.

The Disadvantages of Owning. The disadvantages of owning your own home are the following:

- You have the responsibility for maintenance.
- Capital which is tied up in your home could earn a greater return elsewhere.
- Owning a home is a long-term commitment.
- You always face the potential deterioration of your neighborhood.

Should You Continue to Rent?

If you're a renter, you always have the freedom to change your residence. Moreover, you know the monthly rent, and know whether you can handle it without too much difficulty. At the same time, you should be aware that rents can be raised to meet inflationary pressures. And there is always the threat that your structure may be converted to a cooperative or a condominium.

The Advantages of Renting. Among the advantages of renting are the following:

- The landlord or owner is responsible for maintenance.
- Exterior chores, such as cutting the grass and snow removal, are handled by paid staff.
- You face no unexpected repair costs.
- You have freedom to move or travel.

The Disadvantages of Renting. The disadvantages of renting are the following:

- You build up no equity.
- There is no possibility of long-term capital gain.
- A lease limits your freedom of action.
- Your lease may not be renewed by the landlord.

SELF-STUDY:
MY HOUSING DECISION

1. Check the characteristics of your retirement housing which you consider most important:

   Number of bedrooms _____
   Number of bathrooms _____

   Characteristics:
   ☐ Dining room
   ☐ Living room
   ☐ Den
   ☐ Eat-in kitchen
   ☐ Fireplace
   ☐ Gardens and grounds
   ☐ Modern appearance
   ☐ Terrace
   ☐ Garage
   ☐ Single-level
   ☐ Hot climate
   ☐ Cold climate

2. Check non-housing requirements you consider important:

   ☐ Near a medical building (doctors and dentists)
   ☐ Near a general hospital
   ☐ Recreational facilities
   ☐ Cultural facilities
   ☐ Swimming pool
   ☐ Steam room and sauna
   ☐ Library
   ☐ Churches and synagogues
   ☐ Commuting convenience
   ☐ Large complex
   ☐ Younger families

3. Make the housing decision: Move or stay in present home

List the factors you have considered in making your decision:

a. _____

b. _____

c. _____

d. _____

e. _____

f. _____

g. _____

h. _____

i. _____

j. _____

IF YOU STAY IN YOUR PRESENT HOUSING

If you are a homeowner, for most people it makes sense to keep their homes during retirement years. Your home, lived in for so many years, is an important part of your life and reflects your style of living. If your present home fully satisfies your housing and non-housing requirements, and you have decided to remain there during your retirement years, you should do some advance planning to prepare your home for this time of your life.

Useful Changes in Your Present Home

If you stay where you are, you must evaluate your present home in terms of future needs. Does it provide the facilities you will need in retirement to do all that you are planning? For example, does it provide individual space for you and your spouse in which to relax or to study and to pursue separate hobbies and interests?

Some useful changes in your home include the following:

1. **Remodeling.** You may wish to add a bathroom on the main floor to eliminate the need for using stairs. Or, you may wish to make a major room addition, such as an extra bedroom or den which may be used as a study or hobby room. Such changes can be expensive, but moving costs and refurnishing costs are also costly. Cost savings can result by replacing a bed with a sofa-sleeper, thus converting a spare room into a study or some other type of room.

2. **Safety Improvements.** Older individuals are particularly prone to disabling accidents in the home. Many of these accidents can be avoided if proper precautions are taken. For example, add non-slip surfaces to walkways, driveways, bathrooms; provide hand-grips in bathrooms and bathtubs; install adequate lighting in hallways and stairwells; add non-skid rubber underliners beneath rugs and carpets.

3. **Convenience Improvements.** Some improvements can eliminate many mainte-nance burdens, providing more time to do things you prefer. For example, aluminum or vinyl siding on your exterior walls will eliminate the need for periodic painting; paneling some interior walls will save on painting; tiling or other floor coverings will make for easier care; rearrangement of utilities in the kitchen and laundry room will save steps.

4. **Source of Income Improvement.** Adding a small kitchen and bathroom to a base-ment or spare room area of your home can produce a rental unit that can provide a source of income. Rental income could reduce monthly maintenance costs, help meet mortgage payments, or finance other improvements. A renter may offer com-panionship, or perhaps serve as a housesitter when you're away. Such a change in your home would require approval of your local zoning authority.

Tapping Your Home Equity

Many retired homeowners find themselves in a cash bind each month. The value of their home has grown, but inflation has reduced the buying power of their pensions. To compound the problem, many retirees cannot sell their house because affordable alterna-tive housing is not available. For such individuals a number of options are available which make it possible to get monthly income from their property.

Reverse Mortgage

Assume that the market value of a home is $150,000, that the retirees, a couple, are in their seventies, and that they need additional income. They approach a savings and loan bank. They present the case, and the bank offers to lend them up to 80 percent of the home's current value, or up to $120,000. The bank then will use the money to purchase an annuity which for this couple would pay, for example, about $14,000 a year. The bank subtracts the interest charge from this amount, and pays the remainder to the annuitants in monthly checks. These checks will continue to be paid as long as either of the retirees lives. After both have passed away, the home will be sold. Out of the proceeds the loan from the bank is repaid and the balance goes to the estate of the deceased. The concept of the *reverse mortgage* is relatively new. It was approved by the Federal Home Loan Bank Board in December 1978.

Sale Leaseback

Under the sale leaseback arrangement the homeowner sells his house in exchange for lifetime tenancy and a guaranteed monthly income. An investor buys the home at a discount that can range from 20 percent to 35 percent under the market value. A 73-year-old man might sell his $150,000 house for $112,500, a 25 percent, or $37,500, discount. The investor pays the homeowner a cash downpayment of 10 percent, or $11,250, of the purchase price. The homeowner and the investor reach agreement as to a reasonable rent to be paid by the homeowner; for example, $550 a month. The investor pays all taxes, insurance and maintenance costs, as well as regular monthly payments to the homeowner; for example, $875 a month, over a period of 10 or 15 years. The investor must also purchase a lifetime annuity to take over when his liability ends, that is, when he has completed his payments for the home.

The homeowner is taken care of by the downpayment of $11,250; by the investor's continuing $875 monthly payments; and ultimately by the lifelong annuity payments. Moreover, the retiree has a monthly net income of $325 ($875 - $550). The retiree can continue to live in the home for life at the established rent. The benefits to the investor are notable too. He has purchased a home at a 25 percent discount; he has a regular monthly rental income; and he will probably realize a significant capital gain after the seller has passed away or decided to move.

Charitable Remainder Trust

This arrangement was discussed in Chapter 6. In this case, the property is donated to a worthwhile institution in exchange for a lifetime annuity and the privilege of remaining in the home for life.

SELF-STUDY:
DATA FOR MY RETIREMENT HOUSING

1. If you are planning to stay in your present home at retirement, evaluate the home in terms of future needs. List the changes you would like to make and indicate the estimated cost for each change.

Change	Estimated cost
a. _____	_____
b. _____	_____
c. _____	_____
d. _____	_____

2. Have you considered tapping your home equity?   ☐ Yes   ☐ No
   If yes, which option do you favor?

   ☐ Reverse mortgage
   ☐ Sale leaseback
   ☐ Charitable remainder trust

   Your choice should be discussed with your lawyer and/or accountant.

IF YOU DECIDE TO MOVE

If you decide to make a change, it makes good sense to analyze and evaluate the advantages and disadvantages of the alternative types of housing available. You should also compare housing costs and the suitability of the new location before you sever your ties from your present location. A discussion of alternative types of housing and their pros and cons follows.

Smaller Home

Many people buy a smaller home many years prior to their retirement which they use for their vacations. Generally such a second home is located in the country, possibly near a lake. While working, the people pay off the mortgage, and at the time of retirement, the smaller home is available for them. They like the smaller home, are familiar with the area, and over the years have developed good relationships with their neighbors. When they retire they can rent their old house rather than sell it, and use the rental income to supplement their pension and Social Security income.

This may be ideal for some people, but others want to live closer to the central city with more people around and with urban cultural and recreational activities readily available.

In any case, if your present home is too large, a smaller home offers many *advantages*:

- A smaller home costs less than your present home.
- Surplus capital from the sale of your larger house can be invested.
- A bank would grant a mortgage loan if you needed one.
- Cleaning chores are reduced.
- Lawn cutting and snow shoveling are reduced.
- You retain the privacy and comfort of a home.
- Home ownership is a good investment.
- You can choose your ideal location.

The *disadvantages* of a smaller house are the following:

- It still requires cleaning and upkeep.
- It requires exterior and interior maintenance.
- The house ties up a portion of your investment capital.
- Appreciation in value may be less rapid than you anticipated.
- Your quarters may be more cramped than you had expected.

Rental Apartment

Renting an apartment is another alternative. By living in a rented apartment you can enjoy a carefree lifestyle. This is especially desirable for people who enjoy traveling and do not wish to be burdened with the responsibilities of housing maintenance.

The *advantages* of apartment renting are the following:

- Monthly rent is fixed for the duration of the lease.
- Maintenance cost is included in the rent.
- Lawn care and snow removal services are provided.
- You can enjoy the freedom to move or to travel.
- Renting requires a minimal financial investment, permitting more favorable investments of your capital.
- The trouble and expense of selling are eliminated.
- Renting may provide recreational facilities at no additional cost.

The *disadvantages* of apartment renting are the following:

- Renting generally provides less space than a house.
- The landlord has the right to evict a tenant under certain conditions.
- The landlord may not renew a lease if he wishes to convert to cooperatives or condominiums.
- The tenant builds up no equity, and merely collects rent receipts.
- The tenant enjoys no income tax savings.
- A portion of the rent includes vacancy costs and landlord profit.
- The lease usually restricts tenant activities, such as ownership of pets.
- The monthly rent may include extra charges for garage space or air conditioning units.

The Federal government sponsors subsidized or public housing projects for older people. Rents in these developments are set on a sliding scale based on income. People 62 or older and handicapped people can qualify for a Federal rent subsidy in nonprofit housing projects built under this program.

People planning to retire whose incomes are moderate but too high for public housing should consider rental housing for people over 62 sponsored by nonprofit groups and financed with low-interest government mortgages.

Condominium

Condominium was a strange-sounding word ten years ago, raising questions as to its meaning. Today, the concept has spread into every aspect of real estate. Increasingly, people are choosing to live in condominiums rather than in one-family detached homes or rentals. The U.S. League of Savings Associations estimated that the U.S. had about 85,000 condos in 1970, and three million units nationwide by the end of 1983.

What is a condominium? A condominium is a legal plan of ownership in which you buy a home or an apartment, making a downpayment and borrowing the rest of the cost from a lending institution in the form of a mortgage. You own your housing unit plus a proportional interest in common facilities, such as grounds, hallways, elevators and recreation areas, paying a monthly maintenance fee for their care.

Owning a condominium has both advantages and disadvantages. The *advantages* of condominium living are the following:

- It is a safe investment against inflation.
- Monthly mortgage payments build up equity.
- Condominium ownership provides income tax savings; mortgage interest and real estate taxes are income tax deductions.
- You can enjoy the freedom to make the changes you wish with your property.
- Exterior property maintenance is provided.
- Monthly costs are not related to a landlord's overhead and profit.
- Policies are set by the owners' association, in which you have a vote.

The *disadvantages* of condominium living are the following:

- Buying a condominium requires a significant downpayment with a potential income loss from more favorable investment alternatives.
- The collective judgment of the owners may not be the wisest operating decisions.
- The monthly maintenance fee is usually increased to keep pace with inflation and/or poor management.
- The time and costs of selling are the same as those associated with home ownership.
- The structure or complex may be overcrowded, with a consequent loss of privacy.
- The different lifestyles and interests of your immediate neighbors may be displeasing.

One of the most significant attractions for the individual or couple contemplating retirement housing is the cost-saving potential. The price for a condominium unit is generally less than for a single-family home. Large scale construction of a condominium complex with shared roofs, walls and heating facilities reduce unit costs. Condominium units therefore sell for 8 to 10 percent less than equivalent single-family homes. For this reason condominiums account for about 25 percent of all homes purchased, up from only 11 percent in 1979, according to the U.S. League of Savings Associations.

Cooperative

A *cooperative* differs from a *condominium*. In a cooperative you do not own your living space, but you own shares in the corporation that owns the land and the entire structure or complex. If you leave the cooperative, you sell your shares, either to the corporation or directly to the new shareholder, as required by the bylaws. The corporation is composed of the inhabitants of the building, who together share the responsibility of overall management. The amount of your monthly maintenance fee depends on the size of your dwelling, which may be an apartment, a row house, or an individual home.

The bylaws of a cooperative may give the board of directors the authority to approve or disapprove the buyer of a particular share or dwelling unit. Cooperatives exist almost exclusively in urban areas.

The *advantages* of cooperative living are the following:

- Co-ops are usually located in the best areas of cities.
- Co-op membership motivates pride of ownership.
- Shareholders have a vote in setting management policies.
- Co-ops offer an opportunity for capital gain.

The *disadvantages* of cooperative living are the following:

- Some co-ops are overcrowded, resulting in loss of privacy.
- The bylaws of some co-ops, set by members of the association, do not allow children or pets.
- Decisions on interior and exterior painting are controlled by the board of directors, resulting in loss of control by the co-op owner.
- Inept management can result in rising monthly maintenance costs.

Mobile Home

A *mobile home* is a factory-manufactured housing unit. The unit is transported on wheels from the factory where it was built to a site where the wheels are removed and the unit is set upon a permanent foundation of concrete blocks or poured concrete. Mobile homes are reasonably priced. On a per-square-foot basis the highest quality mobile home costs about half the price of a traditional home. This includes only the cost of the house. After buying the house, you would have to locate a mobile home park where a vacancy exists and then either buy or rent a site.

A mobile home offers a unique opportunity for a retired couple to own a low-cost housing unit and to settle in a mobile home community with other retired people who have chosen a similar lifestyle. A mobile home park contains dozens of units which share a certain look-alike appearance. The residents have access to a recreation building containing swimming pools, sauna, gymnasium, music room, club rooms, and an auditorium.

The *advantages* of a mobile home are the following:

- The cost of a mobile home on a per-square-foot basis is half-or-less than the cost of a traditional home (excluding the land, which is a costly component if purchased).
- A mobile home is frequently taxed as personal property, a low tax, whereas a regular home is taxed as real property.
- Mobile home parks offer outstanding social and recreational opportunities.
- Occupants are usually of similar age and financial position.
- Maintenance costs are low.
- Occupants have the opportunity to live in resort areas without a large investment.

The *disadvantages* of a mobile home are the following:

- The opportunity for appreciation in land value is less in a mobile home park where the land is usually rented.
- As a mobile home becomes older, the costs of repair and maintenance increase.
- The value of the mobile home itself tends to fluctuate. Some homes have depreciated in value.
- While monthly rents in a mobile home park are cheaper than renting a traditional home, rents do go up, and often quite rapidly.
- After a few years, some owners no longer enjoy the lifestyle but find it too costly to make a change.
- It is costly to move a mobile home.
- In case of a resale, a mortgage institution may be unwilling to offer a loan.

Other Housing Arrangements

Individuals planning for retirement have a number of other options. Many retirees now live in retirement communities and the number of people choosing this option is growing. An individual or a couple who is beginning to encounter health problems which require professional help may choose a care facility. Other options include moving in with others or asking someone to live with you.

Retirement Community

A *retirement community* or a *retirement village* is constructed exclusively for retired people to free them from the noise and commotion of living among young families. They provide excellent recreational facilities, including golf courses, tennis courts, and swimming pools, as well as libraries, club rooms, and auditoriums. The physical arrangements and types of services provided vary widely. Some offer a shopping center and hospital on the grounds with full-time doctors and nursing staff. Costs vary depending upon available facilities.

A retirement community is likely to be at least 40 to 80 miles away from a large city, at which distance land costs drop sharply. Property taxes are lower because the communities do not have the large educational expense of areas with many children.

Types of housing available include single-family detached homes, duplexes, townhouses, and high-rise buildings, ranging in size from one to three bedrooms. Units may be rented or purchased. Some retirement villages are sponsored by nonprofit organizations, such as churches, unions, fraternal societies, veterans' organizations, civic associations, and teachers' organizations. Others are sponsored by business corporations as investments.

The *advantages* of a retirement community or village are the following:

- It is a self-contained community which meets all your needs.
- Recreational and social facilities are excellent.
- Planned activities for the residents keep active seniors busy at all times.
- Monthly maintenance costs are low.
- Security guards protect entrances and grounds.
- Good medical attention is readily available.

The *disadvantages* of a retirement community or village are the following:

- The initial entrance cost is high.
- The monthly maintenance fee keeps rising.
- Social contacts which are limited to a group of retirees may become boring.
- The lifestyle requires close living with neighbors.
- The location is usually isolated.
- You may miss the noise and bustle of a big city.

Care Facility

As you grow older, you may find it increasingly difficult to maintain independent living. A *care facility* is designed for the individual or couple beginning to encounter some health problems which require professional help. A care facility provides three different levels of service. A large apartment building in which tenants occupy their own apartments offers cafeteria facilities for meal service when desired, as well as 24-hour nursing service if medical treatment is required. This arrangement offers the lowest level of care, since it is designed for the individual with a greater degree of independence.

At a second level care facility, tenants live two or three to a single room with bathrooms, but without kitchen facilities. All meals are supplied by the care facility and the people living here must be well enough to care for themselves physically. The facility provides around-the-clock nursing to insure that tenants take medications when necessary and that nurses are available for emergencies. Such a facility may be thought of as a retirement hotel.

The third or highest level care facility is a convalescent hospital or nursing home for people who require nursing care. Some may be partially paralyzed as a result of strokes with no bowel or bladder control. Others require special care such as medication or the changing of dressings. The occupants are referred to as patients. Registered nurses are on duty and the patients are in hospital beds or wheelchairs. The patients in a convalescent hospital or nursing home do not require intensive medical care. They are stable, merely requiring personal maintenance.

A level beyond the convalescent hospital or nursing home is the medical hospital where patients go for various forms of surgery or for care of acute illness. Medical hospitals are available to provide intensive care for its patients.

The *advantages* of a care facility are the following:

- It provides housing as well as facilities for personal and medical care at various levels of need.
- An individual or couple requiring personal and medical services can choose a care facility most suitable for his or her needs.
- Many of these facilities are subsidized by the government.

The *disadvantages* of a care facility are the following:

- Costs of living in a care facility are generally high.
- It is difficult to locate the best possible facility.
- Usually a choice has to be made with haste and in a time of stress.
- All the alternative care facilities may not be available in your community.
- License regulations and administrative procedures vary from state to state.
- Abuses in care facilities occur from time to time.

Moving in With Others

How times have changed! When America was a rural economy, it was very common to find three generations of a family living together under one roof. Each member of the family had specific chores to perform to keep the farm functioning. The farm house was spacious, and as parents became older, the chores they performed changed, but living space was always available for them.

Today, in our urbanized economy and with the mobility which characterizes our society, young couples buy a house, live in it for a while, find jobs in other places, sell the house, and buy another. If generations lived together, it would restrict both mobility and easy housing turnover. Today, older parents for the most part are on their own. The children grow up and make their own lives, leaving an empty nest. An older parent who is alone may decide to move in with children or relatives, mainly for companionship. Both generations may benefit from such a relationship.

Other older adults may decide to share a household by pooling their financial resources. In this economical arrangement each adult may have his or her own bedroom, sharing the kitchen and other common space. Each individual should carefully evaluate whether this option is best since it is not a suitable arrangement for everyone. You may wish to move in together on a trial basis before making a final decision.

The *advantages* of moving in with others are the following:

- Both parties in the relationship enjoy companionship.
- Living with others offers a degree of security.
- The arrangement is less expensive than owning a home or renting an apartment.
- House maintenance chores are shared.
- You are free to take periodic vacations without having to close the house.
- It is convenient to have someone nearby in case of illness.

The *disadvantages* of moving in with others are the following:

- You give up your personal privacy.
- Living with another individual or family may bring differences to the forefront.
- The feeling of independence is lost in such a relationship.
- A disruption in lifestyle may occur because of a feeling of responsibility for another individual.

Asking Someone to Live With You

At some time you may wish to ask a friend or relative to live with you so as to provide companionship and/or assistance with day-to-day chores. A formal agreement in writing should be considered which sets forth specific financial arrangements. The agreement should be prepared by a lawyer. In exchange, you may wish to leave such an individual or individuals some portion of your estate in appreciation. If a bequest is to be made, it should be included in your will.

In many cases, the individual involved may be a son or a daughter, making it inappropriate to discuss financial arrangements. Such a situation, however, could create many subsequent problems when an estate is divided up among survivors. For example, the offspring who assumed the responsibilities associated with living with an elderly parent may feel that he or she is entitled to a larger share of the estate.

If you ask someone to live with you, you should address the issue of the disposition of individual and/or joint assets in case of death.

LEGAL AND ECONOMIC IMPLICATIONS

Buying or selling a home, leasing an apartment or a house, or entering into a contract for a care facility have both legal and economic implications. You should consult a lawyer before signing any documents relating to any of these major transactions. An accountant and/or investment adviser should be consulted prior to undertaking negotiations involving a large sum of money.

The following sections present some basic guidance on handling these major transactions.

Leasing an Apartment or a House

Many leases are written in archaic legalese and say things in two or three ways. However, the average person can read a lease and understand it. If you do not understand something, ask the landlord or property manager to explain it. If you still have doubts, you should ask a lawyer to go over the lease with you. The fee will be small.

The simplest kind of lease is an oral agreement. You rent by the month, and either you or the landlord can terminate the contract by giving 30 days' notice. To be safe, put your notification in writing. Most leases, however, are written contracts.

For any lease, whether oral or written, you should check the following points:

- *Term of the lease.* Leases usually run for a year or more.

- *Expiration clause.* You may be able to remain on a month-to-month basis. Or, the lease can be automatically renewed for another term.

- *Move-out notice.* The number of days you must give as notice before moving out is specified. The landlord may be subject to a similar requirement.

- *Legal notice of rent increase, change in lease terms, or eviction.* Do not waive your right requiring legal notification of rent increase, change in lease terms, or eviction.

- *Children and/or pets.* Lease terms state whether you may have children and/or pets in the unit.

Other clauses in a lease which may restrict you include such points as the following: a cost-escalator clause, penalty for late rent payment, subletting your quarters, maintenance of appliances, and a schedule of repainting. Make sure that the lease you sign contains provisions you can accept.

Selling Your Present Home

A home can be sold through a licensed real estate agent, a professional who deals in real estate, or by yourself on your own. At some stage you will need a lawyer for the closing, particularly if you are working with an agent. If you decide to sell your house on your own, you need a lawyer at the outset. As a seller, you have certain legal obligations and financial liabilities. No standard printed sales contract fits every situation. Every property sale is unique and requires a contract which is drawn to suit the particular situation.

If you select a real estate agent to sell your house, you can offer an *exclusive listing* under which only this real estate firm will have the authority to sell your house, or you can use the brokers' *central listing service.* In the central listing service all the realtors in your area are advised by the listing realtor that your house is on the market, and the realtor who sells the property must give a percentage of the commission to the listing realtor.

Selling property involves a number of legal documents, agreements, and tax liabilities. A qualified lawyer can help you avoid mistakes and realize the maximum return.

Economic Implications of Selling Your Home

Effective July 20, 1981, the Federal Economic Recovery Tax Act of 1981 makes it possible to sell your house, make up to $125,000 in profit on the sale, and not pay any Federal taxes on the gain. A married couple filing separate income tax returns can each claim $62,500 in profit on the sale. As noted in Chapter 5, you must be 55 years or older and the home must have been your principal residence for at least three of the last five years.

For homes sold before July 27, 1978, the owner had to be at least 65 years of age before the sale date and was permitted to exclude up to $35,000 of the gain from the adjusted sales price, provided that he or she owned and lived in the home for five of the eight years preceding the sale date. (The *adjusted sales price* is derived by deducting from the sales price the expenses incurred in selling the home, including sales commission, title charges, survey, and other closing costs.) A new law, which became effective July 26, 1978, raised the once-in-a-lifetime exclusion to $100,000 of gain provided that the owner was at least 55 years of age by the date of the sale and had owned and used the property for three of the five years preceding the sale date.

The market is not always advantageous for selling or for buying. The ups and downs of the economy bring with it inflation on one hand and recession and unemployment on the other. Record-high mortgage rates in 1979–1983 made buying and selling difficult. Yet the real estate industry did make adjustments. In some of the new types of mortgages, interest rates rise and fall with changes in the money market.

Buying a Smaller Home or Condominium

Buying a home or condominium involves several transactions, each of which requires an agreement in writing. If your interests are not properly protected, you may suffer significant financial loss and frustration.

First, an offer to buy is usually made in writing and includes a deposit or binder. This sales agreement indicates under what conditions the deposit will be returned if the purchase is not consummated; the purchase price; a legal description of the property; and fees and taxes to be paid. Second, the purchase may involve a mortgage in which the inclusion or omission of a few significant clauses can cost you a large sum of money before you pay it off. For example, is the interest rate fixed or is it flexible to reflect the changing cost of mortgage funds? Is there a penalty for prepayment? These and other contract terms involve thousands of dollars. Third, taking title to your home is more than the mere transfer of ownership. The type of property ownership, as detailed in Chapter 7, could have a significant impact on estate planning. This stage of the transaction also requires a title search, that is, checking conditions which may affect your ownership, as well as other legal details, such as a title insurance policy. And, finally, a purchaser of property may also be party to an escrow agreement which sets forth the conditions that must be fulfilled before any money, held by a third party, can be paid. It is important that the interests of the buyer be protected.

A Care Facility Contract

If you are contracting for a care facility, it is essential that you understand clearly what services you will receive, what the costs will be, and what the rules and regulations of the establishment are. The fine print of many of these contracts is designed to protect the owners rather than the residents.

Among the specific details which should be incorporated into the contract are the following: a description of the premises to be occupied; the services which will be provided and their cost; the procedure for escalation of fees to reflect increased costs; safeguards against overcharges; the forms of recreation available and costs, if any; the rules and regulations which would limit, for example, visitation privileges; hours for watching television; freedom to have a pet; the resident's right to sell or bequeath his or her property.

Before you invest your savings in a care facility, it is wise to consult a lawyer to assist you in interpreting the fine points. The fee involved is well worth it.

SELF-STUDY: COMPARATIVE HOUSING COSTS

1. Before making a decision on retirement housing, it is wise to compare the costs of your present accommodations with the costs of a prospective new location. To assist you in making this analysis, a comparative housing cost worksheet is provided in Worksheet 8.1. The worksheet is also useful in that it suggests ways of cutting costs in your present home.

Worksheet 8.1

Comparative Housing Cost Worksheet: Present Housing vs. Retirement Housing

| | | Average monthly expenses | |
| | Present housing | Retirement housing | |
Cost item		Alternative A	Alternative B
Mortgage payment or rent	$ _____	$ _____	$ _____
Property taxes[1,2]	_____	_____	_____
Insurance on house[1,3]	_____	_____	_____
Fuel[1,4]	_____	_____	_____
Electricity[1]	_____	_____	_____

Cost item	Present housing	Average monthly expenses	
		Retirement housing	
		Alternative A	Alternative B
Gas[1]	_____	_____	_____
Water[1]	_____	_____	_____
Furnace maintenance[5]	_____	_____	_____
Repairs[6]	_____	_____	_____
Services[7]	_____	_____	_____
Painting	_____	_____	_____
Total	$ _____	$ _____	$ _____

1. Total your annual expenses using your bills or check stubs, and divide the year's total by 12 to get your average monthly cost.

2. If your county or town grants a property tax reduction for homeowners over 65, use your senior citizen tax rate to compare with retirement housing costs.

3. Check to determine whether your home insurance premium can be reduced by investigating other companies' rates, taking a policy for a longer period, combining coverages in a homeowner policy, or taking a larger deductible.

4. Can you reduce fuel costs with more adequate insulation; storm doors and windows; weatherstripping of doors and windows; or a more efficient burner?

5. Includes repairs, cleaning, and burner insurance.

6. Includes repairs on roofing, gutters and leaders, plumbing, electrical, and windows.

7. Includes cost of lawn service (seeding, fertilizing, pest control), lawn cutting, shrubs, lawn and shrubbery supplies and tools, and snow-removal.

2. In addition to comparing alternative costs for retirement housing, you must also consider two related factors: furnishings and security.
   Furnishings: Will your present furniture and furnishings fit into your retirement home?
   ☐ Yes   ☐ No
   If no, estimate the cost for new furniture, new draperies, and carpeting in your retirement housing, using the following worksheet:

Furnishings	Retirement housing	
	Alternative A	Alternative B
Furniture	$ _____	$ _____
Draperies	_____	_____
Carpeting	_____	_____
Total	_____	_____

Security: The issue of personal security and safety must be taken into account in planning for retirement housing. Will the alternatives you are considering offer you the security you want, both in your housing unit and in the public areas outside your unit?

☐ Yes   ☐ No

3. If you are planning to sell your present home, list the names, addresses, and telephone numbers of three real estate firms in your community who could serve as your agent:

a. _____

b. _____

c. _____

4. List the locations you are considering for retirement housing and evaluate each in terms of advantages and disadvantages.

Location		Location	
Advantages	Disadvantages	Advantages	Disadvantages
_____	_____	_____	_____
_____	_____	_____	_____
_____	_____	_____	_____
_____	_____	_____	_____

5. To arrange for your retirement housing, will you be involved in buying or selling a home, leasing an apartment or a house, or entering a care facility? ☐ Yes   ☐ No
If yes, have you discussed your plans with your lawyer?

RETIREMENT HAVENS ABROAD

Individuals at all income levels may think about retiring to a country outside of the United States but may not consider it seriously. However, individuals who retire with limited incomes may be surprised to discover that some retirement havens abroad offer gracious living in beautiful surroundings on a meager budget, while retirees with higher incomes can live regally in some of these retirement Edens. The decision to start a new life in another part of the world should not be made hastily but should be based on careful research and planning. The Self-Study on evaluating a retirement haven abroad lists the wide range of factors you should consider in order to make a sound decision.

No place in the world is perfect in every respect. The Garden of Eden was lost early in human history. But some locations offer natural beauty, a climate that is comfortable year-round, and most important, a significantly higher level of living than a limited income would buy in the U.S.A. Retirement Edens at bargain prices can be found in the following brief list of countries: Costa Rica, Greece, Ireland, Israel, Italy, Mexico, Portugal, and Spain. Each of these countries offers distinctive characteristics that make it unique. Retirees with limited incomes may find a retirement paradise within their borders.

In Mexico, for example, $400 a month will provide a couple with a two-bedroom house, ample and delicious food and full-time help. Any money left over from this $400 can be used for travel and entertainment, including trips back to the United States for visits with family and friends. An annual income of $5,000 to $15,000 a year can provide a comfortable life. In Spain, there are about 6,400 retired Americans; about half of them reside in Costa Del Sol (Sun Coast) overlooking the blue Mediterranean. It has been estimated that a couple can live well at this location on about $12,000 a year, or about $1,000 a month, which includes the cost of domestic help.

If the possibility of retirement abroad interests you, contact the embassy of the country you're interested in, and you will receive a wealth of information. Hundreds of thousands of Americans have taken advantage of this option. The Social Security Administration mails about 350,000 monthly checks to retirees living outside the United States.

The *advantages* of retirement abroad are the following:

- You can enjoy a fuller lifestyle on a limited budget in some foreign countries.
- You can experience amenities of life not available to you on mainland U.S.A. because of cost.
- Some of the low cost of living countries offer an ideal year-round climate in beautiful surroundings.
- You may wish to return to your family's roots.

The *disadvantages* of retirement abroad are the following:

- Medicare coverage ends if you live outside the United States.
- You may lose contact with your family and friends.
- A wrong choice of location can be an expensive and time-consuming mistake.
- You may not have access to the same level of medical competence as in the States.

Tips for Retiring Abroad

If you plan to retire abroad, the tips given below may prove helpful.

- Before you make a final decision to move to a foreign retirement haven, spend a couple of vacations there, or perhaps a winter or summer season as a visitor.
- Don't burn your bridges. Try the new living arrangements for a year or two before you abandon your ties to your old neighborhood. You can rent your present home for the time you're away.
- Consider carefully the state of your health and your need for specialized medical and/or hospital services.
- Carefully evaluate all the features and characteristics of a retirement haven using the following Self-Study as a guide.
- If you've made the move and find you've made a mistake, remember that the decision is not irrevocable. Retrace your steps.

SELF-STUDY:
EVALUATING A RETIREMENT HAVEN ABROAD

Economic considerations

1. What is the cost of living as compared with the U.S.?
2. What are the tax consequences of living in this foreign country?
3. Does the haven offer economic freedom to invest, buy and sell property, or set up a business?
4. What are the job opportunities in that country if you should decide to reenter the labor force?
5. What types of housing are available and what are their costs?

Physical aspects

1. What is the climate?
2. Are sanitation and water quality problems?
3. Is the potential location accessible to an international airport?
4. What is the quantity and quality of roads, trains, and buses? Telephone and mail services?

Political structure

1. Is the government stable, or is it subject to revolutionary upheavals?
2. What will be your legal status as a long-term resident?
3. Is your potential location subject to crime and violence?
4. As a foreign resident, can you enjoy personal and property safety?
5. Do the people there enjoy the freedoms of speech, press, religion, and assembly?

Amenities

1. What is the quantity and quality of the following facilities?
    a. Educational: schools and colleges

    b. Cultural and religious: museums, libraries, and houses of worship
    c. Entertainment: theaters and movies
    d. Recreational: sports stadium, television, radio, and nightclubs
    e. Shopping: specialty stores and department stores.

2. What are the food and travel facilities like in the country, including restaurants, bars, and hotels?
3. Is there any language barrier?
4. Is the native population friendly?

Health facilities

1. What is the level of medical, hospital, and dental services in terms of quality and cost? Note that Medicare benefits are not payable outside the United States.
2. Are health facilities accessible to your potential location?
3. Are medical insurance policies available, and what are their cost?

GLOSSARY

Adjustable Rate Mortgage. At specified intervals, such as every six months, or thirty months, or three years, the interest rate may be moved up or down by the lender. (See Conventional Mortgage, Graduated Payment Mortgage, Negative Amortization.)

Amortization. A method of liquidating a debt by making periodic payments of the principal and interest over a fixed period of time.

Binder. A deposit requested by a seller to hold a piece of property for an interested buyer until a set date.

Care Facility. A form of housing for the individual or couple beginning to encounter some health problems requiring professional help.

Central Listing Service. Information on dwelling units for sale or rent is disseminated to all member real estate brokers in a given area. Even though the property may have been listed with one of them, each has the right to sell or rent, splitting the commission with the broker who obtained the listing. Also known as *Multiple Listing Service.* (See Exclusive Listing, Exclusive Right to Sell Listing.)

Charitable Remainder Trust. An arrangement with a charity under which a property is donated to the charity in exchange for a lifetime annuity and the right to remain in the home for life. (See Reverse Mortgage, Sale Leaseback.)

Closing Costs. Costs resulting from the financing and transfer of property ownership in a real estate sale.

Condominium. A legal plan of ownership in which a home or an apartment is bought with a downpayment with the rest borrowed from a lending institution in the form of a mortgage. The purchaser of a condominium owns the space he or she occupies with the right to dispose of this space as he or she wishes.

Conventional Mortgage. A home loan available to good credit risks, with fixed monthly payments covering interest and amortization for the life of the loan, and usually not insured by the Federal Housing Administration or guaranteed by the Veterans Administration. Also known as a *fixed rate mortgage.* (See Adjustable Rate Mortgage, Graduated Payment Mortgage, Negative Amortization.)

Cooperative. A legal plan of ownership in which the purchaser buys shares in the corporation that owns the land and the entire structure or complex. The purchaser cannot get a mortgage but may get a loan to purchase the shares. If the occupant wishes to sell his or her shares, permission must be obtained from the board of directors of the cooperative.

Deed. A written instrument that conveys *title* to real property. (See Title.)

Downpayment. The cash a borrower puts toward a purchase, with the remainder of the purchase cost borrowed from a creditor.

Equity. The dollar value of a property owned by an individual or individuals beyond any mortgage on it; the difference between fair market value and current indebtedness.

Escrow. The deposit of money and documents in the custody of a neutral third party until the terms and conditions of an agreement or contract are fulfilled.

Escrow Account. A segregated trust account used to hold funds pending the closing of a transaction.

Exclusive Listing. A written agreement that gives one real estate agent the right to sell a property for a specified period of time but not restricting the right of the owner to sell the property on his or her own without payment of a commission. (See Exclusive Right to Sell Listing, Central Listing Service.)

Exclusive Right to Sell Listing. A written agreement that gives a real estate agent the exclusive right to sell and entitles him or her to a commission regardless of who sells the property during the period of the agreement. (See Exclusive Listing, Central Listing Service.)

Federal Housing Administration. A U.S. government agency that insures mortgages of qualified buyers against loss due to default, thus encouraging lenders to make mortgage loans on favorable terms.

Fixed Rate Mortgage. (See Conventional Mortgage.)

Foreclosure. A procedure by which property pledged as security for a loan is sold or otherwise used to pay the defaulting borrower's debt.

Graduated Payment Mortgage. A financial arrangement in which the interest rate remains constant but monthly payments start at a low level, rising later to cover the full cost of interest and amortization of the principal. (See Adjustable Rate Mortgage, Conventional Mortgage, Negative Amortization.)

Home Warranties. Given by builders, sellers, and real estate agents to protect homebuyers from defects in a home as specified in the contract.

Lease. A contract that gives a tenant possession and use of a property under the conditions and terms stated. (See Rental Apartment.)

Mobile Home. A factory-manufactured housing unit which is transported on wheels to a site where the wheels are removed and the unit is set up on a permanent foundation of concrete blocks or poured concrete.

Mortgagee. A lender in a transaction involving a mortgage instrument.

Mortgagor. A borrower or owner in a mortgage transaction who pledges property as security for a debt.

Multiple Listing Service. (See Central Listing Service.)

Negative Amortization. An arrangement whereby the mortgage payment does not fully cover the interest due, and the difference is then added to the principal owed. (See Adjustable Rate Mortgage, Conventional Mortgage, Graduated Payment Mortgage.)

Prepayment Penalty. A charge levied by a lender when a mortgage is paid off in part or in full prior to maturity.

Rental Agency. A business specializing in locating rental housing for individuals seeking such accommodations.

Rental Apartment. A dwelling unit that is leased from an owner for which the occupant pays rent in accordance with the terms of a *lease*. (See Lease.)

Retirement Community. A self-contained community offering homes or apartments set in carefully maintained grounds, providing excellent recreational facilities and possibly a shopping center and fully-staffed hospital. Also known as a *retirement village*.

Reverse Mortgage. A monthly payment to a homeowner by a mortgage lender, using the home equity as collateral, where the monthly payment amounts are accumulated as a mortgage against the house, to be repaid when the homeowner(s) dies and the house is sold. (See Sale Leaseback, Charitable Remainder Trust.)

Sale Leaseback. Sale by a homeowner of his or her home in exchange for lifetime tenancy and a guaranteed monthly income. (See Charitable Remainder Trust, Reverse Mortgage.)

Sales Contract. An agreement between two or more parties, containing the terms and conditions of the sale. The contract must be written and signed by both parties.

Second Mortgage. A loan that uses as security a piece of property that is already security for a first mortgage.

Title. A document indicating the legal right by the owner of record to the possession of some real property. *Title* may be acquired through purchase, inheritance, gift, or foreclosure of a mortgage.

Title Insurance. Designed to protect owners and lenders against loss from defects in the *title*.

Title Search. The examination of all public records to disclose all facts pertinent to the *title* of the property.

Townhouses. Dwelling units that have their own front and back but common side walls.

Veterans Administration. A U.S. government agency that protects lenders against loss by guaranteeing loans made to qualified veterans through its home loan guarantee program.

Chapter 9
Interpreting Medicare and Medicaid, Other Health Insurance, and Nursing Homes

You buy health insurance for the same reason you buy any other type of insurance, namely, to protect yourself and your family from financial loss if a dreaded event occurs. Illness and disability strike at all ages, but older Americans are generally more vulnerable to health problems than younger people. Two decades ago the government enacted two programs, Medicare and Medicaid, which promote health benefits for the elderly and the poor. This chapter offers a detailed analysis of Medicare and Medicaid.

As you begin to plan for retirement you should investigate whether your health insurance protection will carry over from your coverage as an active employee to your coverage as a retiree. This chapter analyzes the types of health coverage, the need for each kind of protection, the types of organizations that offer health insurance, and basic advice on health insurance. The chapter concludes with a discussion of the different types of nursing home services, an analysis of nursing care facilities, ways to choose an appropriate nursing home, and a checklist for comparing the different facilities available in each.

MEDICARE

Americans enjoy the comforting thought that starting at age 65 the government pays their medical bills. While it is true that Medicare, a Federal health insurance program for senior citizens, provides significant amounts of financial assistance and some peace of mind, the program was not designed to cover all medical expenses for the elderly. Its benefits were set to provide basic hospital and medical services at the lowest possible cost.

Background

In 1965 Congress approved amendments to the Social Security law which, among other changes, established a health insurance program for individuals 65 years of age and over, popularly known as Medicare. Medicare, along with Medicaid, was one of the Great Society programs enacted in 1965, providing health benefits to the elderly and the poor. President Lyndon Johnson signed the Medicare-Medicaid law on July 30, 1965 in Independence, Missouri with former President Harry S. Truman at his side.

Medicare cost almost $3.5 billion in 1967. In fiscal year 1985 it cost $62.5 billion: $42.0 billion for hospital care and $20.5 billion for physician services. In spite of the cost increase, the Medicare program enjoys strong bipartisan support in Congress. The number of people enrolled in Medicare increased from 19.5 million in 1967 to 30 million in 1985. The program helps not only the elderly but also many severely disabled people. A 1972 law expanded Medicare to cover disabled people under 65 years of age and people with chronic kidney disease requiring a kidney transplant or dialysis. Today, it is estimated that Medicare pays about 48.8 percent of the medical costs of the elderly. Unless supplemented by additional health insurance, paying the rest can mean financial disaster since the elderly expend three times more for health care than younger people.

Present and future beneficiaries should clearly understand exactly who is eligible for Medicare, what Medicare provides and does not provide, how to collect benefits, and what additional insurance is needed for maximum protection. Unless a Medicare member has supplementary medical coverage, a catastrophic illness or injury can be financially devastating.

Basic Parts of Medicare

Medicare is a two-part program: Part A provides hospital insurance protection, and Part B provides supplementary medical insurance protection. Anyone who has reached age 65 and is eligible for Social Security benefits, regardless of whether or not he or she is still working, is entitled to Part A coverage without having to pay any premiums. After certain deductibles and coinsurance payments, Part A of Medicare pays for services as an inpatient in a hospital, in a skilled nursing facility, for home health services, and, effective November 1983, for hospice care.

Part B supplementary medical insurance is voluntary, requiring you to pay a monthly premium directly to the Health Care Financing Administration, or as a deduction from your monthly Social Security check, if you are receiving one. After a deductible and coinsurance payments, Medicare Part B pays a "reasonable and customary" amount of your doctor's charges, outpatient hospital services, and specified medical items and services not covered under hospital insurance.

Part A is financed through Social Security taxes paid by people who are still working and by their employers. Part B is financed through premiums paid by Medicare beneficiaries and, in addition, is subsidized by the Federal government.

Who is Eligible?

More than 98 percent of the nation's 29 million elderly are covered by Medicare. People who have reached age 65 without becoming eligible for Social Security retirement benefits include individuals who have not been credited with a sufficient number of quarters of coverage, as well as non-citizens and people convicted of particular crimes. These ineligible individuals may enroll in Part A and Part B of Medicare by paying a monthly Part A premium: $226 for the 1987 calendar year, and, in addition, a monthly Part B premium: $17.90 for the 1987 calendar year. Federal employees, formerly ineligible, became eligible for the Medicare program in January 1983. They pay a 1.35 percent payroll tax.

When to Enroll

Enrollment in Parts A and B is *automatic* upon application for monthly Social Security benefits. You should apply for Medicare separately if you decide to continue working past age 65. Application should be made at your nearest Social Security office about three months prior to your 65th birthday. If you retire before age 65 and file an application for Social Security benefits, you do not have to file a separate application for Medicare.

Medicare coverage becomes effective in the month in which your 65th birthday occurs, even if you elected to begin receiving your Social Security retirement benefits at age 62. When you apply for Social Security benefits or enroll in Medicare, you have the option of turning down Part B coverage. If you retire at age 65 and decline Part B coverage at that time, you will have to pay higher Part B premiums if you decide to enroll later. The penalty for late enrollment in Part B is a 10 percent increase in premiums for each 12-month period in which you could have enrolled but did not.

If you remain employed past age 65 and continue to be covered by an employer's group health insurance plan, you may wait until age 70, or retirement, if earlier, to enroll in Part B without payment of penalty increases in the future.

If your spouse is under age 65 and is already receiving Social Security benefits, your spouse's Medicare coverage will begin automatically at age 65. If your spouse is not yet receiving Social Security benefits, he or she should file an application for Medicare at the nearest Social Security office three months before reaching age 65.

Medicare Hospital Insurance (Part A)

Medicare insurance (Part A) provides four types of benefits:

1. In-hospital coverage
2. Skilled nursing facility coverage after a hospital stay
3. Home health care coverage
4. Hospice care

Benefit Period

A benefit period is a way of measuring your use of services under Medicare hospital insurance. Your first benefit period starts the first time you enter a hospital after your hospital insurance begins. Each benefit period has a 90-day maximum. In addition to the 90-day Benefit Maximum, you are allotted for your lifetime 60 extra "reserve days" that can be used for any hospital confinement that extends beyond 90 days. Once you have used your 60 "reserve days," future benefit periods are limited to 90 days during any one benefit period. There is no limit to the number of 90-day benefit periods you can have, but in order to be eligible for each benefit period, you must have been out of the hospital for *60 consecutive days*.

After a hospital confinement of more than three days, if you need additional care, Part A insurance provides 100 days of skilled nursing home benefits, in addition to the 90 days of hospital benefits, for each benefit period. When you have been out of a hospital or skilled nursing facility for *60 consecutive days*, you are eligible to begin a new benefit period.

Covered and Non-Covered Services

Medicare hospital insurance will pay for most but not all of the services you receive in a hospital, skilled nursing facility, home health services, or hospice care. There are covered services and non-covered services under each kind of care. Covered services are services and supplies that hospital insurance can pay for. An analysis of these services and payment schedules for each kind of care follows.

Inpatient Hospital Coverage

Medicare hospital insurance can help pay for inpatient hospital care if *all four* of the following conditions are met:

1. A doctor prescribes inpatient hospital care for treatment of your illness or injury,
2. You require the kind of care that can only be provided in a hospital,
3. The hospital is participating in Medicare, and
4. The Utilization Review Committee of the hospital or a peer review organization does not disapprove your stay.

Services covered

When you are an inpatient in a Medicare-approved hospital, the following services are covered:

1. A semiprivate room (2 to 4 beds in a room)
2. All your meals, including special diets
3. Regular nursing services
4. Costs of special care units, such as an intensive care unit, or coronary care unit
5. Drugs furnished by the hospital during your stay
6. Blood transfusions (except the first three pints)
7. Lab tests
8. X-rays and other radiology services, including radiation therapy
9. Medical supplies such as casts, surgical dressings, and splints
10. Use of appliances, such as a wheelchair
11. Operating and recovery room costs, including anesthesia services
12. Rehabilitation services (physical, occupational, and speech therapy)

Services not covered

When you are an inpatient in a Medicare-approved hospital, the following services are not covered:

1. Doctors' fees (These fees are covered by Medicare Part B.)
2. Private duty nurses
3. Personal convenience items that you request such as a television, radio, or telephone in your room
4. Any extra charges for a private room unless it is determined to be medically necessary.

Payment schedule for covered hospital expense

You are entitled to receive up to 90 days of inpatient care in any participating hospital in each *benefit period.* For the first 60 days in any benefit period, Medicare pays for all covered services except for the first $520 (1987 amount). This *deductible* is increased annually. For the 61st through the 90th day, Medicare pays for all covered expenses except for $130 a day (1987 amount). Care in a psychiatric hospital has a lifetime limit of 190 inpatient days.

A reserve of 60 additional inpatient hospital days can be used in any benefit period. Each reserve day you use permanently reduces the total lifetime number of reserve days you have left. For each of these additional days you use, the 91st through the 150th day, Medicare pays for all covered services except for $260 a day (1987 amount).

Beyond the 150th day, or after the 90th day, if all 60 *reserve days* have been used, you must pay all charges while Medicare pays nothing.

Skilled Nursing Facility Coverage

After you have been in a hospital, Medicare hospital insurance can help pay for inpatient care in a participating skilled nursing facility if your condition still requires daily skilled nursing or rehabilitation services which, as a practical matter, can only be provided in a skilled nursing facility.

A *skilled nursing facility* is a specially qualified facility which has the staff and equipment to provide skilled nursing care or rehabilitation services and other related health services.

To be eligible for care in a skilled nursing facility *all five* of the following conditions must be met:

1. You have been in a hospital at least three days in a row, not counting the day of discharge, before you transfer to a participating skilled nursing facility,
2. You are transferred to the skilled nursing facility because you require care for a condition which was treated in the hospital,
3. You are admitted to the facility within a short time, generally within 30 days, after you leave the hospital,
4. A doctor certifies that you need, and you actually receive, skilled nursing or skilled rehabilitation services on a daily basis, and
5. The facility's Utilization Review Committee or a peer review organization does not disapprove your stay.

Services covered

When you are in a Medicare-approved skilled nursing facility, the following services are covered:

1. A semiprivate room (2 to 4 beds in a room)
2. All your meals, including special diets
3. Regular nursing service
4. Rehabilitation services, such as physical, occupational, and speech therapy
5. Drugs furnished by the facility during your stay
6. Blood transfusions (except first three pints)
7. Medical supplies such as splints and casts
8. Use of appliances such as a wheelchair

Services not covered

When you are in a Medicare-approved skilled nursing facility, the following services are not covered:

1. Doctors' fees (These fees are covered under Medicare Part B.)
2. Private duty nurses

3. Personal convenience items you request such as a television, radio, or telephone in your room
4. Any extra charges for a private room, unless it is determined to be medically necessary

Payment schedule for care

You are eligible for up to 100 days of care in each benefit period in a participating skilled nursing facility. Medicare pays all costs for all covered services for the first 20 days. For the 21st through the 100th day of continuous confinement, you pay $65.00 a day (1987 amount) and Medicare pays the balance. Beyond the 100th day, you must pay all costs and Medicare pays nothing.

Home Health Care Coverage

If you need part-time skilled health care in your home for the treatment of an illness or injury, Medicare can pay for covered home health visits furnished by a participating home health agency.

A *home health agency* is a public or private agency that specializes in giving skilled nursing services and other therapeutic services, such as physical therapy, in your home.

The program requires that *all* of the following four conditions are met:

1. The care you need includes part-time skilled nursing care, physical therapy, or speech therapy,
2. You are confined to your home,
3. A doctor determines you need home health care and sets up a home health plan for you, and
4. The home health agency providing services is participating in Medicare.

Services and supplies provided

Services and supplies provided by Medicare-approved agencies for home health care include the following:

1. Part-time skilled nursing care
2. Physical therapy
3. Speech therapy

In addition, if any of the above services are required, Medicare also pays for:

- Occupational therapy
- Part-time services of home health aides
- Medical social services
- Medical supplies and equipment provided by the agency

Services and supplies not provided

Medicare does not provide the following services and supplies for home health care:

1. Full-time nursing care at home
2. Drugs and biologicals
3. Meals delivered to your home

4. Homemaker services
5. Blood transfusions

Payment schedule for home health care

Medicare pays the full approved cost of all covered home health care visits. You pay nothing. However, you may be charged for any services or supplies that Medicare does not cover. The home health agency will submit the claim for payment. You are not required to send in any bills yourself.

Hospice Care

Under the Tax Equity and Fiscal Responsibility Act of 1982, Medicare coverage was extended to hospice care services, beginning in November 1983. A *hospice* is a public agency or private organization that is primarily engaged in providing pain relief, symptom management, and supportive services to terminally ill people and their families. Hospice care in a patient's home provides nurses, medicine, home helpers, counseling, and other assistance for terminally ill patients. Hospice care emphasizes relief of pain and suffering as opposed to hospital technology and cures.

Respite care is a short-term inpatient stay which may be necessary for the patient in order to give temporary relief to the person who regularly assists with home care. Inpatients respite care is limited each time to stays of no more than five consecutive days.

Special benefit periods apply to hospice care. Medicare hospital insurance pays for a maximum of two 90-day periods and one 30-day period. The program requires that *all* of the following *three* conditions are met:

1. A doctor certifies that a patient is terminally ill,
2. A patient chooses to receive care from a hospice instead of standard Medicare benefits for the terminal illness, and
3. Care is provided by a Medicare-approved facility.

Services covered

Hospice services covered by a Medicare-approved facility include the following:
1. Doctors' services
2. Nursing services
3. Drugs for pain relief and symptom management
4. Physical therapy, occupational therapy, and speech-language pathology
5. Home health aide and homemaker services
6. Medical social services
7. Medical supplies and appliances
8. Short-term inpatient care (respite care)
9. Counseling

Services not covered

Hospice services not covered by Medicare include the following:

1. Treatments other than for pain relief and symptom management of terminal illness
2. Five percent of the cost of outpatient drugs or $5 per prescription, whichever is less

3. Five percent of the cost of inpatient respite care, up to à total of $520 (1987 amount), Medicare's initial hospital deductible.

Payment schedule for hospice care

During a hospice benefit period, Medicare pays the full cost of all covered services for the terminal illness. There are no deductibles or co-payments *except for part of the cost of outpatient drugs and inpatient respite care.* The patient is responsible for 5 percent of the cost of outpatient drugs or $5 toward each prescription, whichever is less. For inpatient respite care, the patient pays 5 percent of the cost, up to a total of $520 (1987 amount) during a period that begins when a hospice plan is first chosen and ends 14 days after such care is cancelled.

While receiving hospice care, if a patient requires treatment for a condition not related to the terminal illness, Medicare continues to help pay for all necessary covered services under the standard Medicare benefit program.

Medicare Medical Insurance (Part B)

Medicare medical insurance helps pay for doctors' services, those of your regular doctor as well as those you might need in a hospital, such as anesthesiology, radiology, and pathology. Medicare medical insurance can also help pay for outpatient hospital care; outpatient physical therapy and speech pathology services; an unlimited number of skilled home health care visits each calendar year; medically necessary ambulance transportation to or from a hospital or skilled nursing facility; and other outpatient medical services and equipment.

Medicare medical insurance payments for covered services or supplies are based upon *reasonable charges,* not on your doctor's or supplier's *current charges.* A *reasonable charge* is an amount the coverage will allow for a given health service or supply which is set by the Medicare carrier in your area and based primarily on the usual or customary charge for that service or supply in your locale. Actual or current charges most often are considerably higher than Medicare allows as reasonable. You must pay the full amount of all charges in excess of Medicare's reasonable allowance. In addition, you must pay the first $75 (1987 amount) of the reasonable charge, known as a *deductible,* in each calendar year. Then, Medicare pays 80 percent of the reasonable charge, and you pay the remaining 20 percent, known as the *Part B coinsurance.*

How Medical Insurance Payments are Made

There are two ways Medicare medical insurance payments are made. One way is called the *assignment method.* The second payment method is *payment to you.*

Assignment method

When the assignment method is used, the doctor or supplier agrees that his or her total charge for the covered service will be the charge approved by the Medicare carrier. Medicare pays your doctor or supplier 80 percent of the approved charge, after subtracting any part of the $75 deductible you have not met. The doctor or supplier can charge you *only* for the part of the $75 deductible (1987 amount) you had not met and for the coinsurance, which is the remaining 20 percent of the approved charge. Your doctor or supplier also can charge you for any services that Medicare does not cover.

Payment to you

The *payment to you* method is used if your doctor does not accept Medicare assignment. Under this method of payment the doctor bills you for his or her *actual charge,* which you pay. You then submit a claim to the Medicare carrier in your area. The carrier decides on the reasonable charge, which is generally less than the actual charge. After subtracting any part of the $75 deductible you have not met, Medicare pays you directly the 80 percent of the *approved* or *reasonable charge.*

An American Medical Association survey of payment methods in 1985 indicates that only 37.2 percent of patient care physicians accept Medicare *assignment* 100 percent of the time. In either case Medicare will send you a notice called *Explanation of Medicare Benefits.* This notice shows what services were covered, what charges were approved, how much was credited toward your $75 deductible, and the amount Medicare paid. You have the right to ask the carrier for a review of the decision.

Coverage

Medicare medical insurance (Part B) covers some doctors' services, but not all. A list of services that are covered and those that are not covered follows.

Doctors' services covered

Medicare medical insurance covers the following doctors' services:

1. Medical and surgical services, including anesthesia
2. Diagnostic tests and procedures that are part of your treatment
3. Radiology and pathology services by doctors while you are a hospital inpatient
4. Other services which are ordinarily furnished in the doctor's office and included in his or her bill, such as:
   a. X-rays you receive as part of your treatment
   b. Services of your doctor's office nurse
   c. Drugs and biologicals that cannot be self-administered
   d. Transfusions of blood and blood components
   e. Medical supplies
   f. Physical therapy and speech pathology services

Doctors' services not covered

Medicare medical insurance does not cover the following doctors' services:

1. Routine physical examinations and tests directly related to such examinations
2. Routine foot care
3. Eye or hearing examinations for prescribing or fitting eyeglasses or hearing aids
4. Immunizations (except pneumococcal vaccinations or immunizations required because of an injury or immediate risk of infection)

5. Cosmetic surgery unless it is needed because of accidental injury or to improve the functioning of a malformed part of the body
6. Dental care
7. Services received outside of the United States
8. Acupuncture
9. Chiropractic services
10. Christian Science practitioners' services
11. Custodial care
12. Drugs and medicines you buy with or without a doctor's prescription
13. Homemaker services
14. Injections which can be self-administered, such as insulin

How to Fill Medicare's Major Gaps

Medicare was not designed to cover first-dollar costs of basic health care services. From the outset, it usually paid about half the charges incurred, requiring the recipient of services to pay the balance. These out-of-pocket expenses are referred to as gaps. Following is a listing of Medicare's major gaps and how Medigap insurance covers some of these costs.

Medicare's Major Gaps

Medicare pays part of specified hospital, medical, and surgical costs for people 65 or older. Individuals covered by Medicare insurance must pay some expenses either directly or through private health insurance. It is important therefore for senior citizens and those moving along in that direction to know where the major gaps are in the Federal plan. These gaps are summarized in Table 9.1, using 1987 amounts:

Out-of-Pocket Costs

The hospital benefit for hospital stays that end by the 60th day is reasonable. Your out-of-pocket expense is $520 (1987 amount) plus the cost of private nursing, if needed, and the first three pints of blood, if needed, and the television set in your room. However, if your hospital stay extends beyond the 60th day, say for 90 days, your additional out-of-pocket cost would be $3,900 ($130 x 30) in 1987. To use your lifetime reserve of 60 days would cost you an additional $15,600 ($260 x 60) in 1987. Long-term illness is very expensive and beyond the financial ability of the average person. Of the 10 million hospital admissions of the 29 million people 65 and older, it is estimated that between 100,000 and 200,000 individuals are hospital inpatients beyond the 60th day when copayments begin. The financial problem is significant, indicating that senior citizens should purchase a Medigap insurance policy as well as some form of catastrophe major medical insurance.

Medigap Insurance

Senior citizens are preyed upon by sellers of Medicare supplement insurance, known as *medigap insurance*, to fill the gaps in Medicare. Because the gaps are too well known, senior citizens often do not know which gaps should be plugged or how much supplemen-

Table 9.1

Medicare's Major Gaps

Gap	Description	Amount you pay
1.	Part A: Hospital insurance deductible	$520
2.	Part A: 61st through 90th day in hospital	$130 a day
3.	Part A: 91st through 150th day if you use your lifetime reserve days	$260 a day
4.	Part A: A hospital stay of more than 150 days	Current daily rate in your area
5.	Private duty nursing	Current daily rate in your area
6.	Part A: Post-hospital skilled nursing care facility — 21st through 100th day	$65.00 a day
7.	Part A: Post-hospital skilled nursing care facility — 101st through 365th day	Current daily rate in your area
8.	Part B: Medical insurance: annual deductible	$75
9.	Part B: Medicare's approved or reasonable charge	20 percent
10.	Part B: Amount by which actual charges exceed Medicare's reasonable charges	All costs
11.	Custodial care	All costs
12.	Care outside the United States	All costs
13.	Homemaker services for individuals ill at home	All costs
14.	Prescription drugs and medicines outside a hospital (except if receiving care from a hospice program).	All costs

tary coverage is enough. A comprehensive major medical policy which would close all the gaps listed above is costly. Medicare supplement or medigap insurance that is specially designed to close a set number of gaps is less costly. Nevertheless, it is important to have either medigap insurance or comprehensive major medical coverage. Many employers provide comprehensive major medical coverage into retirement for their retirees and their spouses. If this is not available to you, then you should buy the most comprehensive coverage you can afford from a reliable company, making sure that it is renewable.

The House Select Committee on Aging in the late 1970s recommended some general rules relating to medigap policies. Subsequently, the National Association of Insurance Commissioners drew up a *model state regulation* which has been adopted by almost all the states. Some of the standards suggested for medigap policies require that the policy supplement both Part A and Part B of Medicare; exclude pre-existing conditions for no more than six months; permit cancellation within 30 days without penalty; and be written in simple English. If you buy a medigap policy, be sure that it meets these minimum standards.

More than two-thirds of the elderly have some type of private health insurance to help cover expenses not paid for by the Medicare program.

Basic Advice on Medicare

Eight suggestions to guide you in your acquisition and use of Medicare follow.

1. Apply for Medicare coverage at your Social Security office at least three months prior to your 65th birthday to make sure your benefits start on time.
2. Be sure to purchase Medicare medical insurance (Part B). It requires that you pay a monthly premium, but is one of the best buys available.
3. Buy medigap insurance, which pays for the gaps in Part A and Part B Medicare coverage. This will reduce some of your out-of-pocket costs. If you can afford it, buying comprehensive major medical insurance provides even better coverage.
4. Set up a health emergency fund of your own to cover some of the out-of-pocket expenses in connection with illness even though you have Medicare and supplemental, or medigap, health insurance.
5. In purchasing insurance to fill the gaps in Medicare (medigap insurance) be certain to compare the benefits of at least three companies to be sure you get the coverage you want. Avoid policies with confusing language and overlapping coverage.
6. Avoid exploitive salespeople who seek to make you buy coverage you do not need or cannot afford. If you are in doubt, contact your State Insurance Commissioner.
7. When visiting physicians and surgeons, do not hesitate to ask about the fees and how they are to be paid. If you think they are too high, check with other physicians and surgeons.
8. If your spouse is under 65 and dependent, be sure that your dependent spouse has adequate coverage for hospitalization and medical care, equal at least to the protection of Medicare Part A and Part B.

MEDICAID

Medicaid is a public assistance program designed to provide benefits for those people who are unable to pay for health care. The official name of Medicaid is Medical Assistance. While it has special provisions for persons 65 or older, Medicaid applies to everyone in need of medical services which are unaffordable.

Background

Medicaid is part of the Social Security law, Title 19. This portion of the law provides for aid by local welfare departments to cover medical expenses of people unable to pay for such needed care. The program is financed primarily by the Federal government. For its first full year of operation in 1967, Medicaid cost about $1.5 billion. The cost for fiscal 1985 was about $20 billion. In spite of the cost increase, Medicaid enjoys strong bipartisan support in Congress. Each state designs its own program in accordance with Federal guidelines. With the exception of Arizona, all states as well as the District of Columbia, Puerto Rico, and the Virgin Islands have Medicaid programs.

Medicaid is administered as part of the state or local welfare department. If you, as a retired person, cannot afford the premium for Part B of Medicare and the additional expense of supplementary insurance to close the Medicare gaps, you should apply for Medicaid. Welfare no longer has the stigma it once had. However, where to apply might give you some problems. The best first step would be to contact the local office of the welfare department, the local Red Cross office, or the nearest Social Security office, all of which are listed in the phone book. Or, you can contact your representative in the local or state legislature to find out where to apply.

Eligibility

Your local public welfare office can tell you the qualifications for Medicaid. Basically, low income people can meet the test. While for Medicare you must be age 65 to qualify, Medicaid covers people of all ages, including the 65-or-older group, some of whom are already receiving public welfare benefits. Also eligible are the blind, the disabled, and members of families, both adults and children, who are low income.

Even though your income may fall within the prescribed income limits set by your state's law, the agency will check your savings account and assets. Most states permit you to keep some savings as a reserve and will still consider you eligible for Medicaid.

If you are eligible, the welfare department will give you an identification card which you can use to get the medical services you require. The state's administrative agency will pay the doctors, pharmacists, and others who will serve you. Simply present your card in advance of receiving the service to be sure that the fees set by the state are acceptable to the supplier.

A unique aspect of the Medicaid law is that adult children have been relieved of the legal responsibility for their parents' medical expenses. Even though your grown children may have provided financial assistance or currently are able to help you, this does not affect your eligibility for Medicaid. However, husbands and wives are still legally responsible for each other, and must contribute to each other's support.

Covered Services

If a person is eligible for both Medicare and Medicaid, then Medicaid will cover all the gaps and deductible charges required under Medicare. In many states, Medicaid pays for such additional services as dental care, prescribed drugs, eyeglasses, clinic services, intermediate care facility services, and other diagnostic, screening and rehabilitative services.

A Final Tip

If you need the financial support offered by Medicaid, apply for it. There is no shame or stigma in having inadequate resources. All levels of government are striving to fill people's needs and are available to process your application. With the costs of health care as high as they are, and still rising, it is virtually impossible for an individual or a family to cope with the expense of a catastrophic illness. If your income is low and you need financial support to cover the costs of an illness, it is advisable to apply as soon as the need arises.

SELF-STUDY:
MY MEDICARE COVERAGE AND
ITS MAJOR GAPS

1. To obtain Medicare coverage *you must apply for it* about three months prior to your 65th birthday unless you are already receiving Social Security checks. It is not assigned to you automatically. To help you to remember to do this, enter your 65th birthday:

    _____
    Month   Day   Year

    Enter the date that is three months prior to your 65th birthday:

    _____
    Month   Day   Year

    Visit your local Social Security office on or before the date which is three months prior to your 65th birthday to make your application for Medicare coverage. Failure to apply will cause coverage problems including a 10 percent increase in your Part B premium.

2. If you are already a member of Medicare, enter here your claim number:

    _____, and effective dates of Part A and Part B coverage:

    Part A—Hospital insurance _____
                                         Effective date

    Part B—Medical insurance _____
                                      Effective Date

3. If you are considering the purchase of Medigap and/or comprehensive major medical insurance to supplement your Medicare coverage, use Worksheet 9.1 to compare the details of each company's policy.

Worksheet 9.1

Comparison of Medigap and/or Comprehensive Major Medical Insurance Policies

Medicare's Major Gaps (1987 figures)	You pay	Benefits		
		Company Policy Type	Company Policy Type	Company Policy Type
Part A: Hospital insurance				
1. Hospital Deductible	$520	_____	_____	_____

Medicare's Major Gaps (1987 figures)	You pay	Benefits		
		Company Policy Type	Company Policy Type	Company Policy Type
61st–90th day	$130/day			
91st–150th day	$260/day			
Beyond 150th day	All costs			
Or after 90th day (If 60 reserve days have been used)	All costs			
2. Post-hospital skilled nursing care 21st–100th day	$65.00/day			
Beyond 100 days	All costs			
Part B: Medical insurance 1. Excess charge	All			
2. $75 annual deductible	All			
3. Medicare's reasonable charge	20%			
Care in a foreign country	All costs			
Annual premium				

OTHER HEALTH INSURANCE

Retirement planning for health care is an essential element in enjoying a good life as a retiree. The packages of health insurance programs offered by employers and/or unions may carry over into retirement to provide for your health protection. The types of coverage include basic Blue Cross hospitalization coverage, basic medical/surgical insurance protection, and a comprehensive major medical policy. Some packages also include disability income insurance which usually terminates at retirement.

Other programs designed to benefit active employees as well as retirees include dental insurance, optical expense benefits, coverage for hearing aids, a prescription drug plan, and a blood program. An older population is also concerned about specialized assistance programs such as visiting nurses, homemaker services, and meals on wheels.

Health insurance is available from three types of organizations: Blue Cross and Blue Shield, health maintenance organizations (HMOs), and commercial insurance companies.

Types of Coverage

The principal types of coverage available today for an individual, a family, or a group include those discussed below.

Blue Cross Hospitalization Insurance

Blue Cross is the oldest and most widely held form of hospital expense insurance. Blue Cross plans will cover you for daily room and board and regular nursing services while in the hospital for varying periods of time, usually ranging from 21 to 365 days. Some hospitalization policies also provide for X-rays, laboratory tests, drugs, and medications. Hospitalization is a basic form of health insurance which everyone should have. It is usually provided by employers or unions for their members.

Basic Medical/Surgical Insurance

Basic medical/surgical insurance covers you for doctors' visits in and out of the hospital, including diagnostic and laboratory tests as well as a specified list of surgical procedures. The plan itemizes the maximum benefit it will pay for each. Many of these plans have an annual deductible and coinsurance clause. This basic policy is usually provided by employers or unions in conjunction with Blue Cross hospitalization insurance.

Comprehensive Major Medical Insurance

Comprehensive major medical insurance picks up where basic health insurance protection ends, covering the high costs of serious long-term illness. Some policies have very high deductibles, and provide benefits up to $500,000 or $1,000,000. Other policies provide for first-dollar coverage. Some employers or unions provide this type of insurance on a contributory basis while others are non-contributory. It is an appropriate form of insurance for people to have at any age, including those over 65 on Medicare, instead of Medigap insurance. If this form of insurance is provided by your employer, find out whether it may be carried over into retirement and whether it would be contributory or non-contributory. For an individual 65 or older, the combination of Medicare Parts A and B coverage and Medicare supplementary insurance may still require the additional coverage of comprehensive major medical insurance.

Disability Income Insurance

Disability income insurance policies pay a percentage of your regular monthly income when you become disabled and unable to work because of illness or injury for an extended period. This type of insurance is provided by the Social Security system at no extra cost to you, by commercial insurance companies whose premiums for this type of coverage are usually quite high, as well as by some retirement systems. The best disability coverage begins to pay a monthly allowance after 60 or 90 days of disability and pays benefits until age 65 or retirement, whichever comes first. Provisions vary. Most people tend to pay too much attention to life insurance and too little to disability income insurance during their working years. The need for disability insurance disappears after retirement when you begin to collect a pension and Social Security starting at age 62 or later.

Insurance for Special Needs

Active employees and retirees need a variety of specialized types of insurance coverage that are generally excluded from basic and major medical plans. These include the following: dental insurance, optical expense insurance, coverage for hearing aids, a prescription drug plan, and a blood program.

Dental insurance

At a time when the family budget is under severe strain, the cost of dental care is becoming less of a burden for many American households. The reason for this is the rapid growth of dental insurance, financed wholly or in part by employers as a fringe benefit. Dental expense insurance covers necessary dental health care providing for oral examinations, including X-rays and cleanings, fillings, extractions, inlays, crowns, bridgework, dentures (prosthodontics), oral surgery, treatment of gums (periodontics), root canal (endodontics), and aligning teeth (orthodontics).

The American Dental Association estimates that in 1986 dental insurance covers between 90 and 100 million persons, about 40 percent of the population. One of the reasons for this level of coverage is the fact that labor unions support this type of protection.

The estimated 25,000 plans now in operation pay varying amounts of the cost of dental work. While some pay 100 percent, most pay less, possibly a third or a half of costs. To reduce expenses some dental insurance plans may require workers to pay part of the monthly premium and to absorb an annual deductible and a coinsurance provision, requiring the insured to assume 20 percent of the cost.

Optical expense benefits

An optical expense program provides eyeglasses to eligible members and their eligible dependents including spouse and unmarried dependent children under a specified age, usually 19 or 23. In one such plan each eligible individual is able to obtain a pair of eyeglasses every two years free of charge, either single vision or bifocal lenses of standard prescription with a standard frame, offered by a Participating Optical Outlet. The group administering the program reimburses the participating optician with a set fee for single vision lenses and a higher fee for bifocal lenses. If the member uses an optician not on the Participating Outlet list, the member can be reimbursed for the specified sums directly.

Hearing aids

The process of aging is the most common cause of hearing loss, and about half the purchases of hearing aids are made by people 65 or older. It is estimated that about 3 million Americans use hearing aids. Many older people find the cost of a hearing aid prohibitive. Some employer health insurance packages for employees include a subsidy for the purchase of a hearing aid, and some of the programs carry this benefit over into retirement. This particular fringe benefit has not been widely adopted, and recently a Federal Task Force on Hearing Aid Health Care recommended that the U.S. Department of Health and Human Services consider the possibility of subsidizing the purchase of hearing aids for elderly persons.

Prescription drug plan

Some employers and unions provide a Prescription Drug plan which may be carried over into retirement. The full cost of prescription drugs is covered, provided the prescription is filled by a participating pharmacist. If a non-participating pharmacist is used, reimbursement of charges is made in accordance with a schedule of allowances. Prescriptions may not exceed a ten-day supply, and if the physician so specifies, one or more refills are allowed. Drugs, vitamins, and diet supplements which can be purchased without a prescription usually are not covered. Members are advised to ask doctors to prescribe generic drugs when possible as a substitute for brand name products in order to reduce costs without sacrificing quality. Each covered member is issued an identification card and may be required to use special prescription blanks which request identifying data from the member, the doctor, and the pharmacist.

Blood program

Many large employers, both public and private, offer membership in a blood program to their employees. An enrolled employee or a substitute is required to donate one pint of blood annually. Some of the plans provide unlimited blood credit for the member, spouse, unmarried children regardless of age, unmarried brothers and sisters who live with the member, regardless of age, member's parents and grandparents, and spouse's parents and grandparents, no matter where they live. If you donate more than a pint a year, you can build up credit for future years. Some of these programs carry over into retirement and help in providing the first three pints of blood not covered by Medicare.

Nursing Home Care: A Major Gap

The major gap in health insurance coverage for the elderly is long-term nursing home care. Other gaps include prescription drugs, eye examinations and eyeglasses, dental care, and doctors' fees above levels deemed "reasonable" by Medicare. These costs can quickly erode lifetime savings, often resulting in bankruptcy. In particular, long-term nursing home care costs an average of $22,000 a year per resident. In some parts of the country these costs run as high as $40,000 to $50,000 a year. For the 1.4 million Americans living in nursing homes and the estimated 2.5 million Americans afflicted with Alzheimer's disease, such costs are prohibitive. Current government proposals would provide unlimited hospital days to replace the current limit of 60 days, and would pay for all out-of-pocket medical expenses over $2,000 at a cost of $4.92 added to the already established $17.90 monthly premium . The proposal, however, excludes long-term nursing home care, which is the costliest gap in the entire system of health insurance.

Specialized Assistance Programs

A few specialized assistance programs are of particular interest to an older population. Retirees should be aware of these services if the need should ever arise. They include visiting nurses, homemaker services, and meals on wheels.

Visiting nurses

An important service available to people is provided by the Visiting Nurse Association. On request, this organization will send a nurse to your home to provide certain types of nursing care, such as insulin injections and other services. These associations usually charge a reasonable fee for the services of a nurse on a per-visit basis. However, if you cannot afford the fee, the charge may be waived or reduced. Most cities and larger towns have a Visiting Nurse Association. You can locate your association in your phone book. If none is available in your locality, contact your local health department, which usually employs public health nurses who serve in the same capacity.

Homemaker services

A *homemaker* is a trained individual employed by a health or family agency to assist in a household during illness or when other problems occur. These services are available for active as well as retired people who are in need of assistance in homemaking or physical care on a part-time basis, such as two to three times a week. If you can afford to pay, the fees are moderate, usually on an hourly basis.

Meals on Wheels

The *Meals on Wheels* program is designed to bring hot meals to the homes of older people who are unable to shop or cook. The cost is moderate and while not yet available everywhere, the program is expanding. Some groups supply homebound senior citizens with three hot meals a day while others may supply just one or two meals a day. The meals are delivered by volunteer workers who may be retired individuals or young people. Local senior citizen agencies can advise you as to the availability of this service in your own community.

Sources of Health Insurance Coverage

Health insurance is available from three types of organizations: Blue Cross and Blue Shield, health maintenance organizations (HMOs), and commercial insurance companies.

Blue Cross and Blue Shield

Today, Blue Cross and Blue Shield cover every state and are coordinated through the Blue Cross and Blue Shield Associations. The Blues, as they are sometimes called, protect close to 100 million people in private programs, of whom about 85 percent are members of groups. In addition, the Blues administer Federal and state government health care programs for another 26 million people, making the total covered about half of the nation's population.

Blue Cross plans, initated in 1929, offer hospital expense insurance and have contracts with more than 90 percent of the nation's general, non-Federal, acute care hospitals. The Blue Shield plans, initiated in 1946, offer surgical and general physician expense insurance and have a working relationship with about 80 percent of the nation's practicing medical doctors.

While commercial insurance carriers provide all forms of health care protection, Blue Cross and Blue Shield organizations are the pioneers in this type of insurance coverage, having started more than half a century ago. The basic goal of these plans has been and continues to be to offer high quality, effective, and economical health care services to people. Blue Cross and Blue Shield usually return between 85 and 90 percent of premiums paid, making these plans excellent.

Health Maintenance Organizations (HMO)

Your best coverage can be obtained by joining a Health Maintenance Organization (HMO) if one is operating in your area. The HMO gives you medical care and hospitalization coverage without deductibles and coinsurance. It is all prepaid and there are no out-of-pocket expenses.

A *health maintenance organization* (HMO) consists of one or more hospitals and a group of doctors and other health care personnel who have joined together to provide necessary health maintenance and remedial services to the organization's members. The group practice plans of HMOs offer complete office and hospital care to an optimum number of members for fixed monthly fees. Because of reduced costs and Federal subsidies, the fees are reasonable as compared with other forms of health care delivery systems. Members of an HMO receive all the health care they need, including periodic checkups, X-rays, lab tests, mental health treatment, and 24-hour emergency services, with no additional out-of-pocket costs once the monthly fee has been paid.

The Federal government's financial support for health maintenance organizations began in 1973 in an effort to curb the quickly rising cost of health care. The 1973 law, as amended in 1976, requires that a company with 25 or more workers offer HMO membership as an alternative to any existing health-care program the company might have.

The nation's first prepaid health care plan for physician visits and hospitalization was established in 1929 at the Roos-Loos Clinic in Los Angeles. The second was started by Henry Kaiser in the 1930s in the West to care for the workers at his isolated industrial sites. The first HMO-type organization in New York was established in the 1940s. Known as the Health Insurance Plan of Greater New York, or simply HIP, it was designed to provide complete medical services for employees of New York City, which paid the premiums. Currently, it is known officially as HIP/HMO.

The biggest and best known HMO is the Kaiser Foundation Health Plan, which functions in California and five other Western states. This HMO has more than three million members, operates its own hospitals, and employs more than 3,000 salaried physicians. The smallest HMOs have only a few staff members, most often internists, obstetricians, and pediatricians. If a member needs the services of another kind of specialist, the HMO will send the patient to one and pay the charges.

The main criticisms of the HMO are that the patient has no personal choice of doctor; that the relationship between the patient and the doctor is impersonal; and that HMOs operate on an assembly-line basis. The principal advantage is that the cost of paying for each visit to the doctor is eliminated, thus encouraging people to seek early detection and treatment of disease in its most curable stage. It has been estimated that HMO members are admitted to hospitals 30 to 60 percent less often than nonmembers, helping to reduce overall costs and, presumably, reflecting better health maintenance.

Since July 1, 1973, Medicare beneficiaries have been able to join health maintenance organizations. A recent Harris poll reveals that the nation's 337 HMOs now have about 17 million members and that membership is increasing at a rate of 22 percent annually.

Commercial Insurance Companies

A large number of commercial insurance companies offer a variety of health insurance policies that fill buyers' needs. However, as in any purchase you make, you must be a wise and careful shopper. You must study not only the insurance company but also the policy that is being offered to you. Some questions you should ask about an insurance company include the following:

1. What are the financial resources of this company?
2. What is the rank in size of this company as compared to all the others?
3. Does the company enjoy a good reputation?
4. Is it licensed to do business in your state?
5. Is the company a prompt payer of claims?
6. What is the percentage of premiums that this company returns to its policyholders in benefits? (This is known as the company's *loss ratio*.) Some of these answers may be obtained from your State Insurance Department, your Better Business Bureau, or *Best's Insurance Reports* in your public library.

Questions you should ask about the insurance policy include the following:

1. What does the policy cover?
2. What are the policy's exclusions?
3. Is the policy a *service benefit* contract, paying a percentage of charges and therefore keeping up with inflation, or an *indemnity benefit* contract, paying fixed dollar amounts?
4. What is the maximum that the policy will pay for each service?
5. How does the contract handle pre-existing conditions?

Other Considerations

In your retirement planning you should be aware of special situations related to health insurance coverage that are handled in particular ways. For example, if you are under 65, still working, and not yet covered by Medicare, you must make a special effort to obtain adequate health insurance at a reasonable price. Similarly, if you are 65 through 69 years of age, covered by Medicare, but still working, Federal law requires that your employer's health insurance plan must be the *primary payer* with Medicare serving as *secondary payer.* Finally, if you are retiring and your spouse is under 65, be certain that your spouse has adequate health insurance coverage. A discussion of each of these situations follows.

If You Are Under 65 and Still Working

For those under 65, still working, and not yet covered by Medicare, essential health care coverage should include basic Blue Cross hospitalization coverage, basic medical/surgical insurance, a comprehensive major medical plan to supplement basic coverage, and disability income insurance coverage if it is offered by your employer and/or union on a contributory or non-contributory basis, or if you can afford it on a self-pay basis.

Most people are covered for health insurance to some extent through their jobs. Those not so fortunate have a major problem in getting adequate health insurance at a reasonable price. Private coverage purchased by an individual from a commercial insurance company is very expensive. Moreover, the policy you buy very likely has a deductible and a 20 percent coinsurance provision. An individual or couple without basic health insurance coverage (hospitalization and medical/surgical protection) should either:

1. Join a health maintenance organization which will provide full coverage without deductibles and coinsurance, or
2. Join Blue Cross/Blue Shield, non-profit groups whose premiums reflect actual costs.

If You Are Age 65 Through 69 and Still Working

If you are age 65 through 69 and still actively employed, the Tax Equity and Fiscal Responsibility Act of 1982 (TEFRA) changes health insurance coverage. TEFRA amends the Age Discrimination in Employment Act and the Social Security Act in two ways: First, employers of 20 or more persons must give older workers the same health insurance coverage offered to employees below the age of 65 and under the same conditions, even though they are covered by Medicare. To reduce their benefits in any way is considered age discrimination and therefore illegal. And, second, TEFRA stipulates that Medicare will no longer be the insurer of first resort for older employees. Instead, the employer's plan must be the *primary payer* with Medicare serving as *secondary payer*. An active employee between the ages of 65 through 69 has the right to reject the employer's plan so that Medicare would be the primary payer but then no benefits are paid by the employer's plan. Even though Medicare is the secondary payer between ages 65 through 69, it becomes the primary payer at age 70.

These changes, effective January 1, 1983, save the Federal government hundreds of millions of dollars a year by transferring the primary insurance bill to the private sector.

Health Insurance for Your Spouse

If your spouse is under age 65 and you are retiring, you should check your employer's health insurance coverage to determine whether your spouse will continue to be covered as a dependent if your coverage carries over into retirement. After retirement most employer group health insurance plans continue coverage for the spouse and other eligible dependents. If this is not the case, it may be possible to convert from group coverage to an individual self-pay basis. If this is not possible, it may be necessary to purchase an individual hospitalization and medical/surgical insurance policy from a commercial carrier for your spouse. In any case, make sure that your spouse has adequate health insurance.

A spouse whose status changes from dependent to survivor should check the employer's health insurance coverage of the deceased to determine whether protection is still in effect. If the coverage terminates, it is necessary for the survivor to purchase an individual hospitalization/health insurance policy on a self-pay basis.

Continuation of Health Insurance for Women

Women often lose health insurance coverage if they divorce, if they are widowed, or if their husbands lose a job or retire. For various reasons, an estimated five million American women aged 40 to 65 have no health insurance whatsoever. At age 65 they become eligible for Medicare coverage. The Group Health Insurance Continuation Act (Public Law 99–272), enacted in April 1986, helps women (and other individuals) to retain their health insurance when work or family status changes. The law is effective for health plan years beginning after July 1, 1986. The employer or health plan can tell you when your next plan year begins. If your plan year begins in February, the law takes effect for you in February 1987. This new law does not help you if you have already lost your health insurance before the law takes effect.

- *Retiring workers*—If you have employee health insurance that ends when you retire, you, your spouse and dependent children can continue coverage for up to 18 months after you retire. Your coverage ends when you become entitled to Medicare.

- *Spouses and dependent children of retiring workers*—If you lose group health insurance when your spouse retires, you and your children can continue that coverage for 18 months (36 months if your spouse is entitled to Medicare and you are not). If you elect to continue coverage when your spouse retires and you are then divorced, legally separated, or your spouse dies or becomes entitled to Medicare within 18 months after retirement, you can receive a total of 36 months of coverage. Your right to continue coverage ends when you become entitled to Medicare.

- *Widows, divorced or separated spouses, and dependent children*—If you have health insurance through your spouse's employer, you and your children can continue that coverage for three years after your spouse dies, or if you divorce or are legally separated after the group health insurance law takes effect. Provision for health insurance may be included as part of a divorce decree. But remember that coverage ends if premiums are not paid, so you should pay the premium yourself and be reimbursed by your former spouse. Otherwise, late or missed payments could jeopardize your insurance.

Additional information is available from the Older Women's League, 1325 G Street, N.W., Washington, D.C. 20005, (202) 783-6686.

Basic Advice on Health Insurance

1. If you are under 65 and still working, and you have an individual or group health insurance policy,
   a. Determine what benefits your coverage will provide when you reach 65 and whether you can carry it over into retirement.

   b. Consider buying disability income insurance. Normally you insure your home, your car, and your jewelry, but it is your regular income that makes all the other amenities possible.

2. Consider purchasing a comprehensive major medical policy to cover both you and your spouse.

3. You should be insured for as many of the other health care needs as you can afford, including dental insurance, prescription drugs, optical expenses, and hearing aids.

4. In general, you should avoid the following kinds of health insurance: mail order health insurance policies, cancer or other dread disease insurance, and nursing home coverage. Policies for nursing home insurance do not cover extended stays.

5. Protect your health insurance policies by keeping them in a safe place, and be sure that a close relative or friend knows where they are. In a separate place keep a list of your policy numbers, the companies that issued them, and the name of your agent, just in case the originals are lost.

6. Keep a record of your medical expenditures and reimbursements. This is the only way you can follow up on open items to be sure you receive what is due.

SELF-STUDY:
CHECKLIST FOR MY HEALTH INSURANCE

1. To ascertain the gaps in your overall health care coverage, check what you have or lack, and note whether what you have carries over into retirement.

Type of health care insurance	Do you have the coverage indicated?		If you are covered, will it carry over into retirement?	
	Yes	**No**	**Yes**	**No**
a. Blue Cross hospitalization	☐	☐	☐	☐
b. Basic medical/surgical	☐	☐	☐	☐
c. Comprehensive major medical	☐	☐	☐	☐
d. Disability income insurance	☐	☐	☐	☐
e. Dental insurance	☐	☐	☐	☐
f. Optical expense benefits	☐	☐	☐	☐
g. Hearing aids	☐	☐	☐	☐
h. Prescription drug plan	☐	☐	☐	☐
i. Blood program	☐	☐	☐	☐

2. List the gaps in your present health insurance coverage:

_____

_____

_____

_____

3. List each health insurance coverage you have that will not carry over into retirement:

_____

_____

_____

_____

4. How do you plan to fill the gaps in your retirement health insurance package noted in your answers to questions 2. and 3. above?

_____

_____

_____

_____

5. Personal Record of Medical Expenditures and Reimbursements. It is suggested that you maintain a record of your medical expenditures and reimbursements not only for yourself but also for your spouse and other family members living with you. Worksheet 9.2 contains spaces for the type of information you should have. If you do not receive a particular benefit to which you are entitled within a reasonable period of time, it will show up clearly on this type of record, and you can then follow up. The form provides for Medicare, if you're a member, and for one supplementary policy. If you're not on Medicare, change the heading to the type of coverage you have. If you have additional coverages, such as dental insurance, the form can be expanded by adding one or more columns similar to the two included. You can purchase multi-column worksheet paper in a stationery store.

Worksheet 9.2

Personal Record of Medical Expenditures and Reimbursements

Name of patient _____ Year _____

Date of visit or service	Name of doctor, hospital, lab or other	Illness or treatment	Paid			Medicare				Supplementary policy or other coverage			
			Amt.	Date	Check No.	Claim submitted		Check received		Claim submitted		Check received	
						Date	Amt	Date	Amt	Date	Amt	Date	Amt

SELECTING A NURSING HOME

Anyone who has ever given the subject any thought probably has a preconceived notion about a nursing home. The stereotype, usually negative, pictures a place to locate the elderly when the family can no longer respond to the individual's needs, and the individual is unable to care for his or her own person. Surprisingly, a nursing home is not what most people envision; actually, it is meant for people of all ages who are convalescents, some of whom will recover completely and quickly, as well as for people of any age who are in need of long-term care. The goal of the nursing home is to help the patient recover and to return to routine life and community as soon as possible. Choosing a nursing home for anyone close to you—relative, friend, or even yourself—is a task that requires careful consideration and evaluation. The needs of the patient should be given primary consideration. The requirements of an older patient are different from those of a younger patient; those of an ambulatory patient are different from those of a patient who is bedridden. A family physician or social worker should be helpful in offering guidance.

Types of Services Offered

Nursing homes provide a variety of services to patients requiring care. These include nursing care and personal care, as well as social and recreational guidance, which is referred to as residential service.

1. **Nursing care** requires the professional skill of a registered nurse or a licensed practical nurse. The nurse follows the instructions of the attending physician and may be called upon to administer medications and injections. Additionally, the nursing home provides physical therapy, occupational therapy, dental services, dietary consultation, and X-ray services for post-hospital stroke, heart, or orthopedic cases. Also, a pharmaceutical dispensary is usually available in a nursing home.

2. **Personal care** implies that in a nursing home a patient will receive help getting in and out of bed, bathing, dressing, eating, and walking. Attention will also be given to special diets that are prescribed by the physician.

3. **Residential service** means that a nursing home offers a secure environment in which the patient is comfortable, as well as a program to meet the social and recreational needs of the individual. In some cases, spiritual needs are also provided for.

Types of Nursing Care Facilities

The needs of patients differ. Some patients who are bedridden require 24-hour nursing service. Others who require less intensive care benefit from a different type of facility, and those who require no medical services merely need a secure environment which includes social, recreational, and spiritual guidance. The three types of nursing care facilities are:

1. **Skilled nursing facilities,** often referred to as SNFs, provide registered nurses, licensed practical nurses, and nurse's aides to carry out the instructions of the patient's physician. Physical, occupational, and other therapies are provided to help restore the patient's health. Service is on a 24-hour basis. This type of facility is eligible to participate in both Medicare and Medicaid programs.

2. **Intermediate care facilities,** often referred to as ICFs, are designed for patients or residents who do not require care that is as intensive as that supplied by the SNFs. Nevertheless, for those who are not capable of independent living, the ICFs provide room and board along with medical, nursing, social, and rehabilitative services on a regular basis. This type of facility is also eligible to participate in both Medicare and Medicaid programs.

3. **Residential care facilities,** as the nomenclature suggests, provide secure and healthful accommodations to individuals who are capable of meeting their own basic needs. The emphasis is on the social requirements of the resident, rather than on the medical needs that are emphasized in both the SNFs and ICFs. Residential care facilities give particular attention to the social, recreational, and spiritual requirements of the residents. They also relieve the resident of anxiety and frustration by providing housekeeping services including meals, and medical assistance as required.

Finding a Suitable Place

Locating a suitable nursing home is a time-consuming and painstaking task. You should begin by obtaining a list of nursing homes in your area from your local medical society or health or welfare department. Contact the facilities individually to determine how well they meet the needs of the person you have in mind. Narrow the list you have obtained to those that are most suitable. Arrange to visit each facility you are considering; ask for a tour of the premises as well as an opportunity to talk to the administrator. What you uncover in your search will enable you to decide practically and intelligently what is most appropriate for the person you have in mind.

If you or your spouse needs a nursing home, it is important that you personally inspect the facility, always keeping in mind the individual's specific needs.

Coverage

As indicated earlier, Medicare covers the first 20 days in each benefit period if specified requirements are met. After that you pay $61.50 a day for the 21st through the 100th day of continuous confinement, and Medicare pays the balance. Beyond the 100th day, you must pay all costs and Medicare pays nothing. Medicaid coverage for skilled nursing facilities varies from state to state.

SELF-STUDY:
HOW TO EVALUATE A NURSING FACILITY

If the occasion should arise when you need a skilled nursing care facility, use the following checklist when comparing the facilities that are available. The importance of personal inspection cannot be overemphasized.

Evaluation of a Nursing Facility

Item	Yes	No
1. Is the facility tidy?	☐	☐
2. Does it have a clean smell?	☐	☐
3. Are the food menus acceptable?	☐	☐
4. Does it have cheerful day rooms?	☐	☐
5. Do the patients appear well-cared-for?	☐	☐
6. Is the building fireproof?	☐	☐
7. Are handrails and other safety aids in evidence?	☐	☐
8. Are the physical and occupational programs satisfactory?	☐	☐
9. Is your own physician on ready-call?	☐	☐
10. Are house physicians on ready-call?	☐	☐
11. Is the nursing staff adequate?	☐	☐
12. Have you studied the facility's operating certificate to confirm the services offered?	☐	☐
13. Have you seen the Department of Health inspection report?	☐	☐
14. Is the general atmosphere of the facility pleasant?	☐	☐
15. Have you spoken to a few patients?	☐	☐

GLOSSARY

Actual Charges. The fees billed by doctors and suppliers, sometimes referred to as *current charges.*

Approved Charge. When a medical insurance claim is submitted, the carrier compares the *actual charge* shown on the claim with the *customary* and *prevailing* charges for that service or supply. The charge *approved* by the carrier will be either the *customary charge,* the *prevailing charge,* or the *actual charge,* whichever is lowest. Medicare pays 80 percent of the *approved charge,* sometimes referred to as the *reasonable charge.* (See Customary Charge, Prevailing Charge.)

Assignment. When a doctor or supplier accepts an assignment of the medical insurance payment, he or she agrees that the total charge to you for covered services will be the charge approved by the carrier. The doctor or supplier can charge you only for the part of the deductible you have not met and for the coinsurance, which is the remaining 20 percent of the *approved charge.*

Benefit Period. The period for calculating Medicare benefits that begins when you enter a hospital or skilled nursing facility and ends when you have gone 60 days without being re-admitted to either facility.

Catastrophic Major Medical Insurance. Provides compensation for extraordinary medical costs not covered by hospitalization insurance, or by basic or major medical insurance. One such policy, after a $10,000 deductible, pays up to $2,000,000 for up to 3 to 10 years from the date an initial medical expense is incurred. (See Comprehensive Major Medical Insurance.) In February of 1987, President Reagan endorsed a new health care plan that would improve the Medicare program of health insurance for about 29 million elderly people. By adding $4.92 to the $17.90 monthly premium, the proposal would provide unlimited hospital days and pay all out-of-pocket costs over $2,000. While the plan excludes the costs of long-term nursing home care, it does offer some relief from the specter of enormous hospital and medical bills that may someday accumulate.

Coinsurance. The percentage of an expense covered by a policy that you are required to pay. You pay 20 percent of the *approved charge;* the insurer pays 80 percent.

Comprehensive Major Medical Insurance. Provides coverage for the same types of services that are covered under basic health insurance plans; that is, hospitalization, medical, and surgical, picking up where basic protection ends. Some policies provide for first-dollar coverage of some health care services, and others may have high deductibles, but may provide benefits up to $500,000 or $1,000,000.

Copayment. The specific dollar amount or percentage of an *approved charge* that you must pay. (See Coinsurance.)

Current Charges. (See Actual Charges.)

Custodial Care. Primarily for the purpose of meeting personal needs, such as helping in walking, getting in and out of bed, bathing, dressing, eating, taking medicine, and other services which can be provided by persons without professional skills or training. Medicare does not cover custodial care.

Customary Charge. Generally the fee most frequently charged by doctors and suppliers for specific services and supplies furnished to patients in the previous calendar year.

Deductible. The annual maximum amount you must pay on claims before the insurance carrier begins to calculate benefit allowances due you.

Disability Income Insurance. Provides a percentage of your regular income when you are unable to work for an extended period of time because of illness or injury.

Elimination Period. The first days of confinement in a hospital or other health care facility that are not covered by a health insurance policy.

Exclusion. An expense or condition that the policy does not cover and toward which it will not pay.

Explanation of Medicare Benefits Notice. A report showing what services have been covered, what charges have been approved, how much has been credited toward the patient's deductible, and how much Medicare has paid. If the patient believes any figure on the notice is questionable, he or she may appeal to the carrier for a review.

Health Maintenance Organization (HMO). Any organized system of health care that provides a full range of health maintenance and treatment services to an enrolled population in return for a fixed sum of money agreed upon and paid in advance. Certain HMOs are eligible for Medicare reimbursement. Such eligible organizations provide (1) physicians services; (2) inpatient hospital services; (3) laboratory, X-ray, emergency, and preventive services, and (4) out-of-area coverage.

Hospice. A public agency or private organization that is primarily engaged in providing pain relief, symptom management, and supportive services to terminally ill people and their families, primarily in the home.

Intermediate Care Facility. Designed for patients or residents who do not require the type of intensive care provided by a *skilled nursing facility* but need room and board along with medical, nursing, social, and rehabilitative services. (See Residential Care Facility, Skilled Nursing Facility.)

Meals on Wheels Program. Brings hot meals to the homes of older people who are unable to shop or cook.

Medicaid. A public assistance program, administered as part of the state or local welfare department, which is designed to provide medical benefits for people of all ages who are unable to pay for health care. Application may be made through the local office of the welfare department.

Medicare. A Federal health insurance program for people 65 or older and for certain disabled people which is run by the Health Care Financing Administration and utilizes the services of local Social Security Administration offices.

Medigap Insurance. A form of supplemental major medical insurance which covers some or all of the gaps in Medicare coverage.

Policy. A legal contract that sets forth the rights and obligations of both policyholder and insurance company.

Pre-Existing Conditions Limitation. A limit on benefits allowed for a health condition that one had before becoming insured.

Premium. The amount of money paid to the insurance carrier in return for insurance protection.

Prevailing Charge. For each covered service and supply, the *prevailing charge* is the amount which is high enough to cover the *customary charges* in three out of every four bills submitted to the carrier in the previous year.

Rate of Return. The percentage of premiums that an insurance company returns to its policyholders in benefits.

Reasonable Charge. (See Approved Charge.)

Residential Care Facility. Provides secure and healthful accommodations to individuals who are capable of meeting their own basic needs, paying special attention to the social, recreational, and spiritual requirements of the residents. (See Intermediate Care Facility, Skilled Nursing Facility.)

Respite Care. A short-term inpatient stay in a hospital which may be necessary for a hospice patient in order to give temporary relief to the person who regularly assists with home care. Medicare limits each occurrence of inpatient respite care to stays of no more than five consecutive days.

Skilled Nursing Facility. A specially qualified facility which has the staff and equipment to provide skilled nursing care or rehabilitation services and other related health services. Most nursing homes in the U.S. are not skilled nursing facilities, and many skilled nursing facilities are not certified by Medicare. (See Intermediate Care Facility, Residential Care Facility.)

Suppliers. Persons or organizations, other than doctors or health care facilities, that furnish equipment or services covered by medical insurance, such as ambulance firms, independent laboratories, and organizations that rent or sell medical equipment.

Waiting Period. The amount of time that must pass after a person becomes insured before his or her policy begins to pay benefits for a pre-existing condition or specified illness.

Chapter 10
Preparing for the Inevitable

While many people prefer to ignore or overlook the subject, the fact remains that death is inevitable. Just as you make preparations for every facet of life, so too you must make careful preparations for the final event. It is not easy to do. A death in the family is a deep wound. Survivors invariably react with shock and disbelief, even on those occasions when the dying was anticipated. The grief and sense of loss are overwhelming, and people are not prepared to cope.

It is precisely during this period of suffering that you are required to handle complex and often expensive business arrangements. Under normal conditions this would require calm detachment and presence of mind. Yet, when death occurs, and you become highly emotional, it is difficult to exercise sound judgment. Perhaps it might be sensible at such a time to call upon a close relative, friend, clergy, or your family lawyer to make the decisions that have to be made and to do the things that have to be done.

Thinking people who are concerned about the inevitable should prepare in every way possible for such a time. Planning will insure that you have a voice in your own disposition and will save your loved ones the headaches and problems of making decisions on matters they may be too bereaved to handle effectively.

This chapter provides a checklist of things to consider before and after a death, things to do after the funeral and interment, details of arranging a funeral, funeral ceremonies and costs, and survivors' benefits.

WHEN DEATH OCCURS

The passing of a loved one is deeply emotional. Most people find it difficult to think clearly at such a time. The following checklists of things to do after a death and after the funeral and interment should be helpful. This section also provides background material on the role of the death certificate.

A Checklist of Things To Do After a Death

After a death, some things must be done immediately and some things must be done after the funeral and interment.

Things To Do Immediately

The following things must be taken care of immediately following a death.

1. **Death certificate.** Obtain a *death certificate* from the physician attending at the time of death or from the physician who examines the body after death.

2. **Notify your religious leader.** A member of the clergy can help you to make decisions at this time and can offer spiritual comfort.

3. **Disposal of the body.** Check whether the decedent had any specific wishes for disposal of the body, including possible donation of the body or organs for medical purposes. A Uniform Donor Card may have been prepared in accordance with the Uniform Anatomical Gifts Act. Check the decedent's will or the supplemental letter of instructions, if available.

4. **Burial or memorial society.** If the deceased was a member of a burial society or a memorial society, notify an official of that group. Find out what services the society provides.

5. **Funeral homes.** After comparing the costs of two or three funeral homes, hire one. The first service of the funeral home will be to transfer the body to its facilities.

6. **Cemetery plot.** Determine whether the deceased owns a burial plot. If a *family plot* is to be the site of the burial, obtain the consent of the responsible individual for the interment. If no gravesite is available, it will be necessary to purchase one.

7. **Funeral arrangements.** Make final arrangements for the funeral and interment.

8. **Notify relatives and friends.** Advise relatives and friends of the date, time, and place of the funeral and burial.

9. **Obituary notices.** Prepare an obituary notice and then place it in appropriate newspapers and other publications.

10. **Notify employer.** Notify the decedent's employer. Also, notify fraternal orders or lodges in which the decedent was a member.

Things To Do After the Funeral and Interment

After interment has occurred, the survivor should do the following things.

1. **Contact decedent's lawyer.** Inform the decedent's lawyer about the death. The original will may be in the lawyer's vault or in a safe deposit box. Probate proceedings should be initiated.

2. **Collect official documents.** Collect the official documents left by the deceased and turn them over to the lawyer and/or the executor or executrix so that settlement

of the estate can be started. The locations of these documents may have been listed in the *Supplemental Letter of Instructions,* attached to the will.

3. **Funeral and burial allowances.** Prepare a list of funeral and burial allowances to which the survivors may be entitled. Sources of such allowances are: Veterans Administration, Social Security Administration, a labor union, a fraternal organization, an employer, burial insurance purchased from an insurance company, or other sources. Obtain and prepare the necessary applications.

4. **Tombstone.** Begin to make arrangements for a tombstone or grave marker.

The Death Certificate

A *death certificate* stating the date, time, place, and cause of death is required in all states. The document is prepared by a physician, medical examiner, or coroner who examines the body. It must be filed in the appropriate county office. It is important that you obtain several certified copies of the death certificate. These are required as proof of death in order to arrange for probate of the will and to secure Social Security benefits, life insurance payments, and pension benefits. A *death certificate* is also required to gain access to the decedent's safe deposit box and to obtain possession of the decedent's assets. Additional certified copies of the death certificate can be obtained later if they are required. It is important that the cause of death be correctly entered on the death certificate, since accidental death, if this were the case, may elicit higher life insurance benefits for the survivors.

In most cases death is due to natural causes. Depending upon state laws, the certificate must be filed within a few days of death. However, if death was due to an accident or other unnatural causes, such as murder or suicide, a medical examiner or coroner must determine the date and probable cause of death. An autopsy may be performed if the cause of death is doubtful, or to provide the medical profession with additional information about any illness from which the decedent may have suffered. An autopsy requires the consent of surviving relatives, except in the case of murder or suicide.

SELF-STUDY:
BASIC INFORMATION ABOUT MYSELF

Collect basic information for your obituary and/or eulogy. It will be very helpful for your survivors.

	(Name of husband or individual)	(Name of wife or individual)
1. Full name		
2. Place of birth		

	(Name of husband or individual)	(Name of wife or individual)
3. Date of birth		
4. Schools and colleges attended		
5. Degrees		
6. Honors		
7. Father's name		
8. Father's birthplace		
9. Father's occupation		
10. Mother's maiden name		
11. Mother's birthplace		
12. Mother's occupation		
13. Your occupation		
14. Your place of work		
15. Years in your occupation		
16. Armed services record		
17. Memberships in clubs and/or fraternal organizations		
18. Your children's names and addresses		
19. Number and names of grandchildren		

ARRANGING A FUNERAL

Time is limited in arranging a funeral, but crucial decisions must be made regarding disposal of the body, selection of a casket, the type of funeral service, and other details. A discussion of these arrangements follows.

Disposal of the Body

State laws generally require that a dead body be buried or otherwise legally disposed of within the number of days specified by your state's statute. Generally, these laws further specify that only a licensed funeral director is authorized to move the decedent.

The family or the executor of a decedent's estate is not legally bound to follow the decedent's wishes regarding the funeral and burial, such as cost of the funeral, or how the body should be prepared, or where it should be buried. The law, however, usually does honor a decedent's right to donate the body or specific body organs. Every effort, of course, should be made to satisfy the decedent's wishes as specified in the will or supplemental letter of instructions.

The choices of disposal of the body for the typical family are:

1. ***Earth Burial.*** In the United States and Canada earth burial is the most widely used form of disposition, involving interment in a grave or crypt of uncremated remains, generally in a casket.

2. ***Entombment.*** In entombment the casket with the remains is placed in a mausoleum or in an above-ground tomb.

3. ***Cremation.*** In cremation the body is reduced to ashes which are then buried or scattered, depending on your wishes or local ordinances. While most religious groups approve cremation, some, such as certain Protestant denominations, Islam, Eastern Orthodoxy, and Orthodox Judaism, do not.

4. ***Whole-Body or Organ Donation.*** You may wish to consider donating a particular organ or organs of your body, such as eyes, kidneys, heart, or your entire body for research or educational purposes. Donating a particular organ or organs of your body could help someone who may be in desperate need. Such a donation is probably the most meaningful gift you can make to promote life and happiness for someone else.

   Making this donation through a properly signed and witnessed document is legally binding on the heirs of the deceased. Often, however, some of the survivors object, and medical schools, research foundations, and hospitals are reluctant to go to court to enforce such a gift because when an organ is donated the delays of a court case make the organ useless for transplantation. If you desire to donate your body or any part of it, you should discuss your wishes with your family to obtain their agreement. Be sure that they understand the procedures to be followed after your death. A free Uniform Donor Card can be ordered from the Continental Association of Funeral and Memorial Societies, 1828 L Street, N.W., Washington, D.C. 20036.

5. ***Direct Disposition.*** In direct disposition the body is transferred from the place of death to the place of disposition, either a cemetery or a crematory. Direct disposition

is less expensive than a traditional funeral, because it involves no embalming, no viewing, and no need for an expensive casket.

The two least expensive options are whole-body donation and direct disposition.

Funeral Ceremonies

A funeral ceremony offers an opportunity to commemorate the life of the deceased and to recognize the loss that has occurred. The type of funeral ceremony is determined by personal preferences and religious beliefs. If you wish to plan your own funeral, you should write your preferences as part of your supplemental letter of instructions. Traditional religious funerals vary among different religious groups. Whether you are planning your own funeral or a funeral for a relative or friend, the best guidance you can obtain is your local minister, priest, or rabbi.

A memorial service, at which the body is not present, is becoming increasingly popular. The memorial service is generally held after a burial or cremation and is conducted in a church, a synagogue, a funeral home, a private home or any other meeting place. The service is very flexible and is designed to meet the preferences of the deceased or the family. Other types of services include fraternal ceremonies, such as those conducted by the Masons or Knights of Columbus. These services are supplementary to a regular funeral service.

If you are planning a funeral ceremony, consider whether you desire a religious or a non-religious service; the type of readings and/or music to be included; the number and names of the participants; whether the body will be present or not, and if it is present, whether the casket will be open or closed.

The *Final Report* of the Federal Trade Commission on the Funeral Industry Regulation Rule reveals that 66 percent of funerals held are the Open Casket Service with Ground Burial; 20 percent are Closed Casket Service with Ground Burial; 12 percent involve cremation either before or after a service; and two percent entail above-ground burial.

Funeral Costs

The July 1982 *Final Report* of the Federal Trade Commission indicates that charges billed through a funeral home for the funeral ceremony and burial average $2,500. Cremation cost is considerably less than a ground burial, averaging about $700. Since these are averages, variation in cost is quite wide, with one out of eight funerals with ground burial costing more than $3,500. These figures confirm the high cost of dying. The United States funeral industry consists of about 22,000 funeral homes with an annual volume of $6.0 billion in merchandise and services.

Critics of the funeral industry state that some funeral directors take advantage of grief-stricken and ill-prepared customers who, under the pressures of bereavement, make poor decisions which prove to be very costly. They argue that more government regulation is needed to protect the public. They advise consumers to learn well in advance about the choices that are available.

The FTC funeral rule calls for significant changes in industry practices, requiring the nation's funeral homes to:

1. Make available full disclosure of prices, including an itemized list before the funeral is scheduled;
2. Refrain from misleading advertising and deceptive practices such as advising a prospective customer that embalming is required and that this process will preserve a body indefinitely;
3. Provide consumers with price information over the telephone.

The Federal Trade Commission's rule on funeral trade practices went into effect on April 30, 1984.

The economics of the funeral industry requires high costs. With about two million people dying each year, the 22,000 funeral homes handle an average of fewer than 100 each per year. This number of customers must generate enough income to keep the facility attractive, to maintain a year-round staff, and to provide for new hearses and limousines. The funeral director must generate maximum income out of every funeral conducted to meet overhead costs.

A Complete Funeral

The price of a *complete funeral* includes certain standard items, extra items, and burial or cremation costs.

1. **Standard Items.** Undertakers generally include the following standard items in the price of a *complete funeral:* removal of the body to the funeral establishment; use of funeral home facilities; embalming and restoration; dressing of remains; cost of casket; use of hearse and one limousine; staff services; arranging for religious services, burial permit, death benefits, and newspaper death notices; providing pallbearers; arranging and care of flowers; providing guest register and acknowledgment cards; obtaining copies of the death certificate; and in some cases, extension of credit.

2. **Extra Items.** Extra items which may be purchased include a vault, which is very costly; extra limousines; music, if any; an honorarium for clergy, which may be handled directly by a survivor; flowers; burial clothing; and taxes.

3. **Burial Costs.** Burial costs also add to the cost of a funeral. The undertaker may be called upon to assist survivors with the purchase of a cemetery plot, and will arrange with the cemetery for the opening and closing of the grave. These burial costs are often paid for by the undertaker and then reimbursed by the survivors.

Pricing Systems

Some funeral homes sell each standard item and each extra item separately and then prepare an itemized price list whose sum is the total cost of the funeral. The more popular method of pricing for a conventional funeral is based on the cost of the casket. The cost of the casket selected is multiplied by the ratio of the dollar amount of a year's desired gross sales to the expected cost of a year's caskets, yielding about a five-to-one ratio. The price of the complete funeral, excluding additional items and burial or cremation costs, is generally five times the wholesale cost of the casket.

Price Itemization

Several states, including New York and Florida, require price itemization of each of the standard and extra items purchased for a funeral. The survivors in those states know exactly the price of every item included in the total cost. Price itemization makes it easier to reject those goods and services which are not wanted. In some instances, the funeral director may increase other prices to compensate for the items rejected. The FTC notes in one study that unscrupulous funeral directors switch tags on caskets before prosperous-looking survivors enter the selection room. Another fraudulent tactic is the substitution of a less expensive casket for the more expensive one selected by the survivors. Even when prices are itemized, however, you have no way of knowing whether you are being charged the same prices as everyone else.

The FTC notes that documents obtained from a large California mortuary revealed a compensation system for salespersons which penalized them for low-priced sales and rewarded them for high-priced ones.

Embalming

Second to the coffin in the price of a funeral is embalming, which makes possible the viewing of the body in an open casket. If survivors reject embalming, then the funeral home will add a charge for *preservation*, which is simply refrigeration, and this service may cost as much as embalming.

Vault

A vault is a container which encloses the casket when it is placed in the ground and can be one of the most costly components of a funeral. No evidence is available to prove that a vault prolongs protection for a body. Indeed, the airtight vault may hasten the decomposition of the corpse. Some cemeteries require a vault to keep the ground from collapsing as the casket gradually disintegrates. Some cemeteries sell their own concrete boxes, which are less expensive than the steel or concrete vaults sold by funeral homes. It is estimated that almost three-fourths of all burials include a vault.

Monument

The manufacture and sale of a marker or monument for a gravesite is a separate industry. Markers or monuments are usually granite, marble, or bronze and account for a major expense associated with interment. The monument is selected by the survivors and must then be inscribed, moved to the cemetery, and erected on a concrete foundation on the gravesite. A considerable amount of time elapses after burial before a monument is erected.

Memorial Societies

Memorial societies are nonprofit, cooperative-type organizations created by consumers and designed to help you get the kind of funeral you want at a reasonable price. Over 200 memorial societies have been organized in the United States, with about 1,000,000 members. They are usually affiliated with· churches, senior citizen centers, unions, or civic groups, and are staffed primarily by volunteers. They provide information about low-cost funerals, cremation, bequeathal of the body or organs of the body, and other information on death arrangements. You can join a memorial society by making a one-time membership payment of $10 to $20.

Since the memorial society is operated by volunteers, it has no incentive to earn a profit and it does not provide or sell any funeral merchandise or funeral services. It serves as liaison with funeral directors to provide for the needs of its membership. Generally the price for a funeral arranged by a memorial society is lower than that of a funeral home because the memorial society is a large purchaser of funeral services. While memorial societies are geared specifically to assist its members, most societies will assist nonmembers in obtaining a low-cost funeral. The society may even furnish comparative cost data for your area.

To locate your nearest memorial society, you can contact the Continental Association of Funeral and Memorial Societies, 1828 L Street, N.W., Washington, D.C. 20036.

Cemetery Plots

If you plan to continue to live where you are now living, and if you wish an earth burial, you should buy a burial plot or graves while you are still alive. This will spare your survivors the unpleasant and painful task of having to buy a gravesite quickly after your demise. As indicated previously, state law requires that a human body be buried in an officially designated cemetery or graveyard.

All cemeteries are regulated and supervised by agencies of the Federal, state, or local governments. Depending upon their ownership, cemeteries may be classified into three categories:

1. Those owned and operated by religious, fraternal, and philanthropic groups with private funds;
2. Those owned and operated by private corporations for profit;
3. Those owned and operated by a public authority and supported by tax funds.

When buying a cemetery plot, the factors to consider are

1. **Location.** You must decide whether you wish to be buried where you grew up or spent your adult life or where you are living in retirement. You should also find out whether you have the right to resell your plot if you decide to buy one elsewhere and whether the cemetery will buy it back from you and at what price.

2. **Size.** Cemetery plots are usually sold as single graves (one for yourself), or two gravesites (a plot for you and for your spouse), or a cemetery plot for the entire family. Some cemeteries allow double-depth graves, where one casket can be buried on top of another. This is a cost-saving factor which should be considered.

3. **Maintenance Costs.** Determine what the annual upkeep costs are as compared to the costs of perpetual care of the grave or graves. Costs are also involved in opening and closing the grave at the time of burial.

If you buy a cemetery plot before it is needed, you have the opportunity to look around and to compare prices. You can ascertain the reputation of a cemetery by checking with the local Better Business Bureau or a member of the local clergy.

SURVIVORS' BENEFITS

The two most important benefits generally available to survivors are the Social Security death benefit and the Veterans Administration death benefit. Many people do not realize that they are entitled to one or both of these and often money is lost because the time limit for application expires.

Social Security Survivor Benefit

The benefit is a lump-sum payment to a survivor or the individual responsible for paying the funeral expenses, in an amount up to $255. The application for death benefits must be submitted within two years from the date of death, using Form SSA8.

If the deceased left no surviving spouse, the death benefit may be paid to any other survivor responsible for or who has paid the expenses of the funeral. If the survivor wishes, Social Security will send the payment directly to the funeral home. If a body is donated to a medical facility, the cost of transporting the body is an expense which Social Security will reimburse, not exceeding the maximum of $255. See Chapter 2, Understanding Social Security.

Veterans Administration Survivor Benefit

The Veterans Administration will pay a $300 funeral allowance plus free burial in a national cemetery upon an eligible veteran's death. If the burial is not in a national cemetery, the Veterans Administration will pay an additional $150 as an interment allowance. All veterans are entitled to a headstone and a United States flag. These benefits are available to any veteran who has served honorably in the armed forces in wartime or peacetime, even if the deaths are nonservice-connected.

If the death is service-related, an allowance of up to $1,100 will be paid. VA Form 21-530 must be filed within two years after the death whether the death is service-related or nonservice-related. The payment will be made to the individual who paid for the funeral.

Veterans, their spouses, and minor children are entitled to burial in a national cemetery. If you are a veteran, contact your local Veterans Administration office for further details.

Documents Required for Survivors' Benefits

Survivors will need copies of the following documents when applying for death benefits:

1. ***Death Certificate.*** A copy of the death certificate, certified by the issuing agency.

2. ***Birth Certificate.*** A certified copy of the birth certificate of both surviving spouse and minor children for Social Security and Veterans Administration benefits.

3. ***Marriage Certificate.*** A certified copy of the marriage certificate.

4. ***W-2 Form.*** A copy of the W-2 form or the Federal income tax return for the most recent year as proof of the decedent's recent employment record for the Social Security benefit.

5. ***Veteran's Discharge.*** A copy of the veteran's discharge papers for V.A. benefits.

6. **Receipted Bill.** A copy of the receipted bill from the funeral home for V.A. benefits and for Social Security benefits if the applicant is not the surviving spouse.

7. **Social Security Number.** Survivors should have available the Social Security number of the deceased to claim Social Security benefits.

SELF-STUDY:
INSTRUCTIONS FOR MY SURVIVORS

The following is a sample list of instructions which you should prepare for your survivors. When it is completed, make it available to your spouse, relative or close friend.

Instructions for Funeral and Burial

	(Name of husband or individual)	(Name of wife or individual)
1. Name, address, and phone number of funeral home selected	_____	_____
	_____	_____
2. Type of service preferred: a. At funeral facility?	_____	_____
b. Church or synagogue? Name and address	_____	_____
c. Religious or nonreligious service	_____	_____
d. Type: Private? Public? Memorial service later?	_____	_____
	_____	_____
e. Name of person to conduct service	_____	_____
Phone number	_____	_____
f. Names of speakers	_____	_____
	_____	_____

Instructions for Funeral and Burial (Continued)

	(Name of husband or individual)	(Name of wife or individual)
g. Music? Flowers?	_____	_____
h. Casket flag for a veteran	_____	_____
3. Casket: a. Type and price range	_____	_____
b. Open for viewing or closed	_____	_____
4. Disposition of body: a. Burial. Specify: Earth burial or above ground in a mausoleum	_____	_____
b. Cremation. Specify: Earth burial of urn; Niche in Columbarium; Delivered to survivors; Scattered: land or sea	_____	_____
c. Donation of body or parts. Specify: Entire body; List parts	_____	_____
Name, address and phone number of recipient organization. (Attach authorization)	_____	_____
5. Name and location of cemetery:	_____	_____
a. Individual grave or plot?	_____	_____
b. Location of cemetery deed	_____	_____
6. Memorial contributions: Name and address of charity or organization to receive memorial donations.	_____	_____
7. Organizations to be notified: a. Name of organization	_____	_____

	(Name of husband or individual)	(Name of wife or individual)
b. Person to be contacted		
c. Address and phone number		
8. Membership in memorial society: a. Society name		
b. Person to be contacted		
c. Address and phone number		

SURVIVING A LOSS

Most individuals prefer to avoid the topic of death and dying. The subject is ignored or spoken about only in private. Actually, it cannot be brushed aside and must be confronted honestly. Death does occur. It is a reality you must face because it is the ultimate human experience.

Interest in death has grown significantly over the last several years. A large number of books and articles have been published on the subject, and colleges and universities around the country are offering courses about death and dying. Psychologists are dealing with the complex problems of survivors and their adjustment after the loss of a loved one. Some of the major aspects of survival are discussed below.

The Crisis of Bereavement

The loss of a loved one creates a deep wound. The healing process is often slow and painful. While it may never heal completely, an adjustment to living is ultimately effected. It is natural to think that you cannot live without the deceased, and you feel lost. You function and do what has to be done, arranging the funeral, and finally giving away the deceased's clothing and other items. You are in shock.

After a while, as the shock of the event wears away, the pain becomes more evident. It is difficult to shake off and seems to persist over the weeks and months. You need the support of relatives, friends, and clergy to help you get a grip on yourself once again and come to terms with reality. Eventually, you begin to emerge from this phase of grief and begin to take note of the world around you. The experience helps you to grow. An understanding of the feelings and needs of others emerges. You become wiser and warmer in your relationships.

Living Alone

Now you are alone. The daily chores of running a household persist. Food must be bought and stored; a meal for one must be prepared; the house must be cleaned; laundry must be taken care of; and you may have to report back to work to do your job. Living alone may be a fearful experience. It is important to feel secure in your surroundings, and you worry about locking the door and windows at night. The slightest sound may awaken you. And then, every night you must come home to an empty house which is silent and dark. The reality of your aloneness is devastating.

As a widow or widower, you must now become active in the handling of the details of the will, of probate proceedings, of distributions to children and possibly grandchildren, and of a variety of other financial matters with which you may be unfamiliar.

Questions that will arise require solutions. A change in housing arrangements may be in order, *but do not make any changes until at least one year has elapsed.* You may wish to pursue a second career or a new career. This may require training and career counseling. Other problems will arise: dating, sexuality, remarriage. You may wish to develop new friendships, continue your education, or enjoy new leisure activities.

SELF-STUDY: MY THOUGHTS ON SURVIVING A LOSS

1. From your personal experience, what problems have you observed in the life of an individual who has suffered a loss?

_____

_____

_____

_____

2. If you had the opportunity, what suggestions would you make to this grieving individual in order to alleviate the problems?

_____

_____

_____

_____

3. What plans do you have for dealing with a loss if you should suffer one?

_____

_____

_____

_____

_____

GLOSSARY

Burial. See Cremation; Earth Burial; Entombment.

Burial Society. An organization of individuals that assumes responsibility for all the details of burial and/or cremation.

Burial Vault. An outer receptacle used to enclose a casket or similar container in a grave.

Casket. A coffin or rigid container that encases a body. May be ornamented and lined with fabric. (See Minimal Container.)

Cemetery. A burial ground or tract of land set aside for graves or tombs.

Cemetery Plot. A burial site for one or more graves owned by an individual, family or organization.

Columbarium. A building where cremation urns are stored.

Cremation. The act of incinerating a body. The residue of ashes consists of small bone fragments. (See Earth Burial, Entombment.)

Crematory. An establishment that incinerates a body as the means of disposal.

Crypt. A room or cell that serves as an alternative to earth burial. May be located underground. (See Mausoleum.)

Death Benefit. The two most important benefits generally available to survivors are the Social Security death benefit and the Veterans Administration death benefit.

Death Certificate. A document, signed by a doctor, medical examiner or coroner, giving pertinent information about a deceased person, such as name; age; date; time, place, and cause of death.

Direct Disposition. The act of burying or cremating a body without a ceremony or viewing.

Earth Burial. The act or ceremony of burying the remains of a deceased person in the ground. It is the most widely used form of disposition in the United States and Canada.

Embalming. The process of treating a dead body using chemicals and drugs so as to preserve it to make viewing possible in an open casket. (See Preservation.)

Entombment. The placing of a casket with the remains in a *mausoleum,* an above-ground tomb. (See Cremation, Earth Burial.)

Eulogy. A speech or writing in honor or praise of a deceased person.

Family Plot. A burial site for one or more graves owned by a family.

Funeral Director. A mortician or undertaker who is in charge of arrangements for a funeral and burial or cremation.

Funeral Home. An establishment specifically intended as a place where the body of the deceased may repose before the funeral and where those who knew the deceased may pay last respects. Also known as *funeral chapel, funeral parlor, mortuary.*

Funeral Service. A ceremony that is usually held with the body present.

Funeral Trade Practices Rule. Sets forth rules of operation for the nation's funeral homes. It was approved by the U.S. Federal Trade Commission and became effective April 30, 1984.

Grave Liner. (See Burial Vault.)

Grave Marker. (See Monument, Tombstone.)

Immediate Disposal. (See Direct Disposition.)

Lot. (See Plot.)

Mausoleum. An above-ground building where crypts are located. (See Crypt.)

Memorial Service. A ceremony usually held after a body has been buried or cremated.

Memorial Society. A non-profit cooperative designed to help people arrange for the funeral services they want at a reasonable price.

Minimal Container. A non-metal, alternative container to hold a body, possibly a non-rigid pouch made of canvas that is simple and much cheaper than a casket. (See Casket.)

Monument. A tombstone or structure erected as a marker for a grave. (See Tombstone.)

Mortuary. (See Funeral Home.)

Obituary. A notice of the death of a person, generally in a newspaper, and often containing a brief biographical sketch.

Plot. The cemetery land purchased by an individual for burial in a grave.

Preservation. Refrigeration of the dead body to make viewing possible in an open casket. (See Embalming.)

Supplemental Letter of Instructions. A memorandum of personal details that should be attached to your will with a copy to your executor and one for you and your spouse so that it may be kept up-to-date. The Supplemental Letter of Instructions should include such information as location of the will, location of vital documents, location of assets, employment or business information, and funeral and burial instructions.

Tombstone. A stone marker, usually inscribed, on a grave or tomb.

Uniform Donor Card. A card prepared in advance of death, indicating the decedent's wishes for disposal of the body, including possible donation of the body or specific organs for medical purposes, and prepared in accordance with the Uniform Anatomical Gifts Act.

Urn. An ornamental container used to hold cremated remains.

Will. A legal document, almost always in writing and properly executed, which describes how a person wants his or her property distributed after death. May include funeral and burial instructions.

Chapter 11
Working and Playing in Retirement

At some point in your life you become an older American, perhaps in your fifties or sixties, by retiring from your job and entering into a new lifestyle. You may retire by choice because you have had enough of the work routine, or by the force of circumstances because of ill health, or because your firm goes out of business or changes management, or because your job is no longer necessary. Whatever the reason, you are out of the labor force and have become a retiree. Suddenly, you have at least fifty extra hours a week to spend however you choose. Some enjoy this added leisure and find it to be the most rewarding period of life. Others are unable to cope with all this free time and quickly become bored and restless.

THE ROLE OF WORK IN YOUR LIFE

Some research evidence indicates that if retirees had a choice, most would opt for some kind of work because work contributes something to your life which cannot easily be replaced by anything else. Some of the satisfactions offered by work include:

- A feeling of self-worth stemming from the contribution you are making
- A sense of fulfillment because you enjoy your work and others appreciate and recognize your ability
- A sense of belonging through the social contacts and friendships you make at work
- A structured life which gives order to the day and makes time pass quickly

These satisfactions or goals do not disappear at retirement. Whether you are actively employed or retired, these needs remain the same because they are basic human needs for everyone.

The work options at or after retirement are

1. Work at the same job or in a new career
2. Part-time work with the same employer or elsewhere
3. Unpaid volunteer work in your community
4. Establishing and operating your own business.

A discussion of each of these options follows.

Option 1—Continue Full-Time Work

If you wish to work beyond age 65 or 70 as a full-time, paid employee, you might want to approach your employer to discuss this possibility. With your lifetime experience in your job, you may very well qualify to serve as a consultant on a full-time basis at the same time that you may serve as a company trouble-shooter wherever problems arise; as a trainer for younger staff members who often need guidance and advice; and as an ombudsman to handle individual gripes of employees.

If you can arrange to remain at the same company beyond your retirement date, several work arrangements are possible.

1. *Job Reassignment.* You may be willing to accept less money in a less-demanding job in some other assignment within the company.

2. *Job Redesign.* You may arrange to have your job specifications changed to eliminate those functions causing physical or mental stress.

3. *Compressed Work Week.* You may arrange to work fewer days by doing your week's work in four ten-hour days instead of five eight-hour days.

4. *Flexible Location.* You may arrange to spend part of your week's work time on the company's premises and the other part at home.

5. *Flexitime.* You may arrange a flexible work schedule to fit a new set of job specifications, such as coming in later and leaving earlier, or starting later and leaving later.

Such potential arrangements would yield benefits to both your employer and yourself.

A New Career

You may decide to enter a second career, to work at something you have always wanted to do but for one reason or another could not undertake. Retirement gives you the opportunity to make a fresh start. You may wish to enter a field that requires more traveling, or less. You may want to work with your hands after having spent your first career at a desk. You may enjoy cooking professionally or spending your time at a college or university taking courses you enjoy and/or teaching in your area of expertise. Retirement is the time to take advantage of these options and at the same time to continue to earn an income.

Option 2—Shift to Part-Time

Most people who are planning to retire would like to have a not-too-demanding part-time job which would provide income and keep them in the mainstream. If such thinking is part of your retirement plan, you should approach the quest with the same care and lead time as you did when seeking a new full-time job while still in the labor market. Some occupations offer better part-time job prospects than others. A retired lawyer may wish to continue in his or her profession after retirement by serving a reduced number of former clients. An office worker or factory worker may be able to fill in for those who are ill or on vacation. Your company may be willing to retain you after retirement on a part-time basis.

Hiring part-time and temporary help saves companies from the high cost of paying for fringe benefits. The company does not have to make pension contributions, or offer participation in the profit-sharing plan, or pay for Blue Cross or Blue Shield, or any other health benefits program. This is a significant advantage to the company, at the same time that part-time work fits the needs of people who choose to work fewer hours, particularly retirees who seek to ward off boredom.

The number of part-time workers, those who work fewer than 35 hours a week, continues to grow and currently amounts to about 20 percent of the nonfarm work force. A new concept has been developed in industry, known as *phased retirement,* which appears to be adding more part-time workers to the labor force.

The Phased Retirement Program

Phased retirement means helping older employees retire gradually by reducing present work time without reducing ultimate pension benefits. As you reduce your work time, you also reduce your take-home pay, which helps you adjust to living on less. In addition to helping you make a financial adjustment, phased retirement increases your free time, thus enabling you to increase your leisure time activities. A positive financial advantage to the employer in phased retirement is the gradual reduction in salaries. At the same time, the company derives the benefit of utilizing an employee's job knowledge to train others and of keeping the job functions operative. Variations of the phased retirement program include:

1. Varied part-time schedules such as mornings only, or afternoons only, or alternating mornings and afternoons, or a daily schedule from 10 A.M. to 3 P.M.
2. A regular daily work schedule with a one-month vacation after every two months on the job, or a variation of this arrangement.

If any of these variations of a reduction of work hours is of interest to you, you can pursue it by discussing it with your company management or with your union.

Job Sharing

In *job sharing* two workers divide the hours and responsibilities of a single full-time job between them. For example, one may work from 7:30 A.M. to 1 P.M. and the other from 11:30 A.M. to 4 P.M. For many people, this is the perfect answer. Some job-sharing arrangements are family affairs in which neither party wants to work full-time. A mother and a daughter may operate a small business. One works on Mondays and Wednesdays, the other on Tuesdays and Thursdays, and they alternate on Fridays.

Many businesses are hiring more part-timers because it fits their needs too. Fast-food shops, for example, hire many workers only for peak hours. Partnerships of doctors, lawyers, and accountants sometimes discover that they prefer shorter working hours to larger incomes. In some places the demand for computer specialists is so great that many companies offer part-time positions to attract skilled workers, even though they might prefer full-time employees.

For many people who have been out of the job market for years, part-time work offers a chance to return gradually. Some professionals decide that temporary positions in their own fields are preferable to the regular but less skilled work that is available immediately.

Option 3—Do Volunteer Work

If you wish to participate in a volunteer activity after you retire, retirement planning gives you the opportunity to try out various volunteer jobs in your spare time. This may enable you to find out what group you would like to work with. By sampling several different organizations before you retire, you can make a more intelligent decision as to which gives you the most fulfillment. If you make up your mind sufficiently ahead of your actual retirement, you will have the opportunity to gain a great deal of experience and possibly to qualify for an executive position as a volunteer at the time you do retire.

A variety of groups and organizations utilize volunteers on the local level. These include:

1. *Hospitals.* Every hospital in your community relies heavily on the work of volunteers to operate the institution. All types of jobs are available, but basically you must be capable of working closely with people who need help on the road to recovery. A smile and a helping hand brighten the day for the sick or infirm. If you are interested, contact your nearest hospital.

2. *Cultural Institutions.* Many cultural institutions, such as museums or public television stations, offer opportunities for volunteers. Typical jobs include guiding tours or fund raising.

3. *Schools.* Volunteers serve in schools to assist teachers in the classroom or to tutor weaker students in basic skills. Contact your local school.

4. *Community Service Organizations.* Churches and synagogues offer a variety of volunteer jobs. Charitable organizations, "Y" groups, or improve-your-neighborhood activities are always seeking the assistance of volunteers.

Option 4—Own a Business

You may be interested in starting your own business after you retire. Such a venture offers you the opportunity to be your own boss, to be financially independent, and to be working in a field that you enjoy. The idea is enticing to many who are contemplating work options after retirement. Many small businesses succeed and generate high incomes for their entrepreneurs, but most do not survive for very long. According to the U.S. Small Business Administration which studies mortality rates in small businesses, about 20 percent close in the first year, 20 percent in the second, and another 10 percent in the third year.

The reasons for failure are varied and include poor location, poor management, insufficient capital, ineffective purchasing, and unsuccessful marketing. Each of these areas of failure should be thoroughly checked prior to undertaking a small business. Some of the knowledge required in each of these areas can be learned by working for a few years in the type of business you are contemplating and by supplementing your personal experience with formal education and training. The probability of failure is high for the inexperienced and the untrained. However, there are many resources available for free consultation, such as the U.S. Small Business Administration.

SELF-STUDY: HOW DO I RATE FOR POST-RETIREMENT WORK?

1. A recent Social Security Administration poll reveals that 80 percent of white collar workers and 60 percent of blue collar workers get new jobs in their pre-retirement fields. What are your long-range plans for work after retirement? Check the appropriate box or boxes.

Work Options After Retirement	Full-time	Part-time
Continue at present job	☐	☐
Seek a new position	☐	☐
Do volunteer work	☐	☐
Start a business	☐	☐
No work; enjoy leisure	☐	☐

2. Personnel officers as well as large and small employers have pinpointed the characteristics of employees which they deem most important to the success of their enterprises. How would you rate yourself on each of the following characteristics? Check the appropriate boxes.

Characteristic	Above average	Average	Below average
a. Good appearance	☐	☐	☐
b. Regular and punctual work habits (low absentee rate)	☐	☐	☐
c. Good writing, spelling, and mathematical skills	☐	☐	☐
d. Ability to accept supervision	☐	☐	☐
e. Mature attitude (minimum irritability or anger)	☐	☐	☐
f. Pride in work	☐	☐	☐
g. Thoroughness	☐	☐	☐

Characteristic	Above average	Average	Below average
h. Satisfactory completion of assignments	☐	☐	☐
i. Knowledge and skills	☐	☐	☐
j. Outgoing personality	☐	☐	☐
k. High productivity	☐	☐	☐
l. Company loyalty	☐	☐	☐
m. Motivation	☐	☐	☐
n. Enthusiasm	☐	☐	☐
o. Flexibility	☐	☐	☐

Interpretation of results: If most of your ratings are above average, your employability index is high. Your first step is to find a vacancy.

3. The following are characteristics of people who have succeeded in their own businesses. How do you rate? Check the appropriate boxes.

☐ Willingness to work long hours
☐ High energy level
☐ Initiative
☐ Perseverance
☐ Pleasant attitude
☐ Sincerity
☐ Leadership
☐ Ability to make good decisions
☐ Organizing ability
☐ Industriousness
☐ Responsibility
☐ Financial reserves to keep you afloat in case of set-backs
☐ Emotional strength to cushion possible failure

JOB HUNTING

Job hunting is a difficult and frustrating experience for most people. The rejections appear to pile up all too quickly. But always in the back of your mind you know that your goal is the single acceptance that is out there someplace. The methods used in job hunting include the following possibilities.

1. **Visit personnel departments.** It is estimated that about 27 percent of prospective employees are hired directly by the personnel officers of companies through whose

door they walked. So, choose the company you would like to work for and visit the personnel office. If a vacancy exists, and if you meet the requirements, you have a job. It is always wise to draw up a plan of company visits and to know precisely what type of work you are seeking.

2. **Read classified help wanted ads.** Read the classified help wanted advertisements in all the newspapers in your town or city, and check off those for which you are particularly well-qualified. Answering the ad may require a personal visit or a letter and resumé.

3. **Visit employment agencies.** Two kinds of employment agencies are available: a state employment service, which is a tax-supported agency, and a private employment agency that charges a fee if it helps you land a job. Since private agencies specialize in the type of jobs they fill, select an agency in your own area of expertise. In your job hunt apply to both the public and private agencies.

4. **Follow up on job tips.** When you are in the job market, you talk to personnel officials as well as friends and relatives. Often in the course of a conversation, a job lead may be offered. It is prudent to follow up on each such tip. Leave no stone unturned.

How to Apply: The Resumé

One of the most important tools in job hunting is the *resumé*. While the resumé cannot be relied upon to get you the job you want, it may open the door for an interview. Essentially, a resumé is a summary of your work experience, your education, and your training. If properly prepared, it can indicate to a potential employer that you do indeed have something positive to offer. It should be easy to read and well organized, containing the following information:

1. Name, address and telephone number
2. Job objective
3. Work history
4. Education and/or special training
5. Personal information including references

If you mail a resumé to a prospective employer, include a cover letter explaining why your particular qualifications will satisfy the requirements of the job for which you are applying.

The Interview

When you are called in for an interview, you will have the opportunity to sell yourself and your specialized experience and training to the prospective employer. The two key elements during an interview are your personal appearance and your attitude. Be prepared to answer a variety of questions about your work experience, your education, and your opinions and attitudes. Highlight the special benefits that would accrue to the company by hiring a mature person. Remember that as long as you are under seventy, Federal law specifies that age cannot be a deterrent to employment. Prepare in advance the answers you would give to questions posed by the interviewer, turning a weak point into a strength that would benefit the employer.

Thank You Letter

After you have completed the interview, it is suggested that you send a thank you letter. In addition, you may wish to write again or call periodically to determine if any jobs are open. You have made a contact, and if you continue to display an interest in working for that particular employer, you may eventually land a job.

Where to Look

The job market changes almost daily. Because of this, the mature individual entering the job market in the 1980s may require some retraining and upgrading of skills which would guarantee him or her employment on his or her own terms. For example, clerical jobs are always in great demand. An experienced typist, stenographer, or bookkeeper is still in demand. But the experienced typist/stenographer who learns to handle a word-processing machine would have no difficulty in locating a position. Similarly, with the growth of computer technology, the demand for computer operators is constantly increasing. Mature individuals can learn to operate a computer without knowing the technical details of how a computer functions, and computer operators will be in even greater demand in the future.

With the 65-and-over group expanding more rapidly than the population as a whole, the need for retirement counseling and pension planning consultants will grow. The health-care field will offer enormous opportunities over the next decade since more and more people will be required to provide health care for the aged. Also, younger Americans are increasingly concerned about their health and have more money and health insurance coverage than ever before.

Retail sales always offer opportunities to older individuals. Salespeople or clerks in retail stores account for millions of jobs, and hundreds of thousands of such jobs become available each year. A growing company may suddenly experience the need to increase its staff and a whole network of positions would become available.

The greatest market for part-time work is to be found in the service industries, including jobs in areas such as schools and libraries, food stores, department stores, cafeterias, day-care centers, and other places of employment that have evening hours. About one-third of people over 65 have part-time jobs, and these are more plentiful than full-time jobs. One of the advantages of a part-time job for an individual collecting Social Security is that it enables the person to earn up to the maximum allowed by Social Security without losing benefits.

Opportunities in the 1980s will grow in financial services including banks and brokerage houses. Nurses and medical technicians are in heavy demand. Hotels and spas offer all types of job opportunities, both full-time and part-time. Teachers are in great demand in the sciences, mathematics, and computer technology.

Holding down some kind of job contributes to your physical and emotional health, in addition to providing a financial return. The goal of working at least part-time during your retirement years is worthwhile and definitely worth pursuing. The older worker needs the same sense of usefulness and accomplishment as his or her younger counterpart. A work affiliation offers these benefits.

SELF-STUDY:
MY RESUMÉ

1. An attractive and well-organized resumé can provide an introduction to a company or organization, highlighting your most important qualifications, and leaving an impression of yourself after the interview which is independent of the opinion or impressions of the interviewer. Prepare your personal resumé using the sample below as an outline.

2. A job interview gives you the opportunity to present yourself and your qualifications to a representative of the company or organization. Following are some sample questions that might come up in an interview. To be well prepared for the interview, you may wish to practice your responses in advance.

   a. Work experience
      (1) What type of job are you seeking?
      (2) What did you enjoy doing most in your last job?
      (3) What did you not enjoy doing?
      (4) How did your supervisors describe you as a person?
      (5) For what did they criticize you?
      (6) For what did they praise you?

   b. Education
      (1) How would you describe your educational accomplishments?
      (2) How did you come to choose the kind of work you did?
      (3) Has not having a college degree (or graduate degree) hindered your vocational progress?

   c. Personal
      (1) Talk about yourself.
      (2) How do you spend your leisure time?
      (3) What are your major strengths and weaknesses?
      (4) Why do you want to work for us?
      (5) What salary are you seeking? (full-time or part-time?)

Sample Resumé

Name _____

Address _____ _____
                                  City   State   Zip code

Telephone number (include area code) _____

Job objective: _____

_____

Work history: (List current or most recent employment first)

Dates From To	Job title and duties in brief	Name of supervisor/title Company/organization name and full address
_____ _____	_____	_____
_____ _____	_____	_____
_____ _____	_____	_____
_____ _____	_____	_____

Education:

Dates From To	Name and address of school	Diploma; Degree(s)	Major
_____ _____	(High school)	_____	_____
_____ _____	(College)	_____	_____
_____ _____	(Graduate school)	_____	_____

Special Training:
(Company training courses; armed forces schools;
adult education courses; home study; correspondence courses)

Dates From To	Type of training, name and address of sponsor
_____ _____	_____
_____ _____	_____
_____ _____	_____

Personal information:

Age _____ Date of birth _____ Place of birth _____

Marital status _____ Number of children _____ Health _____

Armed forces record: _____

References:

	Name	Title	Address
1)	_____	_____	_____
2)	_____	_____	_____
3)	_____	_____	_____

LEISURE

The proper use of leisure time in retirement is the basic determinant of whether your retirement will be happy and fulfilling or boring and restless. The transition from full-time work to retiree status adds at least 50 additional hours a week which you can do with as you please. You must begin early to plan to use this extra time in such a way that your feeling of usefulness and contribution to society will continue. Managing your time effectively should be given prime consideration.

Some people turn to _hobbies_ to provide the satisfaction of creativity and recognition resulting from work. Library shelves are filled with books on hobbies and how to select one or more for fulfillment in retirement. Other retirees turn to the world of _education and learning._ Throughout the nation older adults are studying to achieve the never-completed degree or simply pursuing new academic interests and enjoying the excitement and sense of purpose generated by the world of academia. Still others turn to _travel_ in retirement. You definitely will have the time and probably also the money. Add a little imagination and you can satisfy that wanderlust. Some retirees begin _volunteering_ to preserve the sense of identity, self-worth, and usefulness which are derived from work. A carefully selected volunteer job will give you all the job satisfactions you need.

Your leisure plan should include one or more of the leisure activities noted above. The choice or choices you make must be based upon your desire for personal satisfaction and happiness. Do what pleases you.

Hobbies

Hobbies are important to retirees. Those who enjoy a hobby appear to be happier and better adjusted to the retirement lifestyle than those who do not. Deep involvement in a hobby not only offers a focal point for structured living, absorbing countless hours of your leisure time, but also provides the psychological rewards previously derived from your job. If you have not enjoyed a hobby or hobbies prior to retirement, you should explore what is available by reading and by talking to individuals who can guide you. The field of hobbies is vast, offering a wide variety of choices to accommodate individual interests and differences of people. It is essential that you develop a plan for the use of your leisure time in retirement.

The following suggestions are some recommended hobby activities that will help you enjoy your retirement leisure. Of course, the actual possibilities are not limited to the suggestions on the following page.

- **Collecting.** Antiques, autographs, bottles, coins, matchbooks, paintings, postcards, rocks, seashells, stamps.

- **Crafts.** Basket weaving, cabinetmaking, candle making, ceramics, fixing and refinishing furniture, jewelry making, leather tooling, model building, needlecrafts, photography, pottery, quilting, scrimshaw, silversmithing, stained-glass crafting.

- **Games.** Backgammon, bingo, card games (bridge, gin rummy, pinochle, poker), checkers, chess, crossword puzzles, Monopoly, Scrabble.

- **Sports.** Bicycling, boating, bowling, cross-country skiing, fishing, golf, hiking, horseshoes, jogging, ping-pong, tennis, shuffleboard, swimming, walking, weightlifting.

- **Skills.** Acting, cooking, decorating, drawing, entertaining, music, painting, sculpture, sewing.

- **Outdoor Activities.** Birdwatching, camping, gardening, landscaping.

- **Raising Pets.** Bees, birds, cats, chickens, dogs, ducks, fish (tropical), horses, turkeys, other animals.

- **Continuing Education.** Earning a college degree, taking courses, learning a foreign language, writing, geology, philosophy, psychology.

- **Working with Groups.** Cultural, civic, religious, political, club activities.

- **Communicating.** Citizens band (CB), ham radio, letter writing (pen pal).

- **Inventing.** Set up workshop, read relevant literature, join groups.

- **Reading.** Go to your local library and bookstore, join book discussion groups.

- **Visiting.** Develop closer ties with relatives and friends, offer your services to hospitals and community groups.

- **Theater.** Join local theater groups, take courses in speech and theater.

- **Volunteer Work.** See Appendix B (under *Volunteer Work*) for suggested groups to contact.

- **Paid Work.** Read newspaper help wanted ads, contact personnel offices of local businesses and industries.

Leisure-Time Guidelines

The following are suggested guidelines for you to use in planning your leisure:

1. **Variety.** Try to develop a reasonable mix of activities. Take into account the physical slowdown which affects the average individual in later years. Therefore, select some activities that are within your physical ability, some that are intellectual, and some that are creative.

2. **Interaction.** Choose some activities that will enable you to enjoy social contact with other people. Socialization and communication are basic to a sound psychological adjustment. At the same time, each person needs private time for reading, listening to music, watching television, or for contemplation.

3. **Overextension.** In the early enthusiasm of retirement many individuals tend to overextend themselves, trying to do too much. Develop your involvement in your leisure activities slowly, adding or subtracting time as your interest increases or diminishes. Do not take on more than you can handle, and keep your leisure plan flexible.

4. **Lighten the Burdens of Others.** To maintain your feeling of self-worth, choose one activity which gives you the opportunity to spend time helping others who may be less fortunate than you. This is the whole area of volunteer work. Enormous satisfaction can be derived by contributing to the welfare of people in need: spending time with them, providing simple needs, and engaging in conversation.

5. **Pre-Retirement Experimentation.** Try out a few new activities before you retire. See how well you enjoy the activity before making a commitment.

SELF-STUDY:
MY PLAN FOR LEISURE ACTIVITIES

1. To develop a retirement plan for leisure you must first determine the number of hours a week to be considered. Counting time at work and the time consumed getting to and from work, how many additional free hours per week will you have after you retire? _____

2. Which of your *present activities* would you like to continue after you retire? How much of your additional free time would you like to devote to each?

Present activities	Hours per week for each activity	
	Now	After retirement
_____	_____	_____
_____	_____	_____

Present activities	Hours per week for each activity	
	Now	After retirement
_____	_____	_____
_____	_____	_____

3. What *new activities* would you like to pursue after retirement? Are you taking classes or receiving training for these activities?

New activities	Current preparation for these activies
_____	_____
_____	_____
_____	_____
_____	_____

GLOSSARY

Blue-Collar Worker. Anyone whose job requires manual labor and who wears work clothes or other specialized clothing on the job.

Classified Help Wanted Ads. Listings of job opportunities published in newspapers and magazines.

Compressed Work Week. A rearrangement of time so that more hours are worked some days with no hours on other days. For example, five 8-hour days can be compressed into four 10-hour days.

Employment Agency. An organization that helps people find jobs. The services of a public agency are free; private agencies charge a fee. Also known as a *personnel agency.*

Flexible Location. A work arrangement under which part of the time is spent working at home while the rest is spent working on the company's premises.

Flexitime. A work schedule in which time in and time out are arranged to satisfy special needs of an employee.

Interview. A meeting between an employer or an employer representative and a job-seeker to determine suitability for a job.

Job Reassignment. The shifting of an employee from one job to another job with a different set of job specifications.

Job Redesign. A change in job specifications that eliminates unwanted functions and adds desired functions.

Job Sharing. The splitting of hours and responsibilities of a single full-time job between two workers.

Job Specifications. A detailed description of functions required to be performed in a particular job.

Personnel Agency. (See Employment Agency.)

Personnel Department. The department of a business firm that interviews applicants for jobs and that deals with problems affecting employees.

Personnel Officer. An employee with the responsibility of handling personnel decisions and problems.

Phased Retirement. A program to help older employees to retire gradually by reducing present work time without reducing ultimate pension benefits.

Productivity. A measurement of the output of workers in relation to input of resources.

Resumé. A summary of work experience, education, and training. It is one of the most important tools used in job hunting.

Small Business Administration (SBA). A U.S. government agency created in 1953 to aid small business concerns by providing financial, technical, and managerial assistance.

White-Collar Worker. Anyone whose job does not involve manual labor, generally a salaried or professional worker.

Appendix A
Inventory of Personal and Financial Data

Most people are careful about maintaining bits of information and records concerning their personal and financial status. Too often, however, the material is scattered in files or drawers, or recorded in places that may be forgotten, or jotted down on scraps of paper that have become outdated and yellowed with age. When the person or the person's family is suddenly confronted with the need for basic information that is necessary to resolve the myriad of physical and financial situations that inevitably occur, the material is often difficult to locate.

The following Inventory of Personal and Financial Data will preclude the possibility of loss or delay when time is of the essence, and information must be supplied. If you take the time to fill in all the blanks, you will have everything in one place and you will be in a better position to review and evaluate your own personal and financial position. Also, if ever you are temporarily incapacitated or unable to handle matters because of illness, your family will be able to keep things flowing smoothly.

The time that you spend on the Inventory now will certainly be worth the effort. Remember also to check the information from time-to-time to be certain the Inventory is current. This record should be transcribed to worksheets and kept with your important papers.

Personal and Family Information

_____

Date

(Name of husband or individual)   (Name of wife or individual)

Full legal name

Address: Number and Street

    City, State, Zip Code

Personal and Family Information

	(Name of husband or individual)	(Name of wife or individual)
Birth date	_____	_____
Place of birth	_____	_____
Father's name	_____	_____
Mother's name	_____	_____
Social Security number	_____	_____
Current marriage:		
Date of marriage	_____	_____
Place of marriage	_____	_____
Date of termination (Death or divorce)	_____	_____
Divorce:		
Name of previous spouse	_____	_____
Date of divorce	_____	_____
State of jurisdiction	_____	_____
Marital status (Single, married, widowed, separated)	_____	_____
Military service:		
Branch	_____	_____
Serial number	_____	_____
Date of entry	_____	_____
Date discharged	_____	_____
Place discharged	_____	_____
Disability (Service connected)	_____	_____

Children, including those legally adopted

Full name	Full address	Birth date	Place of birth	Extent of dependence
_____	_____	_____	_____	_____
	_____			
_____	_____	_____	_____	_____
	_____			
_____	_____	_____	_____	_____
	_____	_____	_____	_____
_____	_____	_____	_____	_____

Employers (last 10 years)

	Name	Address
Current or last employer	_____	_____
(Dates: From _____		_____
To _____)		
Previous employer	_____	_____
(Dates: From _____		_____
To _____)		
Previous employer	_____	_____
(Dates: From _____		_____
To _____)		
Previous employer	_____	_____
(Dates: From _____		_____
To _____)		

Location of personal and family documents

	(Name of husband or individual)	(Name of wife or individual)
Item(s)	**Location of document**	
Birth certificate		
Marriage certificate(s)		
Divorce papers		
Adoption papers		
Naturalization papers		
Social Security card		
Passport		
Military records		
Will: Original		
First copy		
Second copy		
Paid bills		
Past tax returns		
Cancelled checks		
Stock and bond certificates		
Insurance policies: Life		
Automobile		
Residential		
Health		

Location of personal and family documents

	(Name of husband or individual)	(Name of wife or individual
Item(s)	**Location of document**	
Pension documents		
Bank books		
Real property documents		
Deed to cemetery plot		

Safe-Deposit Box

Every household should rent at least one safe-deposit box for storing important documents and valuable jewelry. Items to be kept in your safe-deposit box include certificates of birth, marriage, divorce, and death; military discharge papers; stock and bond certificates; naturalization papers; copyrights and patents; adoption papers; deeds; mortgages; and jewelry. Your will should be kept in a box rented in your spouse's name and your spouse's will should be kept in a box rented in your name. Usually, a bank seals a box as soon as it learns that the owner has passed away. It is important to note that the contents of a safe-deposit box are not insured. If you wish to insure the contents of your box, you can purchase a separate policy or a rider to one of your other policies. Enter below the information pertaining to your safe-deposit box.

Information About Safe-Deposit Box	Box 1	Box 2
Name of bank where it is located	_____	_____
Address of bank	_____	_____
	_____	_____
Box number	_____	_____
Name of deputy who has access to box	_____	_____
Address of deputy	_____	_____
	_____	_____
Location of key	_____	_____
Inventory of contents	_____	_____
	_____	_____
	_____	_____
	_____	_____
	_____	_____
	_____	_____

Your Professional Consultants

Consultant	Name	Address	Phone
Accountant	_____	_____	_____
		_____	
Lawyer	_____	_____	_____
		_____	
Broker	_____	_____	_____
Banker or trust officer	_____	_____	_____
		_____	
Insurance agent	_____	_____	_____
_____ (Type of coverage)		_____	
Insurance agent	_____	_____	_____
_____ (Type of coverage)		_____	
Doctor (Internist)	_____	_____	_____
		_____	
Doctor	_____	_____	_____
_____ (Specialty)		_____	
Doctor	_____	_____	_____
_____ (Specialty)		_____	
Dentist (General)	_____	_____	_____
		_____	

Consultant	Name	Address	Phone
Dentist	_____	_____	_____
		_____	
_____ (Specialty)			
Minister or rabbi	_____	_____	_____
		_____	

Local Offices: Social Security and Internal Revenue Service

Social Security Office

Enter here the address and phone number of your local Social Security office. If you are in doubt, check your phone book under *Social Security Administration.*

_____

Number and Street

_____

City   State   Zip Code

_____

Phone Number

It is suggested that you phone the Social Security office before you go there. You may be helped on the phone. Even if you must appear in person, your individual circumstances may require specific information which you would then be prepared to provide.

Internal Revenue Service Office

Enter here the address and phone number of your local Internal Revenue Service office. If you are in doubt, check your phone book under *U.S. Government, Internal Revenue Service.*

_____

Number and Street

_____

City   State   Zip Code

_____

Phone Number

Financial Inventory

Savings and Checking Accounts	Savings Account	Savings Account	Savings Account	Checking Account
Name of bank	_____	_____	_____	_____
Address of bank	_____	_____	_____	_____
	_____	_____	_____	_____
Account number	_____	_____	_____	_____
Individual or joint account?* (Name(s))	_____	_____	_____	_____
Location of passbook or check book	_____	_____	_____	_____
Balance as of _____ (Date)	_____	_____	_____	_____

*Many banks freeze a joint account when one of the joint owners dies. If this is your bank's policy, it is suggested that each spouse set up a separate account in his or her name in addition to a joint account.

Individual Retirement Account (IRA)

	(Name of husband or individual)	(Name of wife or individual)
Name of bank or institution	_____	_____
Address of bank or institution	_____	_____
	_____	_____
Account number	_____	_____
Location of passbook or receipt	_____	_____
Balance as of _____ (Date)	_____	_____

Certificate of Deposit (CD)

Name of bank or institution	_____	_____
Address of bank or institution	_____	_____
	_____	_____
Account number	_____	_____
Amount and maturity date	_____	_____

Stock Investments
and/or Mutual Fund Shares

Name of Company or Fund	Number of of shares owned	Serial numbers	Date acquired	Cost per share	Total cost	Owner(s)

(Continue on a worksheet)

Corporate and Government Bond Holdings, U.S. Treasury Bills and Notes

Issuer	Type	Interest rate	Number owned	Serial numbers	Purchase price	Date bought	Maturity date	Owner(s)

(Continue on a worksheet)

U.S. Savings Bonds

Type (Series E,H, EE,HH)	Serial number	Denom- ination	Owner(s)	Location
_____	_____	_____	_____	_____
_____	_____	_____	_____	_____
_____	_____	_____	_____	_____
_____	_____	_____	_____	_____
_____	_____	_____	_____	_____
_____	_____	_____	_____	_____

(Continue on a worksheet)

Real Estate Holdings
(Including Your Home(s)

	Property			
	1	2	3	4
Description of property and address				
Form of ownership (solely or jointly owned)				
Location of property				
Date acquired				
Original cost				
Downpayment				
Current market value				
Original amount of mortgage				
Term of mortgage				
Monthly payment				
Maturity date of mortgage				
Name of mortgagee (lender)				
Name(s) of owner(s)				

Capital Improvements in Your Home

Date	Capital improvement	Cost
_____	_____	_____
_____	_____	_____
_____	_____	_____
_____	_____	_____
_____	_____	_____
_____	_____	_____
_____	_____	_____
_____	_____	_____

Keeping a permanent record of the capital improvements you have made in your home will help to minimize the amount of capital gains subject to tax when you sell your home.

Collectibles and Valuable Possessions

	Item			
	1	2	3	4
Description of item	_____	_____	_____	_____
Original value	_____	_____	_____	_____
Current value	_____	_____	_____	_____
Date acquired	_____	_____	_____	_____
How acquired: purchase, gift, or inheritance	_____	_____	_____	_____
Location	_____	_____	_____	_____

List of My Credit Cards

Issuer's name	Account number	Issuer's address	Issuer's phone

Life Insurance Policy(ies) Inventory

	Policy		
	1	2	3
Name of insured	_____	_____	_____
Name of company	_____	_____	_____
Policy number	_____	_____	_____
Type: term, cash value, endowment, specialized	_____	_____	_____
Face amount	_____	_____	_____
Beneficiary(ies)	_____	_____	_____
	_____	_____	_____
Current loan, if any	_____	_____	_____
Current cash value, if any	_____	_____	_____
Premium amount	_____	_____	_____
Premium due date(s)	_____	_____	_____
Name of insurance agent	_____	_____	_____
Address of agent	_____	_____	_____
	_____	_____	_____
Telephone number of agent	_____	_____	_____
Location of policy(ies)	_____	_____	_____

Annuity(ies) Inventory

	Annuity		
	1	**2**	**3**
Name of annuity owner	_____	_____	_____
Name of company	_____	_____	_____
Address of company	_____	_____	_____
	_____	_____	_____
Premium amount	_____	_____	_____
Premium due date(s)	_____	_____	_____
Payout Plan	_____	_____	_____
	_____	_____	_____
Income per month	_____	_____	_____
Beneficiary(ies)	_____	_____	_____
	_____	_____	_____
Survivor's rights	_____	_____	_____
Name of Agent	_____	_____	_____
Address of Agent	_____	_____	_____
	_____	_____	_____
Telephone number of agent	_____	_____	_____
Location of policy(ies)	_____	_____	_____

Health Insurance Inventory

Medicare
   Claim number   _____   _____

   Hospital insurance (Part A):   _____   _____
                                               Effective date   Effective date

   Medical insurance (Part B):   _____   _____
                                               Effective date   Effective date

Medigap insurance
   Name(s) of insured   _____

   Name of company   _____

   Address of company   _____

                     _____

   Policy number   _____

   Coverage dates: From–To   _____

   Risks covered and amount of each   _____ $ _____

                                       _____ $ _____

                                       _____ $ _____

                                       _____ $ _____

                                       _____ $ _____

   Premium amount $ _____

   Premium due date(s)   _____

   Name of insurance agent   _____

   Address of agent   _____

                     _____

   Telephone number of agent   _____

Other health coverage	Company	Policy number	Premium amount
Basic hospitalization	_____	_____	$_____
Basic medical/surgical	_____	_____	$ _____
Supplementary hospitalization	_____	_____	$_____
Comprehensive major medical	_____	_____	$_____
Catastrophe major medical	_____	_____	$_____
Disability income insurance	_____	_____	$_____
Dental insurance	_____	_____	$_____
Optical expense benefits	_____	_____	$_____
Hearing aids	_____	_____	$_____
Prescription drug plan	_____	_____	$_____
Blood program	_____	_____	$_____

Residential Insurance

Name of company _____

Address of company _____

_____

Policy number _____

Dwelling coverage $ _____

   Deductible $ _____

Other structures $ _____

Personal belongings

   a. _____ $ _____

   b. _____ $ _____

   c. _____ $ _____

Valuable items floater

   a. Jewelry $ _____

   b. Fur coats $ _____

   c. Other $ _____

Personal liability $ _____

Medical expenses $ _____

Other

   a. _____ $ _____

   b. _____ $ _____

Coverage dates: From–To _____

Premium amount $ _____

Premium due date(s) _____

Residential Insurance

Name of insurance agent   _____

Address of agent   _____

                                     _____

Telephone number of agent   _____

Automobile Insurance

Car or cars insured   _____

Name of company   _____

Address of company   _____

                                     _____

Policy number   _____

Coverage dates: From–To   _____

Risks covered and amount of each   _____ $_____

                                     _____ $_____

                                     _____ $_____

                                     _____ $_____

                                     _____ $_____

Premium amount $_____

Premium due date(s)   _____

Name of insurance agent   _____

Address of agent   _____

                                     _____

Telephone number of agent   _____

Inventory of the Contents of Your Home

An updated inventory of the contents of your home should be maintained for insurance purposes as well as for estate planning. Using the format suggested below for the living room, prepare a worksheet for a detailed listing. A similar listing should be prepared for the dining room, master bedroom, second bedroom, third bedroom, bathrooms, den or library, kitchen, basement, and garage. It is also recommended that photographs showing the contents of each area be available. You should also prepare a list for each of the following: jewelry, clothing, silverware, dishes, stemware, table and bed linens, personal belongings, and any other valuable possessions, such as art, antiques, and cameras.

Area	Contents	Date acquired	Cost	Current value
Living room	_____	_____	_____	_____
	_____	_____	_____	_____
	_____	_____	_____	_____
	_____	_____	_____	_____
	_____	_____	_____	_____

Inventory: Your Wills

	(Name of husband or individual)	(Name of wife or individual)
Have you made a will? (Yes, No)		
If yes, date of will		
Executor: Name		
Address		
Telephone number		
Alternate Executor: Name		
Address		
Telephone number		
Have you prepared a Supplemental Letter of Instructions? (Yes, No)		
If yes, note location of the Supplemental Letter*: Original		
First copy		
Second copy		

*Should be attached to original, first copy and second copy of your wills.

Inventory: Trusts

	(Name of husband or individual)	(Name of wife or individual
Have you created a trust? (Yes, No)		
If yes, type (living, testamentary)		
Date created		
Name of attorney		
Address of attorney		
Telephone number of attorney		
I am beneficiary of the following trust		
Name of Trustee		
Address of Trustee		
Telephone number of Trustee		

Inventory: Retirement Plans

	(Name of husband or individual)	(Name of wife or individual
Are you a member of a retirement plan? (Yes, No)	_____	_____
If yes, name of company or plan	_____	_____
Address	_____	_____
	_____	_____
Telephone number	_____	_____
My pension number	_____	_____
I am currently receiving pension benefits from the following company or plan	_____	_____
Address	_____	_____
	_____	_____
Telephone number	_____	_____
My pension number	_____	_____

Appendix B
Resources

Now that you have considered all the elements of a retirement plan, you may wish to utilize the variety of resources that are available. For example, you might join a membership organization, such as the American Association of Retired Persons (AARP). AARP, the nation's largest organization of older people, is for individuals who are 50 years of age or older, and are actively employed, semi-retired, or retired. Its 2,400 chapters around the country offer their members a variety of educational and social programs. Other organizations, listed below with their addresses, can provide you with leads in the areas of education, health, legal services, paid employment, travel, and volunteer work.

MEMBERSHIP ORGANIZATIONS

American Association of
Retired Persons (AARP)
1909 K Street, N.W.
Washington, D.C. 20049
(202) 872-4700

AARP is the nation's largest and most experienced organization of older persons. More than 2,400 chapters work for local community welfare, and provide educational and social programs for their members. Persons who are 50 years of age or older, and actively employed, semi-retired, or retired are eligible to join AARP.

National Retired Teachers
Association (NRTA)
1909 K Street, N.W.
Washington, D.C. 20049
(202) 872-4700

The NRTA is a companion organization of the AARP.

Institute of Lifetime Learning
1346 Connecticut Avenue, N.W.
Washington, D.C. 20036
or
215 Long Beach Boulevard
Long Beach, CA 90802

The goal of the Institute is to provide all older adults with opportunities for continuing education and "lifetime learning."

Action for Independent Maturity (AIM)
1909 K Street, N.W.
Washington, D.C. 20049
(202) 872-4850

AIM offers people between the ages of 50 and 65 and still actively employed a wealth of useful information about money management, health matters, leisure possibilities, and other issues, the successful management of which can make their present life more enjoyable and satisfying. AIM is a division of AARP.

Gray Panthers
3700 Chestnut Street
Philadelphia, PA 19104

Institute for Puerto Rican/
Hispanic Elderly
105 East 22 Street, Room 401
New York, NY 10010

National Caucus and Center for
Black Aged
1424 K Street, N.W.
Washington, D.C. 20005

EDUCATION

Adult Education Association of the U.S.A.
810 18th Street, N.W.
Washington, D.C. 20006

College Level Examination
Program (CLEP)
Educational Testing Service
Princeton, New Jersey 08540

Institute of Lifetime Learning
1909 K Street, N.W.
Washington, D.C. 20049

National Association for Public
Continuing & Adult Education
1201 16th Street, N.W.
Washington, D.C. 20036

National Home Study Council
1601 18th Street, N.W.
Washington, D.C. 20009

University of Kentucky Writing
Workshop for People Over 57
Council on Aging
University of Kentucky
Lexington, KY 40506

U.S. Department of Education
Bureau of Adult, Vocational & Library
Programs
Seventh and D Streets, S.W.
Washington, D.C. 20202

HEALTH

Alzheimer's Disease and Related
Disorders Association, Inc.
360 North Michigan Avenue
Chicago, Illinois 60601

American Association of Homes for
the Aging
1050 17th Street, N.W.
Washington, D.C. 20036

American Cancer Society, Inc.
777 Third Avenue
New York, N.Y. 10017

American Dental Association
211 E. Chicago Avenue
Chicago, IL 60611

American Dietetic Association
430 N. Michigan Avenue
Chicago, IL 60611

American Foundation for the Blind
15 W. 16th Street
New York, N.Y. 10011

American Heart Association
44 East 23rd Street
New York, N.Y. 10010

American Health Care Association
(Nursing Homes)
1200 15th Street, N.W.
Washington, D.C. 20005

American Optometric Association
7000 Chippewa Street
St. Louis, MO 63119

American Podiatry Association
20 Chevy Chase Circle, N.W.
Washington, D.C. 20015

American Speech and Hearing
Association
9030 Old Georgetown Road, N.W.
Washington, D.C. 20014

Arthritis Foundation
221 Park Avenue South
New York, N.Y. 10003

National Association of Jewish Homes
for the Aged
2525 Centerville Road
Dallas, Texas 75228

National Cancer Institute
Office of Cancer Communications
Bethesda, MD 20205

LEGAL SERVICES

American Bar Association
1155 East 60th Street
Chicago, Illinois 60637

National Legal Aid and Defenders
Association
2100 M Street, N.W.
Washington, D.C. 20037

National Senior Citizens Law Center
1709 W. Eighth Street
Los Angeles, CA 90017

PAID EMPLOYMENT

Green Thumb, Inc.
1012 14th Street, N.W.
Washington, D.C. 20005

Mature Temps
Exxon Building
1251 Avenue of the Americas
New York, N.Y. 10020

National Council of Senior Citizens
1511 K Street, N.W.
Washington, D.C. 20036

National Council on the Aging
1828 L Street, N.W.
Washington, D.C. 20036

U.S. Small Business Administration
1441 L Street, N.W.
Washington, D.C. 20549

TRAVEL

BritRail Travel International Inc.
630 Third Avenue
New York, N.Y. 10017

Elderhostel
100 Boyleston Street, Suite 200
Boston, MA 02116

Eurail Pass
c/o French National Railroad
610 Fifth Avenue
New York, N.Y. 10020

Farm and Ranch Vacations, Inc.
36 East 57 Street
New York, N.Y. 10022

Floating Through Europe
271 Madison Avenue
New York, N.Y. 10016

U.S. Department of the Interior
National Park Service
18th and C Streets, N.W.
Washington, D.C. 20240

Golden Age Passport (for age 62 and older)
Golden Access Passport (for blind and
disabled of any age)

Free lifetime entrance permit and discount
on fees to Federal parks, monuments, historic sites, and recreation areas throughout
the U.S. Obtain passport in person at all
National Park Service and Forest Service
offices and National Park system areas
where entrance fees are charged. Proof of
age is required.

VOLUNTEER WORK

ACTION
806 Connecticut Ave., N.W.
Washington, D.C. 20525
(202) 393-3111

ACTION is the principal Federal agency
for sponsorship of volunteer programs. It
administers several programs in which
older volunteers may participate. Among
them are the following:

**Retired Senior Volunteer Program
(RSVP).** The goal of this program is to establish a recognized role in the community

and a meaningful life in retirement by developing a wide variety of community volunteer-service opportunities for persons 60 years of age or over. It provides grants to public and private nonprofit organizations.

Foster Grandparent Program. The goal of this program is to provide part-time volunteer opportunities for low-income persons age 60 and over and to render supportive person-to-person services in health, education, welfare, and related residential settings to children with special needs.

Service Corps of Retired Executives (SCORE), and Active Corps of Executives (ACE). The goal of these programs is to provide advisory and counseling services for the benefit of new and existing small businesses, as well as nonprofit community organizations, by utilizing the management experience of retired and semi-retired (SCORE) and active (ACE) business executives.

Volunteers in Service to America (VISTA). The goal of this program is to provide specialized services, training, advisory services, and counsel to supplement efforts of community organizations to eliminate poverty. VISTA enables individuals from all walks of life and all age groups to perform meaningful and constructive service as volunteers in situations where they help to overcome the handicaps of poverty and secure opportunities for self-advancement.

Senior Companion Program. The goal of this program is to provide part-time volunteer opportunities for low-income persons age 60 and over and to provide supportive person-to-person services to persons (other than children) with special needs, especially older persons living in their own homes, and in nursing homes and other institutions.

If any of the foregoing programs interests you, contact ACTION for further information.

National Council of Senior Citizens
1511 K St., N.W.
Washington, D.C. 20005

Offers part-time work in community-service agencies in activities ranging from child care and adult education to home health and homemaker services.

National Council on the Aging
1828 L St., N.W.
Washington, D.C. 20036

Provides part-time work in Social Security and state employment service offices, public housing, libraries, hospitals, schools, and food and nutrition programs. Also provides escort services, homemaker, and home-repair services.

National School Volunteer Program
300 N. Washington St.
Alexandria, VA 22314

Offers information on how to start or join a school volunteer program.

Appendix C
Suggested Readings

This appendix presents suggested readings for each chapter of the book. The publications enumerated in each subject area were carefully selected to provide the reader with the most informative and up-to-date knowledge. If you wish to delve more deeply into a particular topic, any of the sources suggested would be valuable. The use of this bibliography will help you to expand your knowledge in specialized areas of retirement planning.

CHAPTER 1.
FIRST FACTS ABOUT RETIREMENT AND PLANNING

Blau, Zena Smith. *Aging in a Changing Society.* New York: Franklin Watts Inc., 1981.

Butler, Robert N. *Why Survive? Being Old in America.* New York: Harper and Row, 1975.

Comfort, Alex. *A Good Age.* New York: Crown Publishers, 1976.

Jorgensen, James. *The Graying of America: Retirement and Why You Can't Afford It.* New York: The Dial Press, 1980.

Michaels, Joseph. *Prime of Your Life: A Practical Guide to Your Mature Years.* Boston, Mass.: Little, Brown & Co., 1983.

Schulz, James H. *The Economics of Aging.* 2nd ed. Belmont, Cal.: Wadsworth Publishing Co., Inc., 1980.

CHAPTER 2.
UNDERSTANDING SOCIAL SECURITY

Ball, Robert M. *Social Security: Today and Tomorrow.* New York: Columbia University Press, 1978.

Clark, Robert L. and David T. Barker. *Reversing the Trend Toward Early Retirement.* Washington, D.C.: American Enterprise Institute, 1981.

Ferrara, Peter J. *Social Security: The Inherent Contradiction.* San Francisco, Cal.: Cato Institute, 1980.

Joint Economic Committee. *Social Security and Pensions: Programs of Equity and Security.* Washington, D.C.: 1980.

Social Security Amendments of 1983. 98th Congress, Public Law 98-21, enacted April 20, 1983.

U.S. Department of Health and Human Services, Social Security Administration, Washington, D.C. *Estimating Your Social Security Retirement Check: Using the "Indexing" Method.* Periodic.

————. *Thinking About Retiring?* Periodic.

————. *What You Have to Know About SSI.* Periodic.

————. *Your Social Security.* Periodic.

CHAPTER 3.
CHECKING YOUR PENSION BENEFITS

Allen, Everett T., Jr. and others. *Pension Planning: Pensions, Profit Sharing, and Other Deferred Compensation Plans.* 4th ed. Homewood, Ill.: Richard D. Irwin, Inc., 1981.

Committee for Economic Development. *Reforming Retirement Policies.* New York: 1981.

Hartman, Robert W. *Pay and Pensions for Federal Workers.* Washington, D.C.: The Brookings Institution, 1983.

Kotlikoff, Laurence J. and Daniel E. Smith. *Pensions in the American Economy.* New York: National Bureau of Economic Research, 1983.

Nader, Ralph and Kate Blackwell. *You and Your Pension.* New York: Grossman Publishers, 1973.

Reid, Heddy F. and Karen W. Ferguson. *A Guide to Understanding Your Pension Plan.* Washington, D.C.: Pension Rights Center, 1982.

Tilove, Robert. *Public Employee Pension Funds.* New York: Columbia University Press, 1976.

U.S. Department of Labor, Pension and Welfare Benefit Programs. *Employee Retirement Income Security Act (ERISA) of 1974.* Washington, D.C.: 1974.

CHAPTER 4.
SAVINGS, INVESTMENTS, LIFE INSURANCE, AND ANNUITIES

Chasen, Nancy H. *Policy Wise: The Practical Guide to Insurance Decisions for Older Consumers.* (A project of the American Association of Retired Persons, Re: life, health, residential, and automobile insurance). Glenview, Ill.: Scott, Foresman and Co., 1983.

Hallman, G. Victor and Jerry S. Rosenbloom. *Personal Financial Planning.* 3rd ed. Rev. New York: McGraw-Hill Book Co., 1985.

Lee, Barbara with Gretchen Morgenson. *The Woman's Guide to the Stock Market.* New York: Harmony Books, 1982.

Mayo, Herbert B. *Basic Investments: An Introduction.* Hinsdale, Ill.: The Dryden Press, 1980.

Porter, Sylvia. *Sylvia Porter's New Money Book for the 80's.* Garden City, N.Y.: Doubleday & Co., Inc., 1979.

Quinn, Jane Bryant. *Everyone's Money Book.* New York: Delacorte Press, 1979.

CHAPTER 5.
BUDGETING, CREDIT, INFLATION, TAXES, AND TAX SHELTERS

Budgeting

Sensible Budgeting With the Rubber Budget Account Book. Great Barrington, Mass.: American Institute for Economic Research, 1980.

U.S. Department of Labor, Bureau of Labor Statistics. *Three Budgets for a Retired Couple.* Washington, D.C.: Periodic.

Credit

Federal Reserve Bank of Philadelphia, Department of Consumer Affairs. *How the New Equal Credit Opportunity Act Affects You.* Philadelphia, Pa.: 1981.

Federal Reserve System, Board of Governors. *Consumer Handbook to Credit Protection Laws.* Washington, D.C.: 1982.

Inflation

Advertising Council, Inc. *Dollars and Sense: Inflation: What It Is and What You Can Do To Help Fight It.* New York: 1979.

Case, John. *Understanding Inflation.* New York: Penguin Books, 1981.

Shilling, A.G. and K. Sokoloff. *Is Inflation Ending? Are You Ready?* New York: McGraw-Hill Book Co., 1983.

Taxes and Tax Shelters

Fierro, Robert Daniel. *Tax Shelters in Plain English: New Strategies for the 1980's.* New York: Penguin Books, 1983.

Gordon, Robert D. *Tax Planning Handbook: Strategies and Applications.* New York: New York Institute of Finance, 1982.

Savage, Michael. *Everthing You Always Wanted to Know About Taxes But Didn't Know How To Ask.* New York: The Dial Press, 1979.

CHAPTER 6.
ESTATE PLANNING: WILLS, TRUSTS, PROBATE, ESTATE AND GIFT TAXES

Clay, William C., Jr. *The Dow Jones-Irwin Guide to Estate Planning.* New York: Bantam Books, 1982. Paperback, $2.95.

Dacey, Norman F. *How To Avoid Probate: Updated.* New York: Crown Publishers Inc., 1982. Hardcover: $19.95; Paperbound: $16.95.

Kinevan, Marcos E. *Personal Estate Planning: Financial and Legal Aspects of Accumulating, Protecting, and Disposing of Your Personal Estate.* Englewood Cliffs, N.J.: Prentice-Hall, 1980. Spectrum paperback, $6.95. Cloth, $14.95.

U.S. Department of the Treasury, Internal Revenue Service. *Federal Estate and Gift Taxes.* Publication 448. Free.

Ziegler, Richard S. and Patrick F. Flaherty. *Estate Planning for Everyone: A Basic Guide.* St. Paul, MN: Premier Publishing Co., 1982. Hardback, $11.95.

CHAPTER 7.
HANDLING LEGAL AFFAIRS

American Bar Association. *The American Lawyer: How to Choose and Use One.* 1978. Pamphlet ABA Press.

American Bar Association. *Your Rights Over Age 50.* American Bar Association Press, 1981. Pamphlet.

Center for Financial Management. *Legal Counterattack.* 1980. (The Manual of Do-It-Yourself Law, For the Man Who Wants to Fight Back)

Pomroy, Martha. *What Every Woman Needs to Know About the Law.* Garden City, N.Y.: Doubleday & Company, Inc., 1980.

Reader's Digest Family Legal Guide: A Complete Encyclopedia of Law for the Layman. Pleasantville, N.Y.: The Reader's Digest Association, Inc, 1981.

Sarashik, Steven, and Walter Szykitka. *Without a Lawyer.* New York: New American Library, 1980. Paperback, $5.95.

CHAPTER 8.
MAKING THE RETIREMENT HOUSING DECISION

American Bar Association. *Landlords and Tenants: Your Guide to the Law:* Chicago, Ill.: American Bar Association, 1982. (Booklet, 48 pp., $2.00)

Irwin, Robert. *The $125,000 Decision: The Older American's Guide to Selling a Home and Choosing Retirement Housing.* New York: McGraw-Hill Book Company, 1982. $17.50.

Lee, Steven James. *Buyer's Handbook for Cooperatives and Condominiums.* New York: Van Nostrand Reinhold Co., 1978. (Paperback: $9.95)

Meyers, Joan. *Buying and Selling a Home in Today's Market.* New York: Dell Publishing Co., Inc., 1983. (Paperback: $3.95)

CHAPTER 9.
INTERPRETING MEDICARE AND MEDICAID, OTHER HEALTH INSURANCE, AND NURSING HOMES

Medicare and Health Insurance

American Association of Retired Persons. *Information on Medicare and Health Insurance for Older People.* Long Beach, California: 1983.

Chasen, Nancy H. *Policy Wise: The Practical Guide to Insurance Decisions for Older Consumers.* (A consumer action project of the American Association of Retired Persons). Glenview, Illinois: Scott, Foresman and Company, 1983.

New York State Insurance Department. *Medicare Supplement Insurance in New York State.* Albany, New York: 1983.

U.S. Department of Health and Human Services. *Your Medicare Handbook.* Washington, D.C.: U.S. Government Printing Office, 1982.

Physical Health

Glickman, Stephanie and Judy Lipshutz. *Your Health and Aging.* Produced by the Division of Gerontology, Office of Urban Health Affairs, New York University Medical Center under a grant from the Administration on Aging, Department of Health and Human Services, 1981.

Gordon, Michael, M.D. *Old Enough To Feel Better: A Medical Guide for Seniors.* Radnor, Pennsylvania: Chilton Book Co., 1981.

Taylor, Robert B., M.D. *Feeling Alive After 65: The Complete Medical Guide for Senior Citizens and Their Families.* New Rochelle, N.Y.: Arlington House, Publishers, 1976.

Walford, Roy L. *Maximum Life Span.* New York: W.W. Norton & Co., 1983.

Waldo, Myra. *The Prime of Life and How to Make It Last.* New York: Macmillan Publishing Co., Inc., 1980.

Mental Health

Bradford, Leland P. and Martha Bradford. *Retirement: Coping With Emotional Upheavals.* Chicago, Ill.: Nelson-Hall, 1979.

Butcher, Lee. *Retirement Without Fear.* Princeton, N.J.: Dow Jones Books, 1978.

Eisdorfer, Carl and William E. Fann. eds. *Treatment of Psychopathology in the Aging.* New York: Springer Publishing Co., Inc., 1982.

Reisberg, Barry. *Brain Failure: An Introduction to Current Concepts of Senility.* New York: The Free Press, 1981.

Torack, Richard M. *Your Brain is Younger Than You Think: A Guide to Mental Aging.* Chicago, Ill.: Nelson-Hall, 1981.

U.S. Department of Health and Human Services, Public Health Service, Alcohol, Drug Abuse, and Mental Health Administration. *A Consumer's Guide to Mental Health Services.* Washington, D.C.: 1980.

Vischer, Adolf L. *On Growing Old.* (Translated from the German by Gerard Onn). Boston: Houghton Mifflin Co., 1967.

CHAPTER 10.
PREPARING FOR THE INEVITABLE

Consumers Union. *Funerals: Consumers' Last Rights.* Mount Vernon, New York: Consumers Union, 1977.

Federal Trade Commission. *Consumer Guide to the FTC Funeral Rule.* Washington, D.C. 20580: April 1984. (This free booklet may be obtained by writing to the Federal Trade Commission.)

Loewinsohn, Ruth Jean. *Survival Handbook for Widows (and for relatives and friends who want to understand).* Chicago, Illinois: Follett Publishing Co., 1979.

Mitford, Jessica. *The American Way of Death.* New York: Fawcett World, 1963, updated 1978.

Nelson, Thomas C. *It's Your Choice: The Practical Guide to Planning a Funeral.* (A Consumer Action Project of American Association of Retired Persons) Glenview, Illinois: Scott, Foresman and Company, 1983.

The Office of Impact Evaluation, Bureau of Consumer Protection, Federal Trade Commission. *Final Report.* (In conjunction with Public Sector Research Group, Market Facts - Washington, 1611 North Kent Street, Arlington, Va. 22209), July 1982.

CHAPTER 11.
WORKING AND PLAYING IN RETIREMENT

Dickinson, Peter A. *The Complete Retirement Planning Book: Your Guide to Happiness, Health, and Financial Security.* New York: E.P. Dutton & Co., Inc., 1976. (Paperback)

Gault, Jan. *Free Time: Making Your Leisure Count.* New York: John Wiley & Sons, Inc., 1983.

Hoffman, Ray. *Extra Dollars: Easy Money-Making Ideas for Retired People.* New York: Stein and Day, Publishers, 1977. (Paperback)

Institute of Lifetime Learning. *Second Career Opportunities for Older Persons.* A service of NRTA and AARP. Washington, D.C.: (1909 K Street, N.W., 20049), 1982.

Ledford, Lowell and Jeanne Brock. *Ready or Not: Planning Your Successful Retirement.* New York: Walker and Company, 1977.

INDEX

Actual charges, 220, 242
ADEA. *See* Age Discrimination in Employment Act.
Adjustable rate mortgage, 201, 208
Administrator, 142, 159, 163
Age discrimination, 176, 182. *See also* Credit; Legal problems of retirees.
Age Discrimination in Employment Act (ADEA), 176, 182
Ages 65 through 69 and still working, 233–234
AIME. *See* Average indexed monthly earnings.
Amortization, 208
Annual percentage rate (APR), 120, 129
Annuities, 82–84
Antenuptial agreement, 175, 182
Apartments. *See* Retirement Housing.
Approved charges, 221, 242
APR. *See* Annual percentage rate.
Arizona Governing Committee *v.* Norris, 32
Assets, 101, 129, 133, 140, 137, 163. *See also* Investments.
Assignment (Medicare medical insurance), 220–221, 242
Average indexed monthly earnings (AIME), 24

Balanced mutual funds, 70, 88. *See also* Investments, mutual funds.
Banker's acceptance, 70, 88. *See also* Investments, money market paper.
Bankruptcy, 176–177, 182
Basic medical/surgical, 228
Basis point, 88
Bearer bond, 64, 88
Beneficiary, 135, 136, 137, 140, 145, 147, 163
Benefit period, 215, 242
Bequest, 136, 140, 145, 157, 163
Bereavement, 259
Binder, 201, 208
Blood program, 230. *See also* Health insurance.

Blue Book, 106–107, 129
Blue chip stocks, 88
Blue-collar workers, 279
Blue Cross. *See* Health insurance; Health insurance providers.
Blue Shield. *See* Health insurance providers.
Bonds, 62–67, 88. *See also* Investments.
Budget, 99, 129
Budgeting process, 101–103. *See also* Retirement budget.
    tips, 103
    worksheets, 105–119
Burial, 253, 262
    Society, 262
    vault, 262
Buy-sell agreement, 134, 163

Callable, 62, 88
Call option, 89
Capital, 129
Capital gain, 89
Capital loss, 89
Care facilities, 197–198, 202, 208
Caring for someone else, 176
Cash refund annuity, 89
Cash value, 81, 89
Casket, 253, 262
Catastrophic major medical insurance, 242
Cattle raising. *See* Tax shelters.
CATS. *See* certificate of accrual on Treasury securities.
CD. *See* Certificate of deposit.
Cemeteries, 251, 262
Cemetery plots, 248, 255, 262
Central listing service, 200, 208
Certificate of accrual on Treasury securities (CATS), 89
Certificate of deposit (CD), 69, 89. *See also* Instruments, money market paper.

Charitable remainder trust, 155, 163, 192. *See also* Trusts.

Chattel mortgage, 178, 182

Classified (help wanted) ads, 271, 279

Cliff vesting, 35, 54. *See also* Pension plans, group plans, private.

Clifford trust, 155, 163. *See also* Trusts.

Closed-end mutual fund, 71, 89

Closing costs, 200, 208

Codicil, 145, 163

Coexecutor, 137, 163

Coinsurance, 220, 226

COLAs (cost-of-living adjustments). *See* Social Security.

Collectibles, 74, 89

Columbarium, 262

Commercial insurance companies, 232–233

Commercial paper, 69–70, 89. *See also* Investments, money market paper.

Common stock, 61–62, 89. *See also* Investments, stocks.

Common stock mutual fund, 71, 90

Community property, 170, 173, 182

Compounding, 90

Comprehensive major medical insurance, 228, 242

Compressed work week, 266, 279

Concurrent ownership, 170, 182

Concurrent property ownership. *See* Property ownership.

Conditional sales agreement, 178, 182

Condominiums, 194–195, 201, 208. *See also* Retirement housing.

Conservator, 176–183

Consideration, 183

Consumer Credit Protection Act, 129

Consumer Price Index (CPI), 123, 129

Consumption of savings. *See* Savings.

Contract, 178–179, 183. *See also* Legal problems of retirees.

Contributory pension plans, 34, 54. *See also* Pension plans, group plans.

Conventional mortgage, 205

Convertible, 62, 63, 90. *See also* Investments, stocks, preferred.

Cooperative, 195–196, 209. *See also* Retirement housing.

Copayment, 220, 243

Corporate bonds, 63. *See also* Investments, bonds, mutual funds.

Corporation, 177, 183

Cosigner, 129

Cost of housing, 202–204

Cost-of-living adjustments (COLAs). *See* Social Security.

Coupon bond, 62, 90

CPI. *See* Consumer Price Index.

Credit, 119–122, 129

    age discrimination, illegality of, 119

    borrowing against what you own, 120

    use of credit cards, 120–121

    using credit in retirement, 119

Credit cards, 120–121, 129

Credit life insurance, 129

Credit scoring, 120, 129

Credit unions, 121, 130

Cremation, 251, 252, 254, 262

Crematory, 256, 262

Crypt, 251, 262

Cumulative preferred stock, 62, 90. *See also* Investments, stocks, preferred.

Current charges, 220, 243

Curtesy, 163

Custodial care, 230, 243

Customary charges, 220, 243

Death, assisting survivors

    basic information, 249–250

    instructions for survivors, 257–259

Death, funeral arrangements

    checklist of things to do after a death

        immediately, 247–248

        after funeral and interment, 248–249

    choosing a casket, 253

    death certificate, 249

    disposal of the body, 251–252

        embalming, 254

        monument, 254

        vault, 254

    funeral ceremonies, 252

    funeral costs, 252–253

        complete funeral, 253

        price itemization, 254

        pricing systems, 253

Death, surviving a loss

    crisis of bereavement, 259

    living alone, 259–260

    thoughts on surviving, 260–261

Death, survivors' benefits, 262

    documents required, 256–257

    Social Security, 256

    Veterans Administration, 256

Death benefits, 18, 24

Death certificate, 248, 249, 262

Death taxes, 160, 163

    minimizing, 160

Debenture bond, 63, 90
Deductible, 220, 243
Deed, 209
Deferred annuity, 83, 90
Deficit, 116, 119, 130
Defined benefit plan, 33, 54. *See also* Pension plans.
Defined contribution plan, 33, 54. *See also* Pension plans.
Deflation, 130
Dental insurance, 229. *See also* Health insurance.
Direct disposition, 251, 262
Disability, 17, 24
Disability benefits, 37, 41–42, 54
Disability income insurance, 228, 243
Disability insurance, 24. *See also* Social Security.
Dividend, 61, 90
Doctors' services. *See* Medicare medical insurance.
Do-it-yourself will, 137
Donee, 164
Donor, 164
Dower, 164
Down payment, 201, 209
Dialysis treatment. *See* Medicare, Medicare aid.

Early retirement, 24. *See also* Pension benefits, types.
Early retirement benefits, 37, 54
Earnings limitation for employees (retirement test), 24
Earth burial, 251, 262
Economic implications, housing transactions. *See also* Legal implications, housing transactions.
  comparative housing costs, 202–204
  living abroad, 203–206
  selling your home, 201
Economic Recovery Tax Act of 1981 (ERTA), 126, 130, 133, 145, 160. *See also* Estate Tax.
Elderly population, 1
Elimination period, 243
Embalming, 253, 263
Emergency savings fund, 59, 90. *See also* Savings.
Employee Retirement Income Security Act (ERISA), 31, 54. *See also* Pension Plans.
Employment agency, 271, 279
Employment of retirees, 2, 85

Endowment insurance policy, 80–81, 90
Entombment, 251, 263
Equity, 90, 191–192, 209
ERISA. *See* Employee Retirement Income Security Act.
ERTA. *See* Economic Recovery Tax Act of 1981.
Escrow, 201, 209
Estate, 133, 135, 160, 164
Estate planning, 3, 9, 133–167
  conference, information for, 146–148
  data for, 136
  objectives, 133–134
  steps in, 134–135
  tools of, 134
Estate tax, 160, 164
  Economic Recovery Tax Act, 1981, 160
  maximum rate reduced, 161
  minimize payment of, 133, 160
  tax free transfers aside from spouse, 161
  unlimited marital deduction, 160–161
Eulogy, 249, 263
Exclusion, 221, 243
Exclusive listing, 200, 209
Exclusive right to sell listing, 209
Executor (executrix), 137, 140–141, 145, 147, 164. *See also* Wills.
Explanation of Medicare benefits notice, 221, 243

Family plot, 248, 263
Fannie Maes, 66, 90
Federal civil service pension plan. *See* Pension plans, public.
Federal Housing Administration, 209
Federal Insurance Contributions Act (FICA), 13–14, 25
Federal National Mortgage Association (Fannie Maes), 66, 90
Fiduciary, 140–141, 218. *See also* Wills.
Finance charge, 120, 131
Financial independence, 131
Financial planning, 3, 9. *See also* Annuities; Budgeting; Credit; Inflation; Investments; Life insurance; Pension benefits; Pension plans; Social Security; Tax(es); Tax shelters.
Fixed dollar annuity, 84, 91
Fixed premium annuity, 82, 91
Fixed rate mortgage, 209
Flexible location, 266, 279
Flexitime, 266, 279
Foreclosure, 209

Form of business organization, 177, 183
Full-time work. *See also* Working in retirement.
Fully funded pension plan, 37, 54. *See* Pension plans, group plans, funding.
Fully insured, 14, 25
Funding of pension plans, 37–38, 43, 54, 56
Funeral. *See* Death, funeral arrangements.
Funeral director, 251, 252, 255, 263
Funeral home, 252, 255, 263
Funeral service, 252, 263
Funeral Trade Practices Rule, 252, 253, 263
Futures contract, 91
General mortgage bond, 63, 91.
General obligation bond, 67, 91
Gifts, 134, 158, 164
Gift tax, 161, 164
    increase in annual exclusion, 161
    maximum rate reduced, 161
    taxable gifts, 161–162
Ginnie Maes, 66, 91. *See also* Investments, bonds.
Goals of planning. *See* Retirement goals.
Gold, 74
Gold checks, 25
Government bonds, 63–64. *See also* Investments, bonds.
Government National Mortgage Association (Ginnie Maes), 66, 91
General power of attorney, 175
Graded vesting, 35–36, 55
Graduated payment mortgage, 209
Grave liner, 254, 263
Grave marker, 254, 263
Growth and income funds, 70. *See also* Investments, mutual funds.
Growth funds. 70. *See also* Investments, mutual funds.
Guardian, 135, 141, 147, 164, 176, 183. *See also* Wills.
Group pension plans. *See* Pension plans, group plans.

Handwritten will. *See* Wills.
Health
    mental, 3
    physical, 2
Health assistance programs
    homemaker services, 231
    meals on wheels, 231, 244
    visiting nurses, 230
Health insurance, 227–230, 236–238
    basic advice, 235–236

basic medical/surgical, 228
Blue Cross hospitalization, 228
comprehensive major medical, 228
disability income, 228
special needs
    blood program, 230
    dental, 229
    hearing aids, 229
    nursing home care (gap), 230
    optical expense, 229
    prescription drugs, 230
Health insurance providers
    Blue Cross and Blue Shield, 231
    commercial insurance companies, 232–233
    health maintenance organizations (HMO), 232, 242
Health insurance, other considerations
    health insurance for your spouse, 234
    if you are under 65 and still working, 233–234
    if you are age 65 through 69 and still working, 234
Health Maintenance Organization (HMO), 232, 242. *See also* Health insurance.
Hearing aids, 229. *See also* Health insurance.
Heirs, 133, 134, 135, 136, 137, 138, 164
HMO. *See* Health maintenance organization.
Hobbies, 275–276
Hobby income, 86
Holographic will, 137–138, 164. *See also* Wills.
Home equity. *See* Retirement housing, tapping your home equity.
Home health care, 218–219
Home ownership, 128. *See also* Housing; tax shelters.
Home warranties, 209
Homemaker services, 231. *See also* Health assistance programs.
Hospice, 219–220, 243. *See also* Medicare hospital insurance.
Hospital insurance (HI), 25. *See also* Medicare hospital insurance.
Houses, 73. *See also* Economic implications, housing transactions; Investments; Legal implications, housing transactions.
Housing. *See* Economic implications, housing transactions; Legal implications; housing transactions.

Immediate disposal, 251, 263
Immediate pay annuity, 83, 91
Income, 2

Income mutual fund, 70, 91. *See also* Investments, mutual funds.

Income tax assistance, 127. *See also* Tax(es).

Indexing, 25

Individual pension plans. *See* Pension plans, individual plans, private.

Individual proprietorship, 177, 183

Individual Retirement Account (IRA), 44–47, 53, 127. *See also* Pension plans, individual plans, private; tax shelters.
   rollover, 48, 55, 128

Inflation, 123–125, 130
   annual rate (1960–1986), 124
   coping with, 123
   impact on retirees, 124
   measures against, 125

Inheritance tax, 162, 164
   minimize, 133, 160

Inheritances, 86. *See also* Retirement income.

In-hospital coverage. *See* Medicare hospital insurance.

Irrevocable living trust. *See* Trusts.

Installment refund annuity, 83, 91

Insurance, health. *See* Health insurance.

Intangible personal property. *See* Personal property, intangible.

Integrated pension plan, 33, 55. *See also* Pension plans, group plans.

Interest, 62, 63, 64, 65, 66, 67, 91, 120, 121, 131

Intermediate care facility, 240, 243. *See also* Nursing homes, types of facilities.

Interview, 271–272, 279. *See also* Job hunting; Working in retirement.

Inter vivos trust, 153, 164. *See also* Trusts.

Intestate, 140, 142, 144, 165. *See also* Wills.

Investments
   assets, distribution and current value, 79–80
   bonds, 62–67
     corporate, 63
     government, 63–64
     municipal, 66–67
     U.S. agency (Ginnie Maes), 66
     U.S. Savings, series EE, 65
     U.S. Savings, series HH, 65
     U.S. Treasury, 64
   collectibles, 74
   gold, 74
   house, 73
   money market paper, 67–70
     banker's acceptances, 70
     certificates of deposit, 69
     commercial paper, 69–70
     repurchase agreements, 71
     U.S. Treasury bills, 67–68
     U.S. Treasury notes, 68–69
   mutual funds, 70–73
     advantages, 71
     objectives, 70
     structure, 71
     types, 71–73
   real estate, 73
     real estate investment trust (REIT), 73
   risk quotient (RQ), 77–79
   silver, 74
   stocks
     common, 61–62
     preferred, 62
   strategy for the small investor with limited resources, 77
   tips, 74–77
   unit investment trusts, 72–73

IRA. *See* Individual Retirement Account.

Irrevocable living trust, 154, 165

Job hunting. *See also* Working in retirement.
   methods used in, 270–271
   interview, 271
   resumé, 271, 273–274
   thank you letter, 272
   where to look, 272

Job reassignment, 266, 279

Job redesign, 266, 279

Job sharing, 267, 279

Job specifications, 266, 279

Joint and survivor annuity, 55, 83, 91

Joint ownership, 170–173, 174

Joint tenancy with right of survivorship, 158, 165, 170–172, 183
   advantages, 171
   disadvantages, 172

Keogh plan, 49, 55, 127. *See also* Pension plans, individual plans, private; Tax shelter.

Kidney transplant. *See* Medicare, Medicare aids.

Late marriage. *See* Legal problems of retirees.

Late retirement, 25

Lawyers. *See also* Wills.
   choosing and using, 179
   evaluating, 181
   legal fees, 180

Lease, 200, 210

Legacy, 165

Legal implications, housing transactions, 199–202. *See also* Economic implica-

tions, housing transactions.
   buying a smaller home or condominium, 201
   care facility contract, 202
   leasing an apartment or a house, 200
   selling your present home, 200–201
Legal problems of retirees, 174–179
   age discrimination, 176
   bankruptcy, 176–177
   caring for someone else, 176
   expenditure involving a contract, 178–179
   tips on contracts, 178–179
   second or late marriage, 175
   setting up a business, 177–178
   someone to care for you, 175–176
Legally valid will. *See* Wills.
Leisure, 276–277. *See also* Playing in retirement.
Liabilities, 101, 131, 133, 140, 165
Life annuity with a term certain, 83, 92
Life cycle, 9
Life expectancy, 1, 83
Life insurance, 80–82, 92, 134, 158, 165. *See also* Probate, transferring property; Trusts.
   changing role, 81
   need for, 80–81
   reviewing your needs, 81–82
Limited liability, 177, 183
Limited payment life insurance, 80, 92
Limited power of attorney, 175
Living trusts, 153–154, 158, 165. *See also* Probate, transferring property; Trusts.
Living will, 138–139, 165. *See also* Wills.
Load mutual fund, 71, 92. *See also* Investments, mutual funds.
Lot, 255, 263

Margin account, 92
Marital deduction, 160–161, 165. *See also* Estate tax.
Mausoleum, 251, 263
Maximum family benefit, 25
Maximum taxable amount, 13, 25
Meals on Wheels program, 231, 244
Medicaid, 244
   background, 224–225
   covered services, 225
   eligibility, 225
   final tip, 225
Medicare, 244. *See also* Medicare hospital insurance; Medicare medical insurance.

background, 213–214
basic advice, 223–224
basic parts, 214
   Medicare hospital insurance (Part A), 215–220
   Medicare medical insurance (Part B), 220–222
major gaps, 222–223, 226
   out-of-pocket costs, 222
   Medigap insurance, 222–223, 226–227
Medicare aid, 25
Medicare hospital insurance (Part A)
   benefit period, 215
   covered and non-covered services, 215–216
   home health care
     payment schedule, 219
     services and supplies provided, 218
     services and supplies not provided, 218–219
   hospice care
     payment schedule, 220
     services covered, 219
     services not covered, 219–220
   in-hospital coverage
     payment schedule, 216–217
     services covered, 217
     services not covered, 217
   skilled nursing facility coverage
     payment schedule, 218
     services covered, 217
     services not covered, 217–218
Medicare medical insurance (Part B)
   doctors' services covered, 221
   doctors' services not covered, 221–222
   how payments are made
     assignment method, 220–221
     payment to you, 221
Medigap insurance, 222–223, 244. *See also* Medicare.
Memorial Service, 252, 263
Memorial Society, 254–255, 263
Mental health, 3
Minimal container, 263
Mineral excavation. *See* Tax shelters.
MMDA. *See* Money market deposit account.
Mobile home, 196, 210. *See also* Retirement housing.
Money market, 67–70, 92. *See also* Investments, money market paper.
Money market deposit account (MMDA), 58, 92. *See also* Savings.
Money market instruments, 67–70, 92. *See also* Investments.

Money market mutual funds, 72, 92. *See also* Investments, mutual funds.

Money market paper, 67–69. *See also* Investments.

Monument, 254, 263

Moody's Investors Service, 63, 93. *See also* Investments.

Mortgagee, 210

Mortgagor, 210

Mortuary, 252, 255, 263

Moving in with others, 198–199

Multiple listing service, 210

Municipal bond mutual fund, 72. *See also* Investments, mutual funds.

Municipal bonds, 66–67, 93, 128. *See also* Investments, bonds; Tax shelters.

Mutual fund, 70–73, 93. *See also* Investments, mutual funds.

NASDAQ (National Association of Securities Dealers Automated Quotations), 93

National Association of Securities Dealers Automated Quotations. *See* NASDAQ.

Negative amortization, 210

Negotiable Order of Withdrawal Account (NOW account), 58, 93. *See also* Savings.

Nest egg. *See* Savings, lifetime nest egg.

Net worth, 101, 130, 136, 165

No-load mutual fund, 71, 93. *See also* Investments, mutual funds.

Noncontributory pension plan, 34, 55. *See also* Pension plans, group plans.

Non-cost services, 86–87. *See also* Retirement income.

Normal retirement benefits, 36, 55. *See also* Pension benefits, types.

NOW account. *See* Negotiable Order of Withdrawal Account.

Nursing homes. *See also* Health insurance.
    evaluating a facility, 240–241.
    finding a suitable place, 240
    Medicare coverage, 240
    selecting, 239
    services offered, 239
    types of facilities
        intermediate care facilities, 240
        residential care facilities, 240
        skilled nursing facilities, 239–240

OASDI (old-age, survivors, and disability insurance), 26

Obituary, 248, 263

Oil and gas drilling. *See* Tax shelters.

Old-age, survivors, and disability insurance. *See* OASDI.

Open-end mutual fund, 71, 93

Optical expense, 229. *See also* Health insurance.

Options, 93

Oral will, 138, 165. *See also* Wills.

Organ or whole-body donation, 251, 254

Owning a business. *See* Working in retirement.

Par value, 62, 93

Participating preferred stock, 93

Part-time work. *See* Working in retirement.

Partnership, 177, 183

Passbook savings account, 58, 93. *See also* Savings.

Pass-through securities, 66

Pay-as-you-go, 13, 26

Payment to you. *See* Medicare medical insurance.

PBGC. *See* Pension Benefit Guarantee Corporation.

P/E ratio, 94

Penny stocks, 94

Pension, 55. *See also* Pension benefits; Pension plans; Tax shelters.

Pension Benefit Guarantee Corporation (PBGC), 38, 55

Pension benefits. *See also* Pension plans.
    applying for benefits, 39, 43–44
    computations, 41
    survivors, 37, 42–43
    types, 41
        early, 37
        disability, 37, 41–42
        normal, 36
    what is a good pension, 39

Pension plans. *See also* Pension benefits.
    group plans, private, 30–44, 128
        Arizona Governing Committee v. Norris, 32
        background, 30–31
        contributory, features of, 34
        defined benefit plans, 33
        defined contribution plans, 33
        eligibility, 34
        Employee Retirement Income Security Act (ERISA), 1974, 31
        funding, 37–38, 43
        integrated, features of, 33
        noncontributory, features of, 34
        qualified, features of, 34
        Retirement Equity Act, 1984, 31–32

services, years of, 34–35, 40
sex discrimination, 32
Summary Annual Report, 38
Summary Plan Description, 38, 43
terminations, 38, 43
types of plans, 29, 33
vesting, 35–36, 40–41, 56
vesting, cliff, 35, 54
vesting, graded, 35–36, 55
individual plans, private, 44–51
advantages, 50–51
Individual Retirement Account (IRA),
44–49
Keogh plan, 49
Simplified Employee Plan (SEP), 50
public plans, 51–53
Federal civil service plan, 52
other Federal plans, 53
Pension reform, 53
Personal property, 169, 183
intangible, 169
tangible, 169
Personnel agency, 271, 279
Personnel Department, 270, 280
Personnel Officer, 270, 280
Phased retirement, 267, 280. *See also* Working
in retirement.
Physical health, 2
PIA (primary insurance amount), 26
Planning. *See* Retirement planning.
planning process, 4
Playing in retirement
hobbies, 275–276
leisure-time guidelines, 276–277
planning for, 277–278
proper use of leisure, 275
Plot, 248, 255, 264
Plural ownership, 170, 183
Policy, 244
Population (U.S.), elderly, compared to total, 1
Power of appointment, 165
Power of attorney, 175, 184
general power of attorney, 175
limited or special power of attorney, 175
Pre-existing conditions limitation, 244
Preferred stock, 62, 94. *See also* Investments,
stocks.
Premarital agreement, 175, 184
Premium, 244. *See also* Annuities; Life
insurance.
Prepayment penalty, 201, 210
Prescription drugs, 230. *See also* Health
insurance.

Preservation, 254, 264
Prevailing charge, 220, 244
Price/earnings ratio (P/E ratio), 94
Primary insurance amount (PIA), 26
Probate, 154, 165
advantages, 159–160
criticisms of, 158
disadvantages, 160
transferring property outside probate
gifts, 158
joint tenancy with right of survivorship,
158
life insurance, 158
living trusts, 158
Probate Court, 159, 165
Productivity, 280
Profit on the sale of a home, 127. *See also*
Tax(es).
Property, 133, 134, 135, 136, 137, 138, 165,
169–174, 184
Property ownership
concurrent (plural) ownership, 170
community property, 170, 173
joint tenancy with right of survivorship,
170–172
tenancy in common, 170, 172–173
tenancy by the entirety, 170, 172
sole ownership, 170
which is best, 173–174
Public pension plans. *See* Pension plans,
public.
Public welfare, 87. *See also* Retirement
income.
Put option, 94

Qualified Pension Plan, 34, 55. *See also*
Pension plans, group plans.
Qualified terminable interest property trust
(Q-TIP), 154, 166. *See also* Trusts.
Quarters of coverage (QC), 14, 26

Rate of return, 25, 244
Real estate, 73. *See also* Investments, real
estate; Tax shelters.
Real Estate Investment Trust (REIT), 73, 94.
See also Investments, real estate.
Real property, 169, 184
Reasonable charge, 220, 244
Registered bond, 64, 94
Rental agency, 210
Rents, 86. *See also* Retirement income.
Replacement ratio, 26

Repo. *See* Repurchase agreement.
Repurchase agreement, 70, 94. *See also* Investments, money market paper.
Residential care facility, 240, 244. *See also* Nursing homes, types of facilities.
Residuary, 136, 166
Respite care, 220, 244
Resumé, 271, 273–275, 280
Retirees, profile of
  employment, 2
  housing, 2
  income, 2
  life expectancy, 1
  mental health, 3
  numbers, 1
  physical health, 2
  social relationships, 3
Retirement age, 4
Retirement budget. *See also* Budgeting process.
  need for, 99–100
  typical expenses, retired couple, 100–101
Retirement community, 197, 210. *See also* Retirement housing.
Retirement decision
  reasons for retiring, 7
  reasons for continuing to work, 8
Retirement Equity Act, 1984, 31–32. *See also* Pension plans, group plans.
Retirement goals
  artistic, 7
  cultural, 7
  educational, 6
  employment, 6. *See also* Working in retirement.
  health, physical, 5
  housing, 6. *See also* Retirement housing decision.
  religious activities, 6
  social relationships, 5
Retirement housing, 2, 4
  care facility, 197–198
  condominium, 194–195
  cooperative, 195–196
  decision to move, 193–199
  housing requirements, 186
  mobile home, 196
  moving in with others, 198–199
  process, 189–190
  rental apartment, 188, 194, 200, 210
  retirement community, 197, 210
  smaller home, 193
  moving or staying where you are, 187

  non-housing requirements, 186–187
  owning or renting, 188
  staying where you live, 190
    asking someone to live with you, 199
    changes in your home, 190
  tapping your home equity, 191
    charitable remainder trust, 192
    reverse mortgage, 191
    sale leaseback, 191–192
  where to live after retirement, 185–186
Retirement income, miscellaneous sources. *See also* Annuities; Investments; Life insurance; Pension benefits; Pension plans; Savings; Social Security.
  employment, full-time or part-time, 85
  hobby income, 86
  inheritances, 86
  non-cost services, 86–87
  public welfare, 87
  rents, 86
  reverse mortgages, 85
  royalties, 86
  veterans' benefits, 86
  workers' compensation, 85
Retirement benefits. *See* Social Security.
Retirement insurance, 26
Retirement planning, 9
  estate planning, *See* Estate planning.
  financial planning, 3, 9. *See also* Annuities; Budgeting; Credit; Inflation; Investments; Life insurance; Pension benefits; Pension plans; Social Security; Tax(es); Tax shelters.
  goals, 5–7
  health, physical and mental, 3, 5
  housing. *See* Retirement housing.
  legal affairs, 3. *See also* Legal implications, housing transactions; Legal problems of retirees.
  major categories, 3–4
  preparing for the inevitable, 3. *See also* Death.
  retirement lifestyle, 4, 6. *See also* Playing in retirement; Working in retirement.
  role of law, 169
  timetable for, 4–5
Revenue bond, 67, 94. *See also* Investments, bonds, municipal.
Reverse mortgage, 85, 94, 191, 210
Revocable living trust, 153, 166. *See also* Trusts.
Rights of retirees, 180–181
Risk quotient (RQ), 77–79. *See also* Invest-

ments.
Rollover, IRA, 48, 55, 128. *See also* Tax shelters.
Royalties, 86. *See* Retirement income.

Sale leaseback, 191–192, 210
Sales contract, 200, 210
Savings
    consumption of, 60
    emergency fund, 59
    lifetime nest egg, 57
    money market deposit account, 58
    negotiable order of withdrawal (NOW) account, 58
    passbook account, 58
    super NOW account, 58
Savings bond(s), 65, 95, 128
SBA. *See* Small Business Administration.
Second marriage. *See* Legal problems of retirees.
Second mortgage, 121, 131, 210
Self-Employment Contributions Act, 13, 26
Selling your home, 201. *See also* Economic implications, housing transactions.
SEP. *See* Simplified Employee Pension.
Series EE bonds, 65
Series HH bonds, 65
Setting up a business. *See* Legal problems of retirees.
Settlement costs, 133
Sex discrimination. *See* Pension plans.
Silver, 74
Simplified Employee Pension (SEP), 50, 56. *See also* Pension plans, individual plans, private.
Single premium annuity, 82, 95
Skilled nursing facility, 239–240, 244. *See also* Medicare hospital insurance; Nursing homes, types of facilities.
Small Business Administration (SBA), 269, 280
Smaller home. *See* Retirement housing.
Social relationships, 3
Social Security
    background, 11
    benefits package, 15–16
        disability, 16–18
        retirement, 16
        survivors, 18. *See also* Death, survivors' benefits.
    calculation of benefits, 21
    COLAs (cost-of-living adjustments), 22, 24
    filing an application, 15
    legal status of benefits, 22
    other aspects
        earnings limits, 21
        retire at 62 or 65, 20
    payroll deductions, 11, 13–14
    requirements to qualify, 14
    statement of earnings, 12, 14
    Supplemental Security Income (SSI), 18–19
    tax rates, 13
    tax status of benefits, 22
    tips, 23
    work credit required, 15
Social Security program, 26
Sole ownership, 170, 173–174, 184. *See also* Property ownership.
Someone to care for you, 175–176. *See* Legal problems of retirees.
SPD. *See* Summary Plan Description.
Special power of attorney, 175
Specialized mutual fund, 70, 95. *See also* Investments, mutual funds.
Specialized policy, 81, 95
Spousal health insurance, 234
Sprinkling trust, 154, 166. *See also* Trusts.
SSI. *See* Supplemental Security Income.
Standard & Poor's Corporation, 63, 95
Stock mutual fund, 71. *See also* Investments, mutual funds.
Straight bankruptcy, 177, 184
Straight life annuity, 83, 95
Straight life insurance, 80, 96
Strategy for investment, 77. *See also* Investments.
Students' benefits, 26
Successor (alternate) guardian, 137, 141, 147, 166
Successor (alternate) trustee, 147, 156, 157, 166
Summary Annual Report, 38. *See also* Pension plans.
Summary Plan Description (SPD), 38, 43, 56. *See also* Pension plans.
Stocks, 61–62. *See also* Investments.
Super NOW account, 58, 95. *See also* Savings.
Supplemental letter of instructions, 142–143, 148–151, 166, 249, 251, 264. *See also* Wills.
Supplemental Security Income (SSI), 18–19, 26. *See also* Social Security.
Suppliers, 245
Surplus, 116, 119, 131
Survivors' benefits, 37, 42–43, 56. *See also* Pension benefits; Social Security; Vete-

rans Administration.
Survivors' insurance, 26
Survivorship. *See* Joint tenancy with right of survivorship.

T-bill, 67–68, 96
Tangible personal property. *See* Personal property, tangible.
Taxable gifts. *See* Gift tax.
Tax deferred annuity, 84, 95, 128. *See also* Tax shelters.
Tax Equity and Fiscal Responsibility Act of 1982 (TEFRA), 126, 131
Tax credit for the elderly, 126
Tax free transfers, 161. *See also* Estate tax.
Tax(es), 125–127, 131
    additional exemption for age, 126
    benefits for older Americans, 125
    income tax assistance, 127–128
    minimizing personal income taxes, 126–127
    special gross income requirements, 126
    profit on the sale of a home, 127
Tax rate, 13, 27
Tax shelters, 128–129, 131
    home ownership, 128
    IRA (Individual Retirement Account), 128
    Keogh plan, 128
    municipal bonds, 129
    other tax shelters
        cattle raising, 129
        mineral excavation, 129
        oil and gas drilling, 129
        real estate, 129
    pensions, 128
    rollovers, 129
    tax deferred annuity, 128
    U.S. Government savings bonds, 129
TEFRA. *See* Tax Equity and Fiscal Responsibility Act of 1982.
Tenancy. *See also* Joint tenancy with right of survivorship; Property ownership.
    in common, 172–173, 184
    by the entirety, 172, 184
Term life insurance, 80, 95
Terminations. *See* Pension plans.
Testamentary Trust. *See* Trusts.
Testate, 142, 166. *See also* Wills.
Testator (testatrix), 135, 136, 166
Thank you letter, 272. *See also* Job hunting; Working in retirement.
Three Cs of credit, 120, 131

Tips
    Budgeting, 103
    Contracts, 178–179
    Health insurance, 234–236
    Inflation, 123, 125
    Inheritance tax, 133, 160
    Investments, 74–77
    Lawyer, 179, 181
    Life insurance, 81–82
    Medicaid, 225
    Medicare, 223–224
    Property ownership, 173–174
    Social Security, 23
    Wills, 143–145
Title, 170, 178, 184, 201, 211
Title insurance, 201, 211
Title search, 201, 211
Tombstone, 249, 264
Totten trust, 155, 166. *See also* Trusts.
Townhouses, 211
Transferring property outside probate. *See* Probate.
Trustee, 147, 156, 157, 166. *See also* Trusts.
Trusts, 134, 136, 166. *See also* Wills.
    examples
        charitable remainder, 155
        Clifford, 155
        life insurance, 155
        qualified terminable interest property trust (Q-TIP), 154
        sprinkling, 154
        Totten, 155
        Uniform Gifts to Minors Act, 155
    trustee, choosing a, 156–157. *See also* Wills.
        role of, 156
    types
        living trusts
            revocable, 153
            irrevocable, 154
        testamentary, 154–155
    uses, 152–153
    what is a trust, 152

Underfunded pension plan, 37, 56
Unfunded pension plan, 37, 56
Unified tax credit, 160, 167
Uniform Donor Card, 251, 264
Uniform Gifts to Minors Act, 155. *See also* Trusts.
Unit trust, 72–73, 95. *See also* Investments.
Universal life insurance, 96
Unlimited liability, 177, 184
Unlimited marital deduction, 160–161, 167.

See also Estate tax.
Urn, 251, 264
U.S. agency bonds, 66. *See also* Investments, bonds.
U.S. Government savings bonds, 128. *See also* Savings bond(s).
U.S. Savings bonds, 65. *See also* Investments, bonds.
U.S. Treasury bill, 67–68, 96. *See also* Investments, money market paper.
U.S. Treasury bond, 64, 96. *See also* Investments, bonds.
U.S. Treasury note, 68, 96. *See also* Investments, money market paper.

Variable annuity, 84, 96
Variable life insurance, 96
Variable premium annuity, 82, 96
Vault, 254
Vesting, 35–36, 40–41, 56. *See also* Pension plans.
Veterans Administration, 211. *See also* Death, survivors' benefits.
Veterans' benefits, 86. *See also* Retirement income.
Visiting nurses, 230

Wage earner's plan bankruptcy, 177, 184
Waiting period, 245
Ward, 141, 167, 176, 184
White-collar worker, 280
Whole life insurance, 80, 96
Widowers' benefits, 27
Wills, 136–151, 167. *See also* Trusts.
    basic advice on, 143–145
    basic content of, 136–137
    beneficiaries, 136, 145, 147
    bequests as percentages, 145
    data for, 145–148
    distribution of assets *by intestacy,* 143
    lawyer, role of, 144, 145
    leaving a valid will (testate), 142
    review periodically, 144
    risks of dying without a valid will (*intestate*), 142
    supplemental letter of instructions, 142–143, 148–151
    types of fiduciaries
        alternate executor, 145, 147
        alternate guardian, 141, 147
        alternate trustee, 147, 156
        executor (executrix), 140, 145, 147
        guardian, 141, 147
        trustee, 147, 156
    types of wills
        do-it-yourself, 137
        handwritten (holographic), 137–138, 164
        legally valid, 138
        living, 138–139
        oral, 138
    what makes a will invalid, 159
    where to keep original, 141–142, 144
    why make a will, 137
Work credit for Social Security, 15. *See also* Social Security.
Workers' compensation, 85, 96. *See also* Retirement income.
Working in retirement. *See also* Job hunting.
    job sharing, 267
    phased retirement program, 267
    post-retirement checklist, 269–270
    role of work in your life, 265
    work options at or after retirement
        continuing full-time work, 266
        owning a business, 268–269
        shifting to part-time, 266–267
        starting a new career, 266
        volunteer work, 268
Work options at or after retirement. *See* Working in retirement.
Wraparound annuity, 83, 96

Years of service. *See* Pension plans.

Zero Bracket Amount (ZBA), 131
Zero coupon bond, 97